THE COLOMBIAN STAND FOR FREEDOM had as its pre-cursor Antonio Nariño. As military leader his tactics were cunning and his courage matchless. As architect of the Colombian constitution, his concept of republican government and his speeches in defense of freedom, as translated in this volume, grant him a sure place among the founders of independence in the New World.

In this volume, many English-speaking readers will meet this great American for the first time. As the meaning of America has broadened and deepened among the variety of human beings on the two continents, the heritage of American history no longer stands complete without the record of several American republics who fought for independence over the past two centuries. In their annals are struggles whose leaders were as noble and visionary as the great men who freed the United States from British domination.

So that he could continue to wage both war and peace for Colombia, Nariño spent almost twenty years in pris-ons, wasting in illness, but alert as a hawk for the chance to fight again for his country. His personal ambition was submerged in patriotism, even as military dictator and civilian president of the young republic. A measure of success was to him simply a spur to continue the struggle for freedom which he saw as eternally linked to respon-sibility. The lofty level of his sentiments and his eloquent determination show in such warnings as he addressed to his colleagues in the government in 1813:

NARIÑO

Hero of

Colombian Independence

NARIÑO

Hero of
Colombian Independence

by
THOMAS BLOSSOM

THE UNIVERSITY OF ARIZONA PRESS
TUCSON, ARIZONA

About the Author —

THOMAS BLOSSOM studied Antonio Nariño most intensively during 1962 in Colombia under the joint auspices of the Pan American Union and the University of Florida, extending the research into its Spanish background in 1964, at the National Archives in Madrid and the Archives of the Indies in Seville, under sponsorship of Duke University's Hispanic Foundation. He received his A.B. at Amherst, M.A. at Columbia University, Ph.D. at Duke, and spent a year in graduate study at the Royal University in Florence. In World War II he served as a Navy liaison officer before starting a teaching career which took him to Western Carolina College, the Citadel in Charleston, Southern State College in Arkansas, and the University of Florida previous to joining the faculty at Old Dominion College in Norfolk, Virginia. Professor Blossom's survey for Latin America has provided the background for Prentice Hall's junior high school history text, *The Americas*. He also has served as co-editor of *Alas*, the Journal of the Association of Latin American Studies.

To John Tate Lanning of Duke University
and Mildred Underwood Blossom

———

Their patience and encouragement
made the long journey shorter

PREFACE

Antonio Nariño, although eloquent, valorous, and long suffering, is relatively little known, even today. In the process of setting this matter to rights, Professor Blossom has done service to a neglected hero with many facts and episodes heretofore unrevealed.

Colombian history seems peculiarly resistant to scholarly siege. There seem to be three reasons for this resistance: first, the provincialism intensified by Colombian topography and poverty; second, the turbulence of Colombian population in its cultural and racial heterogeneity; and third, the long continuing uncertainty with regard to the new nation's boundaries.

Against a backdrop both disordered and ambiguous, the figure of Nariño is striking in its leadership qualities as they emerge in this volume. Born wealthy, he poured all his talents and his wealth into the independence movement. His health and life itself were consumed in years of vile imprisonment from which he emerged fatally ill. Yet he lived to see the emancipation of Colombia.

It may be predicted that the general reader, previously unacquainted with the character of Nariño or the story of Colombian independence, will be surprised at the stature of the military man, the statesman, and the democratic lawgiver that emerges from Nariño the rebel, the general, and the president. Specialists in the field of Latin America will surely be pleased with the abundance of documentation from secondary sources to support this stature, and with the extensive bibliography. Colombians themselves will undoubtedly be grateful to Professor Blossom for his vigorous hand to the task of bringing their Precursor into the mainstream of Latin American history.

J. FRED RIPPY
Professor Emeritus
The University of Chicago

ACKNOWLEDGMENTS

A grant from the Southern Fellowships Fund of Chapel Hill, North Carolina, made possible two summers of writing uninterrupted by teaching duties in June and July of 1955, and 1958. Their help at that critical stage of revision is much appreciated.

A Pan American Union travel grant and a University of Florida Graduate School summer study grant made possible three months of travel and study in Colombia in June, July, and August, 1962.

A Duke University Hispanic Foundation grant made possible the author's travel to Spain in April, May, and June of 1964.

Since this book is the story of a Colombian hero, I want especially to thank the many Colombians whose insights were of value in discussions of Nariño which I found both profitable and enjoyable. Many of these people, as scholars who have written about Nariño or his times in the Spanish language, have been eager to see a book about the Precursor in English. I hope to visit with all of them again in Colombia some day: Dr. Guillermo Hernández de Alba of the Casa Del Florero, Dr. Alberto Miramón of the National Library and Archives in Bogotá, Dr. Carlos Restrepo Canal, Colombian Consul in Sevilla, Spain, Dr. Leopoldo Uprimny of the Colegio Mayor de Nuestra Señora del Rosario in Bogotá, Dr. Osvaldo Díaz y Díaz, secretary of The Colombian Academy of History, Dr. Porras y Troconic, Historian of Cartagena, Dr. Arboleda y Llorente, Historian of Popayán, who went with me to Calibío and Palacé, Don Carlos Simmonds, owner of Calibío, Dr. Roberto Cortázar of the Colombian Academy of History, Sra Kathleen Romoli de Avery, authoress of the best book in English on Colombia, Padre Lee, Archivist of the Colombian Academy of History, Señorita Carlotta Bustos, Archivist of the National Archives, my two students and friends Hernan Franco of the University of Florida, Gainesville, and Severiano Valenzuela of Old Dominion College, Norfolk, and last, but by no means least, my mentor and friend in Bogotá who generously gave me office space, letters of introduction, much good advice, and many hours of wonderful insight into

Colombian history and personality, Dr. Gerardo Paredes Fandiño, who was then, in 1962, director of the Servicios Bibliotecarios of the Colombian National Department of Education.

In the United States I want to thank in addition to Dr. John Tate Lanning of Duke, the following professors, mostly historians, who have discussed Nariño with me:

Dr. A. Curtis Wilgus, Dr. David Bushnell and Dr. Lewis F. Haines of the University of Florida; Dr. Harold Bierck of the University of North Carolina at Chapel Hill, Dr. Robert S. Smith of Duke University, Dr. Leon Helguera of Vanderbilt University, Dr. E. Taylor Parks of the U.S. Department of State, and of course, my professors at Duke University in the years 1947–1956 — especially Dr. Harold T. Parker who looked for some hard-to-find items in the French National Archives for me.

While each of these persons had much more than a passing interest in Nariño, none of them is to shoulder responsibility for the views expressed here, but simply to receive the grateful acknowledgment of the author.

THOMAS BLOSSOM

CONTENTS

INTRODUCTION

To understand the revolutions which led to the independence of Colombia, one must first have some understanding of the Spanish colonial system which produced not only the abuses leading to revolt but the leaders of independence. Such a leader was Antonio Nariño.

The first efforts to hold in check the excessive individualists who fought and conquered the Americas — for example, Cortez in Mexico and Pizarro in Peru — led to the development of the *audiencia*. This body often combined legislative and executive duties with its principal function as judicial court. By the 1550's, the need for stricter laws to control the conquistador and the large landowner, or *hacendado*, led to the establishment of two viceroyalties — the first in Mexico City and the second in Lima, Peru. The character of these vice-kings — noble, well paid and, on the whole, efficient — began to decline in honesty and efficiency by 1700. The accession of the French Bourbons in 1700, however, acted as a corrective and a stimulant. The ancient mercantilist exclusiveness of Spanish trade, after 1588 actually a sieve rather than a protective barrier, was made more realistic after 1700. Up-river Seville, long since impractical as an ocean port due to overgrazing and consequent silting, had its *Casa de Contratación*, nerve-center of monopolistic imperial control, moved to Cádiz in 1718. The Guipúzcoa company of 1728, a Galicia company of 1734, and a Barcelona company of 1753 indicated a breakdown of the monopolistic principle, and a spreading out of once restricted trading privileges. By 1765, nine different Spanish ports were allowed to trade with Cuba, Santo Domingo, Puerto Rico, Margarita, Trinidad, and after 1763, with Louisiana. By 1778, the nine Spanish ports allowed in the American trade had increased to thirteen. In the meantime, ships traveled independently, free of the supervision by the fleet system of convoys which was abolished in 1748. Tremendous increases in trade followed these more liberal policies.

Eighteenth-Century Reforms

The eighteenth century saw another reform which weakened the Spanish empire in America: the expulsion of the Jesuits in 1767. While it is true that in Paraguay they had represented an empire within an empire, powerful enough to ignore the kings in Spain, elsewhere they were missionaries and dedicated, successful teachers; their sudden and complete expulsion left a gap not easily filled, and destroyed a force supporting Spanish monarchical rule at a time when other forces were already undermining monarchies and empires.

Another change of the eighteenth century, meant to strengthen the administration, was the adoption of the French intendancy system in 1767. The new intendants took over many of the viceregal duties of enforcing and collecting taxes and thus tended to leave the viceroy largely a social figurehead and weakened in authority. New Granada, however, did not acquire this superimposed official.

Since the leaders of the successful revolutions which led to independence came from the *criollo* (creole) class, their complaints provide a major clue to the underlying causes of the wars of independence (1809–1826). Next to the Peninsular-born Spanish officials, they were the highest in the political, social, and economic scale and were enjoying a rapidly increasing prosperity by 1800, yet they were continually and increasingly discontented. Why was this so? Their chief grievance was that they could never aspire to be viceroys, bishops, abbots, or judges in the *audiencia*. All other high government and church posts were open to them and usually to them alone. But they felt frustrated and insulted by the peninsular Spaniards who monopolized the highest posts. By 1800, an unhealthy division and rivalry existed between the *ayuntamientos* or city councils, sometimes called *cabildos,* and the *audiencias.* The American-born Spaniard or creole largely monopolized the *cabildo* just as the peninsular Spaniard monopolized the *audiencia.* It was thus the *cabildo* that provided the experienced leaders of the revolution and the nucleus of the governmental structures of the later republics. Its creole members, excluded from the regular army, officered the growing colonial militia, ran the businesses and large estates, and in the universities they absorbed the new learning of the eighteenth century which made them admirers of Newton, Locke, Voltaire, Rousseau, Franklin, Washington, Jefferson, Paine, and, finally, of the French Revolution itself. Through their literary societies or *tertulias,* they were able to talk of hoped-for reforms and give vent to their jealousy of the Peninsulars and their dissatisfactions with the slowness of reforms. There, ultimately, they planned the revolutions, although these would not have succeeded without some support from the *mestizo,* the Indian, and the Negro. Manual labor and the lack of shoes were often the determining criteria in classifying the half-white as Indian instead of *mestizo.* Consequently social climbers aspired to shoes and avoided manual labor. Since a cardinal tenet of the *criollo* was also abhorrence of manual labor, the *mestizo* aspiring to be considered *criollo* was similarly apt to be purposefully idle. Some minor government jobs were open to him as were the universities. The excess of lawyers and the lack of engineers in Latin America today has often been ascribed to this concept that manual labor is degrading, to be performed solely by the lowest classes of society — the Indian and the Negro. Under such a system the tax load and the work load bore heaviest on the Indian and the Negro. The *mita* system kept the Indians working and dying young in the mines. Under the *hacendados,* the Negroes worked the sugar, the tobacco, and the cotton plantations and somehow survived both the work and the slave-drivers' whip. Both groups built the churches and supported them with their pittances. While creole and *mestizo* complained of the *alcabala* or sales tax, in the long run, the Indian and the Negro paid the taxes in cash, in kind, and in labor. Next to forced labor and head taxes, however, the levies most apt to arouse Indian and Negro revolts were the brandy and tobacco taxes.

Some time during the eighteenth century, while prosperity was rapidly increasing for the twelve million colonists of Spanish America, a few fusing element appeared which showed signs of acting as a catalyst to the Negroes, *mestizos,* and creoles. The agent was the word *American.* To be American was the one thing which united solidly all those in opposition to Spain. As all Spaniards were privileged to be superior, all Americans were forced to be inferior, though in varying degrees, and the complaint of being treated as inferiors to Spaniards was the one thread which could briefly draw together all discontents against Spanish rule. Jorge Juan and Antonio de Ulloa tried in vain to warn their Spanish rulers of this rising sentiment of Americanism in their *Noticias secretas,* written after their extensive trip of 1735 to America.

The Early Revolts

The first revolts in New Granada against Spain were by Indians, Negroes, and *mestizos.* The American-born Spaniard, or creole, as he was called, was seldom sympathetic to any of these abortive revolts. Either actively or passively, he assisted the Spanish government in suppressing such uprisings. A Negro revolt attempted to establish a Negro monarchy at Santa Marta in 1555; a mulatto was declared king in Venezuela in 1711, and *mestizo* leaders, followed largely by *mestizos* and Indians, led the briefly successful *Comunero* revolts of New Granada in 1780–1781. None of these movements bore much similarity to the North American Revolution of 1776 nor to the French Revolution of 1789, for independence was seldom mentioned. They were race uprisings and demands for tax modification, with no plan to overthrow the government of Spain.

The first creole-led revolutions of any importance in Spanish America took place outside of New Granada, in Venezuela, Paraguay, and Quito. In 1733 and 1751, some Venezuelan creoles revolted unsuccessfully against the exclusive monopoly of the Guipúzcoa company. In 1721, the *cabildo* of Asunción, Paraguay, led by a creole, José de Antequera, successfully ousted a Spanish governor and viceroy but was finally jailed and executed, as was his successor, Mompo, in 1732. The Quito revolt of 1765 was also creole-led. Opposition to the *alcabala,* or sales and transfer tax, was the cause of the revolt. After four hundred revolutionists had died in battle, an amnesty was granted, and the revolt quickly subsided with no noticeable change in the tax or governmental structure.

Although the *Comunero* revolt in New Granada (1781) received little or no support or leadership from the creoles, it served as a dress rehearsal for later revolts leading to independence.

While the Spanish government was busy fighting a war with England, and suppressing the Indian revolt of Tupac-Amaru in 1780–1783, a large-scale revolt focused on taxes and bad government broke out against the viceroy of New Granada and his tax collector, Gutiérrez de Piñeres. Indirectly, this uprising was a consequence of the North American Revolution, since the new taxes were to be used to help Spain support the United States against England. The *alcabala* was raised to 6 per cent. In New Granada, there was an *alcabala* on the sale of everything, even "on the wind," which traveling salesmen with no permanent domicile were obliged to pay.

The royal investigator, Gutiérrez de Piñeres, increased the tax on such goods as salt, tobacco, and playing cards, sold in the *estancos,* or government commissary monopolies. He also put new taxes on comparatively unburdened industries, such as the cotton cloth industry of northern New Granada, and finally a tax on roads traveled by merchants. In order to gain even more revenue, all citizens were divided into two classes for the purpose of assessing a head-tax: the rich, the two-peso class; the poor, one-peso. Tax collectors were accused of pillaging, stealing, and violating women, in addition to collecting (and sometimes not collecting when bribed) all the odious, onerous taxes. At this point rebellion broke out and spread rapidly.

The rebellion began with verses and diatribes against the government, printed on leaflets and smeared on walls. As in the earlier Paraguayan revolts, the leaders demanded justice in the name of the residents of each commune, hence were called *Comuneros,* this name reminiscent, also, of the city dwellers who fought in vain against the rising power of the central government of Charles V in Spain from 1517 to 1520.

In Socorro, the spontaneous outburst soon produced a flaming, passionate leader named Manuela Beltrán. She was soon leading a shouting, hooting, cheering mob with cries of lower taxes and "death to bad government." Shouting, singing, and brandishing clubs, slings and other primitive weapons, a mob of some twenty thousand Indians and *mestizos* soon gathered for a march on Santa Fé. Meanwhile, in Santa Fé, the guard of one hundred soldiers, aided by some creole militia, broke and fled before the mob, as did the royal tax collector, Piñeres. Left to their own devices, the creole leaders of Santa Fé hastily appointed a commission, headed by Archbishop Caballero y Góngora, to treat with the rebel leader, Juan Francisco Berbeo. After agreeing to lower taxes and swearing to keep the agreement, at a special High Mass held in the open in order to accommodate all of the vast multitude, the mob went home satisfied that their petitions would soon be granted.

On June 4, 1781, at Zipaquirá,[1] the solemn oath was given in the parochial church. The archbishop then marched north, preaching peace and promising redress of grievances. Everywhere he was well received. Meanwhile, the royal tax collector had conferred with the viceroy on the coast and raised some militia and they soon declared their sacred oaths null and void[2] and dashed out after the leaders of the revolt, Don Juan Francisco Berbeo and José Antonio Galán. In January, Galán and a second revolt were defeated. Galán and four leaders were tried, executed, decapitated, and chopped up into pieces.[3] Their trunks were burned. Their heads and limbs, stuck on poles as warning to future leaders, were distributed to the communes. Their houses were razed and sprinkled with salt and their descendants declared infamous forever. All the odious taxes were soon reinforced. Some creoles, including Antonio Nariño, were unfavorably impressed with this sample of Spanish justice.

Revolts and threats to the great Spanish empire again subsided in 1783. Santa Fé, cradled in its high plateau between encircling ranges of

---

1. Briceño, Manuel, *Los Comuneros,* Historia de la Insurrección de 1781, Bogotá, 1880, p. 137, hereafter cited as *Briceño.*

2. Friede, Juan, "¿Sabia el Arzobispo que al Ceder Ante los Comuneros Engañaba al Pueblo?" *El Tiempo,* July 8, 1962, p. 1 of Sunday Supplement. "Yes," says Friede. Archbishop Caballero y Góngora did *not* intend to keep his promise to the leaders; 15 Oct., 1782, letter to Galvez proves this.

3. *Briceño,* pp. 180–182 and 259 also 183.

the central and eastern cordilleras, settled back under Spanish rule, outwardly as unchanging, inaccessible, and invulnerable as it had been ever since the arrival in 1538 of Gonzalo Jiménez de Quesada. However, the reforms begun under Charles III in 1765 and continued after his death in 1788, were rapidly closing the gap between far-away Santa Fé and eighteenth-century reforms and revolutions in Europe. Population increased rapidly; the city grew and improved its physical appearance; schools were founded; printing presses appeared; a theater was built and echoes of the North American and French revolutions were freely discussed by the wealthy, educated creoles of Santa Fé. Prosperity and the examples of the United States and France bred discussion, criticism, and a few tentative dreams and plans for revolt in New Granada in the Eighties and Nineties.

Conspiracy Against Empire

Meanwhile, adventurers and plotters in England, France, and the United States urged these three powerful neighbors of a weakened Spain to carry out the logical consequences of 1588 and strip Spain of her great empire in the Americas. The partitions and dismemberment of an immense but feeble Poland in 1773, 1793, and 1795, provided a model. The important help expected from wealthy, powerful creoles, however, might hinge on the granting of semi-independent status, and England, at least, was prepared to make such concessions — particularly after failure to reconquer the United States.

One of the first creoles to attempt a workable combination of English greed and creole discontent was Juan Bautista Morales, chosen by Berbeo in 1781 to get help for the *Comunero* revolt. With his associate, Antonio Pita, he arrived in London in February, 1784, prepared to buy British supplies. He was too late. In the meantime, peace had been negotiated between England and Spain at the treaty of Versailles in 1783. England felt obliged to warn Spain of the plans of Morales and Pita. The next year, in May, 1784, Luis Vidalle arrived from Curaçao to get English support for a revolt which he declared was ready to break out in Santa Fé, Maracaibo, Santa Marta and Cartagena.[4] Vidalle claimed that the *Comunero* revolt of New Granda had been closely associated with that of Tupac Amaru in Peru,[5] and that it had the hearty support of the masses who looked forward eagerly to their separation from Spain. The rebels were even reported as eager to switch

---

4. *Briceño,* op. cit., p. 92.
5. *Briceño, p.* 93, 234–235.

their allegiance to England[6] — all they asked was money and supplies. Spain was allowed to arrest Vidalle,[7] and Morales was not able to secure any promises of help. The next five years were outwardly calm, discouraging to revolutions.[8]

The French Revolution of 1789 and the Nootka Sound crisis of 1790 between Spain and England prepared the stage for the next major revolutionary attempt in Spanish America. This time, a better plan developed, with independence as one of its objectives.[9] In 1789, within the *tertulia* meeting at Nariño's house in Santa Fé, there was an inner group of discussants called the "Casino," and within that, a still smaller group called "El Santuario." Some of the members of the "Santuario" constituted another and secret group, the "Arcano Sublime de la Filantropía," which had as one of its primary aims, independence, to be gained through revolution.

The overall plan of these groups, their methods of operation, and their objectives of reform and revolution, closely paralleled the plan of the juntos and subsidiary juntos of Benjamin Franklin as revealed in his *Autobiography*. The similarity was no accident, for Franklin was Nariño's model and the patron saint of these clubs. Adorning the inner clubroom were his statue, his electrical experiment, and his motto which read: "He snatched the lightning from the skies and the sceptre from the tyrant's hand."

About this time, there arrived from Quito an educated Indian, Francisco Javier Eugenio de Santa Cruz y Espejo, to be tried for slander because of radical pronouncements favoring the French Revolution. Somehow, between 1790 and 1792, Nariño, then treasurer of tithes, and a close friend of the viceroy, Ezpeleta, communicated to Espejo his plan for organizing the literary and patriotic societies as revolutionary cells. Espejo also met (probably through Nariño), Francisco Antonio Zea, later to serve as New Granadan representative at the British court, and Juan Pío Montúfar, who led the Quito revolt of 1809. Upon returning to Quito, Espejo and Montúfar founded "La Sociedad Patriótica o Escuela de la Concordia" to encourage intellectual development and in 1792, Espejo founded a fortnightly review to serve as mouthpiece, and to spread the views of the club. The *Primicias de cultura de Quito,* though

---

6. *Briceño,* p. 93.

7. *Briceño,* p. 94.

8. *Briceño,* p. 94.

9. *Briceño,* says "the Comuneros were the precursors of the independence of Spanish America."

not openly radical, became suspect, and was suppressed after the seventh issue. In the meantime, Nariño had established a press in Santa Fé, *La Patriótica,* and he soon took over the printing of a similar literary and scientific journal, the newly-founded *Papel periódico.*

Miranda's Plan of Attack

The machinery for a cooperative revolt for independence from Spain was already in existence, though in an elementary stage, when Francisco de Miranda, a discontented creole colonel from Caracas, presented the English with his plan of attack of 1790. Since 1783, Miranda had been a fugitive from Spanish justice, traveling in the United States and Europe, sounding out the two nations most likely to profit from a Spanish collapse in the Americas, and seeking to arrange a triangular alliance between England, the United States, and Spanish America. Such an alliance was increasingly favored by the Nootka Sound crisis of 1790. The trouble began when Captain Estevan José Martínez, acting under orders of the Spanish viceroy in Mexico City, captured Captain Colnett of *H.M.S. Argonaut,* in Nootka Sound on the northern edge of the Spanish claims to "California." This boundary dispute made war appear very likely in 1790, and made most attractive Miranda's offer to align creole forces with England against Spain in case of war.

Robertson, the authority on Miranda, says Pitt was definitely interested in Miranda's plan — at least, until the threat of war had passed. With Holland, Prussia, and the creoles of America as allies, England hoped to hold its own against Spain, France, Austria, and Russia, and hoped also perhaps to gain a huge new trade area in Spanish America. On February 14, 1790, Miranda presented to Pitt his plan based on freedom and independence. Provided with maps, an enumeration of forts, and a list demonstrating the slim military forces holding the Spanish empire from California to Cape Horn, Miranda felt sure it would be easy to set up the new state. Panama, the Orinoco, the west coast of Peru and Mexico, and the Venezuelan coast nearest to Trinidad would all make good points for the initial attack. Jesuits exiled from America to Rome in 1767 provided Miranda with accurate maps, lists of forts, and the names of discontented creoles. In his bad French, Miranda described Panama, key to success and control of America, as defended poorly by "fortifications mauvaises et mal entretenue. La Place ne serait pas susceptible d'une longue resistance." As for the people of Santa Fé, richest and most populous province: "Les individus devoués au gouvernement Espagnol ne pourraient être que le vise-roy, les membres de l'audience et quelques officiers, se voyant sur le point d'être abandonnés par la force armée comme ils fûrent en 1781."[10] The refusal of a disturbed and divided France to support Spain against England in 1790 dissolved the war threat and postponed Miranda's plan to free America from Spain.

England had no more forgotten her hopes of attacking Spain than the United States had forgotten its hopes of gaining control of New Orleans in order to assure the growing West of free access to the Mississippi Valley. There must be no bottleneck to this great avenue of trade. American leaders clearly understood the vital nature of the outlet, and watched for a chance to make a final and more favorable settlement. Similarly, England bided her time for attack on a weakening Spanish America. The opportunity came in 1797, when a new war against the Franco-Spanish alliance led to the capture of Trinidad as preliminary to a coordinated attack on all Spanish America. By 1797, the likelihood developed rapidly that England would be joined by the United States in such an attack. The United States began an undeclared naval war against France, and only the determination of President Adams kept Alexander Hamilton from becoming a hero in the liberation of Latin America. Governor Simcoe of Canada and Senator William Blount of Tennessee were also involved. Louisiana and the Floridas were to be attacked by United States frontiersmen. England was to blockade the mouth of the Mississippi and send aid to Canada. Much of this plan aborted when Senator Blount's intrigues were uncovered, and he was expelled from the Senate. The Spanish ambassador to the United States was well informed of the plot. On December 24, 1796, warnings were sent out from Spain to America to be on the lookout for Miranda.[11] The warnings did not prevent Thomas Picton's capture of Trinidad, but probably did account for the failure elsewhere in Spanish America of such revolts as those of Caracas and Santa Fé. In was during the collapse of the Santa Fé plot that Nariño surrendered and was reimprisoned by the Spanish government (See Chapter III).

The master planners were not easily discouraged by these partial defeats. Hamilton wrote to Rufus King in London, August 22, 1798, that Miranda could count on twelve thousand troops from the United States, that Great Britain would provide the fleet, and that he, Hamilton, as

---

10. Miranda letter of September 20, 1798, reviewing his 1790 plans from the Archives of the Indies, Seville, Spain, Estado, Legajo 61, 125/10. Typescript copy in possession of the author.

11. William Spence Robertson, *Francisco de Miranda and the Revolutionizing of Spanish America* (Annual *Report* of the American Historical Association for the year 1907, vol. I), Washington, 1908, p. 312.

second in command, expected to lead the liberating army. Independence under a moderate government supervised by a joint United States-British guarantee was planned, along with equal commercial privileges to the two liberating nations. Shortly thereafter, King wrote to Pickering in Paris that England would furnish the fleet and military stores and the United States would furnish the army. Even as late as June 27, 1799, Hamilton dreamed of an attack on Louisiana and the Floridas, and a "squint at South America."[12] The revolt in the British navy of 1797, Adams' desire to end the war with France, and the Napoleonic peace gestures after the coup of 1799, combined to kill the grand plan of Miranda in which Nariño, Caro, Pedro de Vargas, and many other prominent creoles were deeply involved.

Miranda's Next Attempt

Miranda's next attempt, the *Leander* expedition of 1806, lacked the full support of England, and was neither prevented nor abetted by Jefferson, upon whom the pressure for attack on Spanish America had been considerably eased by the acquisition of Louisiana in 1803. The attempt was also hindered by the accurate and prompt reports of the Spanish intelligence system in America. Thanks to Henry Stoughton, Spanish consul in New York, Miranda was carefully trailed in all his moves there during 1805 and 1806, while fitting out the *Leander*. In Caracas, the authorities were so fully warned that they had little difficulty in repulsing Miranda's abortive attack on Coro in 1806. Since the attack coincided with the somewhat more impressive Beresford-Popham attack on Buenos Aires, in which General Beresford succeeded in capturing the city, June 27 and 28, 1806, some coordination seems likely of these simultaneous attacks on Spanish America. The large number of American adventurers aboard the *Leander* has tended to obscure the fact that the attack was considerably more British than American, and so planned that in case of success there would be no doubt of its British origin and support. British naval forces in the Caribbean protected all the *Leander's* moves to and from Coro against Spanish naval attack, and more than half of the landing forces, according to Robertson, were British marines and seamen. Popham was court-martialed for leaving his station at the Cape of Good Hope to attack Buenos Aires. However, Robertson thinks this can be accounted for by the replacement of the Pitt ministry with that of Pitt's rival, Grenville. The resulting change of policy also accounts for the delay in sending General Whitelocke to Buenos Aires in 1807.

---

12. *Ibid.,* p. 333.

Further insight into the joint nature of the operations seems to have been afforded by a handkerchief of English manufacture found at the site of the Coro attack. The finding bears out the Spanish belief that Popham and Miranda had a secret agreement, the full development of which awaited their mutual successes. On the handkerchief were portraits of Sir Home Popham, General Beresford, Washington, and Miranda, surrounded by sketches of naval battles and bordered with four inscriptions: "Not commerce but union," "Let arts, industry and commerce flourish," "Religion and its holy ministers be protected," and "Let persons, conscience and commerce be at liberty."[13] Christopher Columbus adorned the center, British colors adorned the sides, and England was depicted as goddess of the seas with the lion of Spain at her feet. A young man was pictured rolling up the French colors while poking the lion with his sword. Under the youth was an inscription: "The Dawn of Day in South America." All this symbolism proved to the captain-general of Caracas that the rebel Miranda had been working in connivance with the British as the result of a comprehensive plan made by England for the conquest of Spanish America.

Nariño avoided complicity in the Miranda attacks of 1806, but was closely associated with later movements leading toward Colombian independence. The battle of Trafalgar in 1805 placed England in a position to cut off both Spain and France from their American possessions.

As a consequence of the Spanish civil war of 1808 against Joseph Bonaparte, the "Intruder King," Britain did an about-face in her fight against Spain to become an ally of the Spanish regency and junta governments in the desperate struggle against the imposed Napoleonic puppet. This reversal of British alliance killed the nearly completed British-creole master plan of 1807. Just as the key forces destined for America were assembled in Britain and ready to sail, they were diverted to Spain and Portugal. The aborted "master plan" for the liberation of Spanish America had been quite different. In February, 1807, Sir Arthur Wellesley proposed to attack Tierra Firme (Venezuela and Colombia) where he estimated Spain had about 13,000 troops, most of them in Venezuela. The attacking force was to consist of 6,000 British infantry, 2,600 black infantry (Barbadians), and 1,400 British cavalry. Rendezvous was set for Barbados where the forces would divide for joint simultaneous attacks on La Guayra, Caracas, Cumaná, and Angostura and the valley of the Orinoco. A pincer movement then would

---

13. *Ibid.,* pp. 397, 398.

entrap and defeat the Spaniards caught between Caracas and the Orinoco. At this juncture, an independent government was to be set up, having close commercial ties with England. Castlereagh favored the plan since the new political entity would provide markets to replace those in Europe cut off by Napoleon. Mexico was a secondary target which might require 17,000 troops to be assembled on Jamaica. Santa Fé was mentioned also as a secondary target.[14]

Kidnaping of the Royalists

The kidnaping of Manuel Godoy and the Spanish royal family by Napoleon at Bayonne in May, 1808, radically changed British plans. Wellesley's army for the liberation of South America was rerouted to aid the Spanish and Portuguese against Joseph Bonaparte in Madrid. The popular rising of "Dos de Mayo" (May 2), in Madrid, against the "Intruder King" Joseph, soon led to the formation of guerilla *juntas* loyal to Prince Ferdinand and a central *junta* which retreated behind the protection of the British navy on the island of León in Cádiz harbor. There they were able to round up a few creoles to sit in a new *cortes,* or parliament, which, however, granted only twelve representatives to all America, while the Peninsula received thirty-six.

Not only the kidnaping of the royal family, but the French occupation of Spain itself, created a power vacuum into which the creoles quickly stepped, although they did not usually declare for independence. Their first move usually consisted of declaring loyalty to Ferdinand VII, followed by the setting up of *juntas,* usually composed of wealthy creoles who had traditionally monopolized the city *ayuntamiento* or *cabildo.* By thus avoiding the direct issue of independence, they hoped to gain help from Spain's ally, England — or at least a form of benevolent neutrality. This multiple ambiguity, however, led instead to confusion, to rival governments, and to civil wars throughout Spanish America. In New Granada, an added problem soon appeared as a result of the rivalry between centralists and federalists. Nariño, and after 1815, Simón Bolívar, both believed that the federalist constitution of the United States would constitute too weak an instrument of government to hold together the ancient rival cities of New Granada — like Cartagena and Santa Marta, bitter seacoast rivals, Santa Fé and Tunja, and other lesser mountain cities — all jealous of Santa Fé's wealth, power, and ancient traditions as the viceregal capital.

---

14. *Ibid.,* pp. 405–408.

Nariño and his centralists finally won in 1812 and 1813 against the congressional federalists in Tunja, but not until the forces which should have been used for independence against Spain had been greatly weakened by civil war. It was these weakened forces, however, which under the leadership of Nariño were able to clear southern New Granada from Santa Fé to Popayán, but were finally defeated in May, 1814, at Pasto, near the Ecuadorean frontier. Further tragic division in the face of the enemy resulted from Bolívar's union with the Tunja federalists and his successful attack on centralist Santa Fé in 1814–1815.

Reaction and Reconquest

The concession of thirty delegates to the colonies, or other realms as they are more properly called, for the liberal Cortes of September, 1810–1811, might have kept the American *juntas* truly loyal to Spain, but the rise of a strong conservative element, opposed to concessions to America, in the Cortes of 1812 led to a reversal of policy whereby seventy-seven delegates were to be Spanish and only thirty were to be Americans. This action made it clear that nothing less than independence could gain for Americans their desired equality and recognition. This they might have won, and appeared to be winning, especially under Miranda's leadership in Venezuela in 1812 and that of Nariño in Santa Fé. Then came the earthquake of March 26, 1812, blamed on sinful republicans since it was mostly their cities which fell down, while royalist strongholds were largely unharmed. Not long after the earthquake came defeat, the attempt of Miranda to arrange a truce and his betrayal by Bolívar to the Spanish, Bolívar's successful march south and capture, for congressional federalists, of Nariño's centralist Santa Fé while Nariño was away being defeated at Pasto.

The collapse of Napoleon in Spain and in Europe in 1814 cleared the way for a restored Ferdinand to recapture the revolted colonies in America. Royalists like Domingo de Monteverde in northern New Granada and Melchor Aymerich and Juan Sámano in Pasto were soon reinforced by the veteran army of ten thousand from Spain under General Pablo Morillo.

Most of the early creole leaders in New Granada were executed or decapitated during the Spanish reconquest of 1815–1816 (*see* Caballero Diary). Federalists and centralists alike, who had been fighting each other only a few months before, fell dead, victims of the bloody executioners from Spain. Some were shot but many were hanged, decapitated, and mutilated. The famous botanist, Caldas, was decapitated as was the former president, Torres, and their heads were displayed on poles. Some three hundred of the wealthiest and best educated citizens were similarly killed by order of Morillo and Sámano. (Note: *see* Plaques in Panteón, Bogotá; 1962). Confiscation of property of the widows and children was further aimed to crush forever the spirit of independence. Santa Fé, occupied without the firing of a shot on May 5, 1816, was literally forced to dance at its own funeral.[15] Santander and a small body of patriots, retreating to the trackless jungles of the upper Amazon, were further defeated on July 10, 1816, leaving only the wild state of Casanare as a jungle exile for patriots. Officers of Morillo were ordered to take very few prisoners. Even with the few they took, jails were rapidly filled and had to be emptied by mass executions. By the end of 1816, Morillo considered independence permanently dead in Santa Fé, left Sámano in charge and moved north to Venezuela, bragging that he had not left alive enough individuals of sufficient influence or talents to conduct a revolution.[16]

The Victories of Bolívar

If England had truly wished to aid Spain with her impressive naval power, American independence would certainly have died at this point. Instead, thousands of unemployed British veterans and not a few North American ship captains aided Bolívar in his return to power from his enforced exile in Haiti and Jamaica. By 1816, Bolívar and Gregor McGregor had set up a government at Barcelona, two hundred miles east of Caracas. Morillo forced them to move out but they re-entered Venezuela from behind — up the Orinoco River, making Angostura their capital in 1817. By the middle of 1818, in spite of British proclamations forbidding enlistments, several thousand British subjects made possible Bolívar's daring attacks on Morillo of 1819. Santander and Santiago Mariño in the meantime cut off reinforcements while José Antonio Páez, the wild *llanero* cowboy, drove the Maracaibo royalists back into the lake. Then it was that Bolívar began his incredible march through flooded lowlands and up over the jagged, snow-covered Andes to victory at Boyacá on August 7, 1819. This victory at Boyacá led to the Riego revolt in Spain of early 1820, to the truce of November 25, 1820, and to Bolívar's second victory at Carabobo on June 24, 1821.

---

15. José María Caballero, Diary entitled "Días de la independencia," on pp. 75–274 in *La patria boba* (Biblioteca de Historia Nacional, vol. I, Bogotá, 1902), pp. 148–260. (Hereinafter Caballero, Diary).

16. Frederick L. Paxson, *The Independence of the South American Republics* (Philadelphia, 1916), p. 82.

It was at this point that Bolívar appointed the returned prisoner, Nariño, to preside over the history-making Congress of Cúcuta in May and June of 1821. It was at Cúcuta and at the second constitutional congress of Santa Fé of 1823 that the ancient rivalry of Santander and Nariño erupted. Stemming from Santander's support of the federalists in 1812, it led to the unfortunate verbal battle between the Precursor and "The Man of Laws," Santander. This rivalry ended in 1823, for Nariño with his death, but the dragon's teeth sowed by these two great men originated a series of civil wars over the question of federalism versus centralism which lasted down to the twentieth century.

Nariño's centralism, modeled on that of France, finally has replaced today the unworkable federalist system which both Nariño and Bolívar felt would never unify New Granada. There was no Hamilton and no John Marshall in early Latin American history, and no amount of civil war was ever able to make federalism workable.

This, in general, is the setting in which Nariño — Precursor of Colombian independence — lived, fought, and died.

Antonio Nariño, in a portrait painted by the soldier-artist José María Espinosa Prieto, who was the General's flagbearer during the campaign in the south, bitter aftermath of the victory at Bogotá.

CHAPTER I

FROM ROYAL OFFICIAL
TO REVOLUTIONARY LEADER

Given a young man who is noble, rich, popular, successful in business, highly placed in government, and happily married, one asks: under what conditions will this man write, work, plan, and conspire to overthrow the very system of government to which he owes his position?

Although Crane Brinton in *The Anatomy of Revolution*[1] did not concentrate on the revolutions which divorced Latin America from the Iberian Peninsula, some of his statements about the nature of revolutions and revolutionists seem to apply in the case of Antonio Nariño, Precursor of Colombian independence.

In the world beyond his native New Granada, this rich creole of Santa Fé was best known and is still known primarily for the daring act of translating, for the first time into Spanish, and printing, in 1794, the New World edition of the French Revolutionary *Declaration of the Rights of Man and the Citizen*. It was this important deed that changed his life dramatically, that threw him, in fact, into the cauldron of revolution. But this was only the beginning of a long and colorful career which cast Nariño in many roles.

Nariño was one of those rare transitional figures who manage to play prominent parts in all the stages of revolution — beginning, middle, and end. He initiated the revolution, he led it, and he helped to consolidate it.

A Man of Action and Ideas

Nariño was a remarkable leader, a man of action and of ideas as well. A lofty and sometimes stubborn idealist, he was not averse to compromise, once convinced of its necessity. He had the mental capacity to analyze defeat and to alter preconceptions when they proved wrong

---

1. Crane Brinton, *The Anatomy of Revolution* (New York, 1938), *passim*.

or inadequate in the reality of experience. Since half his life was spent in exile and at least seventeen years of it in nine or more Spanish jails, he had time to think carefully and plan in seclusion. And somehow he always managed to escape to fight for his supreme vision — a free, independent republic.

The most outstanding aspect of the Precursor's life was its rapid fluctuation. His victories (1812–1813) were tempered with defeat (Pasto, May 11, 1814); his place in high office alternated with long years in jail. His years of acclamation were followed by years of oblivion. His moments of happiness were sharpened by misfortune. Petty enemies slandered and blasphemed him, and dogged his footsteps to the end. When he died in 1823, a few months after his famous speech on the senate floor, he was still trying to guide the republic of Colombia toward wisdom.

The little that is known of Nariño's early life does not indicate that the destiny of a tough, determined, revolutionary leader was being forged. Even the year of his birth is not beyond dispute. Most historians give April 9, 1765, as Nariño's birthday. It is known, however, that a José Antonio Ignacio Vicente Nariño was baptized on March 20, 1760, and married on March 27, 1780.[2] A description given on July 18, 1797, in Santa Fé de Bogotá, to aid in his apprehension, described him as "well-built in body, some freckles on his face, eyes prominent and piercing, skin clear and fair to ruddy in color, mouth small, lips rather thick and blubber-like *(belfo),* speech quiet and mellow and somewhat inclined toward stuttering and stammering; age, thirty-four years."[3]

Nariño was typical of the group of wealthy, educated, creole leaders whose careers flourished under Spanish rule and reached their summit during the revolution and in the early days of the independent republics. Nariño himself, during the Spanish regime, rose to the lucrative,

---

2. Eduardo Posada and Pedro M. Ibáñez, comps., *El Precursor; documentos sobre la vida pública y privada del General Antonio Nariño* (Biblioteca de Historia Nacional, vol. II [Bogotá, 1903]), pp. 2, 3. Baptismal certificate, 1760, taken from book of baptisms of Spaniards of the parish of the cathedral, vol. 26, p. 48 *verso.* Matrimonial record, 1780, archives of the parish of Las Nieves, vol. 2, marriages. April 9, 1765, see appendix of Soledad Acosta de Samper, *Nariño,* Pasto, 1910.

April 9, 1965, marks the official 200th anniversary of Antonio Nariño's birth. But the year of his birth was long a matter of argument. As late as 1902 two Colombian historians said he was born in 1760, and married in 1780. However, that apparent error was explained away in 1910, and April 9, 1765 was reconfirmed as his birthday. In 1958, Dr. Hernández de Alba printed copies of Spanish documents in Madrid and Sevilla, written during Nariño's first trial and imprisonment in 1794 and 1795. These definitely and finally established 1765 as the year of his birth.

3. *Ibid.,* p. 238. Description which was to be observed in the imprisoning of D. Antonio Nariño and D. Pedro Fermín de Vargas, Santa Fé, July 18, 1797. Nariño's actual age at this time was thirty-two years. How accurate the rest of the description is, would be hard to say.

honored posts of royal treasurer of tithes and royal monopolist of the quinine export of New Granada, owner of the official press, and close friend of Viceroy José Ezpeleta. In the Colombian period, Nariño became president (1811), dictator and general (1813), and was briefly presiding vice-president of Colombia, appointed by Simon Bolívar to be in charge of the Congress of Cúcuta (1821). As most Colombian presidents since, he was owner and editor of a newspaper, *La Bagatela,* published from July 14, 1811, to April 12, 1812,[4] and through this publication vaulted into the presidency. He was also the owner of a large library.

The Pre-Revolutionary Society

The career of Nariño points up Brinton's description of the intellectual reaction to conditions prevalent in pre-revolutionary societies. Such conditions were increasing in number and importance in eighteenth-century New Granada.

Some of the more easily recognized symptoms of societies approaching a climax of violent action include fermenting ideas and ideals, increased verbal attempts (written and spoken) to find methods for speeding up the material realization of a better world; economic changes and the subsequent dissatisfaction of the newly rich with the failure of the older aristocracy to accept them; and finally the tendency of the dissatisfied to arouse the lower classes, discontented in their own right, against the establishment. Brinton applied this analysis primarily to the English Revolution of 1640, the French Revolution of 1789, and the Russian Revolution of 1917, and secondarily, with less correlation, to the American Revolution of 1776.[5] The same analysis could be applied to Antonio Nariño's revolt against Spain.

On July 23, 1789, Nariño was recommended for the post of treasurer of the tithes by Viceroy José Ezpeleta.[6] During the years of

---

4. Antonio Nariño, *La Bagatela* (reprinted in Biblioteca Popular de Cultura Colombiana, vol. CXII [Bogotá, 1947]).

5. Brinton, *op. cit.,* p. 63.

6. Posada and Ibáñez, *El Precursor,* pp. 3–16. Notarized testimony and deposition of the cathedral chapter and official minutes of the venerable *cabildo* of Santa Fé concerning the nomination made by his excellency the viceroy of Don Antonio Nariño to the post of treasurer of tithes and communications of the viceroy to the *cabildo* and documented certification of the aforesaid *cabildo,* etc., July 23, 1789, July 27, 1789, August 3, 1789, August 7, 1789, August 8, 1789, August 9, 1789. Also similar letters to Viceroy Josef *(sic)* de Ezpeleta, countersigned and receipted by Licenciado Castillo, Madrid, September 12, 1780, and Madrid, October 5, 1780, specifying the right of the cathedral chapter to make the appointment to treasurer of the tithes without previous presentation to the president and *audiencia* in Santa Fé. Also reply of José de Ezpeleta to the venerable dean and *cabildo* of the Holy Metropolitan Church dated Santa Fé, August 12, 1789, basing his nomination of Nariño to the post of treasurer of tithes upon similar nominations of his immediate predecessor in the viceroyalty.

Nariño's growth to manhood and responsible public office, Spain had been making extensive changes in the social, economic, and political structure of her American empire: the Jesuits had been expelled in 1767, modified "free trade" was adopted for the colonies in 1778; and the French intendancy system was superimposed upon the viceregal organization after 1765.[7]

Primarily intended to keep the Spanish empire abreast of the trend of "enlightened" European monarchies, these reforms were reported by the viceroys in their official "Relaciones de Mando."[8] Other changes and reforms, lesser known but more subtly important, were carried out in Latin America by Viceroy José de Solis and Viceroy Pedro Messia de la Cerda, according to a predetermined policy. Roads, bridges, hospitals, and missions were constructed. The first systematic census was taken. A commission was created to plan and divide up the work. A budget and plans were set up to aid the production of tobacco, cocoa, and cotton. Taxes on these items would bring in revenue to replace the large tax income from the over-used and dangerous *aguardiente de caña* (rum).[9] Recommendations were made for the development of an Atrato River canal at sea level from the Atlantic to the Pacific.[10]

On all sides, there were many such improvements in business and

---

7. J. M. Henao and Gerardo Arrubla, *History of Colombia,* trans. by J. Fred Rippy (Chapel Hill, 1938), pp. 143–145. Clarence H. Haring, *The Spanish Empire in America* (New York, 1947), pp. 340–345. Herbert L. Priestley, *José de Galvez, Visitor-General of New Spain, 1765–1771* (Berkeley, 1916), *passim.*

8. Eduardo Posada and Pedro M. Ibáñez, comps., *Relaciones de mando* (Biblioteca de Historia Nacional, vol. VIII [Bogotá, 1910]).

9. *Ibid.,* p. 95. Between 1564 and 1718, seventeen persons commanded the presidency of New Granada. In 1718 it was decided to raise New Granada to the status of viceroyalty. After three false starts in as many years, New Granada reverted to a presidency for the years 1722–1740 but the viceroyalty again replaced the presidency in 1740 and operated with a few gaps during the revolution until 1818.

Of the seventeen viceroys who ruled New Granada in the two epochs of its existence, only seven carried out their legal obligation of writing a report for the guidance of their successor. Those who failed in their duty to make a report were usually too busy fighting in defense of their realm against civil war, English sea attacks and finally against the leaders of independence movements. The following viceroys reported in the years indicated:

Don José de Solís to Don Pedro Megía de la Zerda, 1760.
Don Pedro Messía de la Cerda to Don Manuel Guirior, 1772.
Don Manuel de Guirior to Don Manuel Antonio Flores, 1776.
Archbishop Antonio de Córdova to Don Francisco Gil y Lemus, 1789.
Don José de Ezpeleta to Don Pedro Mendinueta, 1796.
Don Pedro Mendinueta to Don Antonio Amar y Borbón, 1803.
Don Francisco de Montalvo to Don Juan de Sámano, 1818.

The longest and most complete report was that of Viceroy Ezpeleta. See also the original *Relaciones de los vireyes del Nuevo Reino de Granada* of José Antonio García y García (New York, 1869).

10. Posada and Ibáñez, *Relaciones de mando,* p. 106.

government, pointing up the paradox that both the *Comunero* revolt of the masses in 1781, and the independence movement of the classes took place in an era of accelerating change for the better. Not only was there help for business, agriculture, and highways, gold mining in the Atrato River area was increasing, the population was growing, and education was on the move. But war with England, in 1779, brought not only higher taxes, but also familiar curtailment of civilian improvements and channeling of expenditures to the activities of a nation at war. Money earmarked for highways, merchant ships, schools, and hospitals went instead to fortifications, cruisers, militia companies, and generals' and admirals' salaries.[11] Murmurs were heard in the capital against rising prices and taxes, but at the same time the viceregal guard roster was unaccountably diminished "until it comprised a ridiculously small handful of fifteen or twenty old men who scarcely knew how to raise a halberd."[12] Tax collectors, customarily dishonest, became tactless and ruthless as well, stirring up an angry flood of lampooners who printed anonymous criticisms and threats inciting the mob to open revolt.[13]

Reform as the Cause of Revolt

The conscientious administrations of Viceroys Manuel Guirior and Manuel Antonio Flores, though part of a continuous improvement in colonial government in New Granada, were indirectly the cause of the *Comunero* revolt. Taxes on tobacco and *aguardiente* were not appreciably increased, but they were for the first time efficiently collected, and the masses revolted in consequence.

Unfortunately, neither Viceroy Flores nor Visitador José Piñeres made an official *Relación* of the critical period of *Comunero* revolt. But their successor, Archbishop and Viceroy Don Antonio Caballero y Góngora played a major role in suppressing the revolt, and wrote a full *Relación* in 1789, emphasizing that more efficient collection of old taxes had aroused the masses. Although the mob shouted "death to bad government and long live the king," ironically, it was not bad government, but the meticulous consciences of enlightened viceroys that had brought distress.[14] The addition of one new tax simply served as hair-trigger to set off the riot.

---

11. *Ibid.,* pp. 199–205.

12. *Ibid.,* p. 205.

13. Raimundo Rivas, *El andante caballero Don Antonio Nariño; la juventud (1765–1803)* (Biblioteca de Historia Nacional, vol. L [Bogotá, 1936], p. 33.

14. Eduardo Posada and Pedro M. Ibáñez, *Los Comuneros* (Biblioteca de Historia Nacional, vol. IV [Bogotá, 1905]), *passim.* See also *Briceño* for documents.

It is not entirely clear what part Antonio Nariño played in the *Comunero* revolt. The Archbishop spoke confidently in his *Relación* of highly placed persons within the capital directly the revolting masses in Socorro.[15] Certainly the anonymous ridicule and criticism of the government in the "pasquines" which preceded the actual revolt of 1781 closely resemble the "pasquines" that were contemporary with Nariño's publication of the *Rights of Man and the Citizen* which accompanied the abortive revolution of 1794. It also appears that the young creole requested permission to resign his commission as second lieutenant in the city militia after witnessing the brutal hanging and quartering of the *Comunero* leaders. These men had quietly disbanded their victorious armies following the sacred oath of the archbishop, given to them at a special High Mass, and promising that *Comunero* requests for lower taxes and an end to government monopolies would be immediately granted.[16]

The thirteen years between the *Comunero* revolt of 1781 and Nariño's printing of the *Rights of Man and the Citizen* in 1793 were prosperous ones for New Granada and for Nariño. Under Viceroy Ezpeleta (1789–1797), friend and patron of Nariño and of the Enlightenment, schools were improved and secularized; a school for girls was established; Buffon and Linnaeus were taught for the first time; epidemics of smallpox were reduced by the first cowpox vaccination;[17] the Atrato River gold fields were opened to direct navigation to Europe, and the government sponsored the first local periodical, the *Papel periódico de la Ciudad de Santa Fé de Bogotá* which was almost entirely devoted to spreading the most advanced ideas of the Enlightenment.[18]

The Cells of Revolution

The introduction of a printing press, the building of a new theater, the encouragement of the new learning, new ideas, and new hopes all fostered a desire for fewer restrictions, more improvements, and faster evolution of reform — in a word, revolution. The leaders who were to organize the revolution had, besides a theater and a printing press, a

---

15. Posada and Ibáñez, *Relaciones de mando,* p. 205.

16. Rivas, *El andante caballero,* p. 33. Also *El Tiempo,* July 8, 1962, article by Juan Friede, proves Archbishop a trickster who never intended to keep his word to the leaders.

17. Posada and Ibáñez, *Relaciones de mando,* pp. 332–337.

18. Gustavo Otero Muñoz, *Historia del periodismo en Colombia* (Bogotá, 1936), pp. 14–19.

medium for organizing and propagating their plans — the *tertulia.*[19]

The potential revolutionary cells, the *tertulias,* were usually social gatherings somewhat comparable to French "salons." They had as their objective the improvement of literature, agriculture, industry, or just *buen gusto* (good taste). Besides wishing to improve "Man" in his varied aspects — the sooner the better — they wished to express their ideas in print. Thus freedom of the press became an absolute necessity in a fast-changing world, something to fight for if necessary. If a *tertulia* was one aspect of growing organization, the printed journal proved another. In fact, each journal was usually the printed voice of a particular *tertulia.* It is thus not surprising to find that Nariño, once in a high position of authority as treasurer of the tithes and monopolist of the quinine export, was also leader of a *tertulia* and owner of a press called the *Imprenta Patriótica,* authorized by the viceroy to print the *Papel periódico* for the Eutropélica *tertulia* of Manuel Socorro Rodríguez. This press took over the printing of the *Papel periódico* beginning with the eighty-sixth weekly issue, April 19, 1793.[20]

The Eutropélica *tertulia,* operating openly as to members and purpose, included many men who were to be leading revolutionists in the wars of independence, but who were known chiefly at this time as outstanding scientists. Dr. José Celestino Mutis was one of the most prominent members.[21]

About 1789, an open *tertulia,* known as the Casino and having a somewhat different character, began to meet in the home of Nariño. Prominent among the members was a recently arrived Frenchman, Luis de Rieux, who helped to set up an inner or secret *tertulia* called "El Santuario."[22] The purpose of the Casino was "to establish in this city a club of learned men following the example of some of those they have in the casinos of Venice which include the following purposes: the members meet in a comfortable room, and having read published papers, they spend the rest of the evening in searching for the best newspapers, foreign gazettes, encyclopaedic periodicals and other publications of this sort, as the members may decide. At predetermined hours they will get together, read to each other, criticize each other's papers and converse

---

19. José M. Vergara y Vergara, *La historia de la literatura en Nueva Granada* (2 vols., Bogotá, 1931).

20. Eduardo Posada, *Bibliografía bogotana* (Biblioteca de Historia Nacional, vol. XVI [Bogotá, 1917]), p. 17.

21. Otero Muñoz, *Historia del periodismo,* p. 18.

22. Rivas, *El andante caballero,* p. 39.

about other authors. In this fashion they can pass a few hours well-entertained and with self-improvement."[23] Descriptions of the first ten young men to join Nariño's society show them to be most unlikely candidates for two-hour armchair sessions. Seven were bachelors, six were nobles, and only three of the ten were over thirty.[24] In all, they seemed more fitted to fight a revolution against Spain than to read papers, and indeed that is what they were planning behind the camouflage of a learned society.

Two of Nariño's inner group were ardent admirers of the French Revolution, perhaps Masons and apparently anti-church.[25] These two, Luis de Rieux and Don Pedro Fermín de Vargas from the old *Comunero* center of San Gil, were apparently on good terms with Viceroy Ezpeleta, who, like many eighteenth-century Spanish officials, was lax in suppressing the entry of forbidden books which soon began to pile up in great numbers at Dr. Rieux's hacienda of "La Egipciaca" in La Honda, and at Nariño's home in the capital. While talking openly of the plays of Racine, the members secretly admired the French Revolution and laid plans to imitate it through their inner organization called "El Santuario." Part of the plan called for the creation of an independent republic of New Granada.[26]

Within the membership of "El Santuario" there was established an even more secret society called "Arcano Sublíme de la Filantropía" whose constitution was carefully locked up in the desk of Nariño's friend and relative, Dr. José Antonio Ricaurte. This group clustered around two axial units designated as "power" and "wealth." Its three leaders — director, censor, and warden — directed members who never even knew each other but knew only the leader to whom they were responsible and swore blind obedience. Also members swore blind obedience directly to the cause which, though never stated, was probably independence.[27] The principal cell in the capital had the sole right of establishing subsidiary cells of the "Arcano Sublíme" in provincial cities of the vice-royalty. The members were to understand that they must maintain the most absolute secrecy about the real purpose of the society which was different from the advertised purpose. Nariño's *tertulia* was also to serve as meeting place for like-minded foreigners, such as the Quiteño, Francisco Eugenio de Santa Cruz y Espejo, who suggested a coordinated revolution to establish the independence of the whole continent as outlined in an "Escuela de Concordia."

23. Posada and Ibáñez, *El Precursor,* p. 17.
24. *Ibid.,* p. 119.
25. Rivas, *El andante caballero,* pp. 86–87.
26. *Ibid.,* pp. 88–91.
27. *Ibid.,* pp. 92–93.

The Decision to Print

It was apparently in the latter part of 1793, while the French Revolution was approaching the bloody climax of the Terror, that Nariño decided on the daring and perhaps foolhardy plan of committing his revolutionary plans to print by translating and publishing a copy of the French *Declaration of the Rights of Man and the Citizen.* Up to this point, the enlightened viceroy had been on the best of terms with his collector of tithes, and had apparently permitted the importation of forbidden books — perhaps so he could read them himself. But to put such anti-royalist ideas in print was another matter and could not be ignored. The printing of the incendiary document was a turning point, in the life of both Nariño and Spanish America. It therefore deserves minute inspection.

Just as one sees in Nariño the phenomenon which Brinton calls "the desertion of the intellectual,"[28] Ezpeleta seems to fit the pattern of the enlightened but uncertain ruling-class official who alternated between attempts at reform from above and suppression by force of revolts emanating from below. Ezpeleta not only permitted Nariño to collect a vast library of "heretical" and "revolutionary" books, he further aided the cause of republicanism, independence, and revolution by permitting his captain of the guard, Cayetano Ramírez de Arellano, to read and pass on to Nariño the third volume of Salart de Montjoie's Paris edition of the *History of the Constitutional Assembly.*[29] Here Nariño found that most concise statement of the natural right of man to equal justice, liberty, and property, and the right to upset any government unable or unwilling to support its citizens in these matters. The famous document is conveniently brief, occupying only two and one-half printed pages in Eduardo Posada's *El Precursor,* and it was its very briefness that inspired Nariño to attempt to print and distribute three or four hundred copies among his friends and fellow revolutionaries.

Neither Nariño's specific purpose in printing the statement, nor the precise circumstances of the printing are entirely clear. José Manuel Pérez Sarmiento has gathered together seventy-four documents from the Archives of the Indies at Seville, covering the judicial records of the lawsuit initiated against Nariño during the years 1794–1807.[30] From these and other sources emerges a picture of what actually happened on which writers generally agree.

Having read the *Rights of Man and the Citizen,* Nariño withdrew to his inner study, the "Santuario," to translate it into Spanish. He knew that both the Supreme Council of the Indies and the Tribunal of the

---

28. Brinton, op. cit., pp. 52–63.
29. Rivas, *El andante caballero,* pp. 97–98.
30. José Manuel Pérez Sarmiento, ed., *Proceso de Nariño* (Cádiz, 1914), p. 19.

Inquisition of Cartagena had prohibited reading of the document and had ordered its destruction if found in New Granada. But, having translated the *Rights of Man and the Citizen,* Nariño proceeded to print about one hundred copies of it on his press, "La Patriótica," the same press which printed the government-sponsored *Papel periódico.* His instructions for buying paper indicate that he had intended to print five hundred copies.[31] The printer, Don Diego Espinosa de los Monteros, would give no trouble for two reasons; he was a young and enthusiastic admirer of the republican, Nariño; second, most of his pay came directly from Nariño's personal funds.

All was quiet in the printing office during an early Sunday morning late in December, 1793. An Indian boy had brought the paper, and Don Antonio was quieting the qualms of the easily convinced Espinosa. He argued first that he, Nariño, would be solely responsible and, second, that as owner of the government press he could print anything without previous censorship if it were not more than one page, quarto fold.[32]

When the translation was finished, the two aristocratic printers added, on page four, comments in praise of the French doctrine, and finished the whole in the same elegant style used for viceregal documents — expensive paper, good ink, broad margins — truly a work of art. All but two of the copies of this priceless document were destroyed and those treasures have not yet been found! Eduardo Posada gives Nariño's testimony in full in his *defensa,* in which he explains how he sold one copy, gave one away, and burned the rest when he discovered that their possession might cost him his life.[33]

Why the projected four or five hundred copies were not printed on that fateful Sunday can easily be understood from a glimpse of the primitive handpress with which the revolutionaries did their work.[34] It may also be true that the printers had decided that the planned revolution would break out successfully before the government could start a lawsuit or take other action to silence the press.[35] In this they were mistaken. Their action was to lead to endless lawsuits, jailings, and martyrdoms. Their dream of revolution and independence was realized only after a generation of bloodshed.

---

31. Rivas, *El andante caballero,* p. 100.
32. *Ibid.,* p. 101.
33. Posada and Ibáñez, *El Precursor,* p. 95. José Toribio Medina accepts this testimony as true, basing his reasoning on the failure of all *pesquisas* of the Holy Office in their attempts to locate a copy. (José Toribío Medina, *La imprenta en Bogotá* [Santiago de Chile, 1904], p. 45.)
34. Pérez Sarmiento, *Proceso de Nariño,* p. 72.
35. Rivas, *El andante caballero,* p. 102.

CHAPTER II

THE LIBRARY OF
A REVOLUTIONARY LEADER
The Enlightenment On Trial

The long-drawn-out trial resulting from the printing of the *Rights of Man* marks the turning point in Nariño's life. Until 1794, he had been a high-ranking royal official. After 1794, he was almost continuously the revolutionary, always suspect, and usually under surveillance when not actually in jail or beyond the reach of Spanish power.

Nariño's library of two thousand books[1] played a major role in converting the wealthy creole from a royal official into a revolutionary republican leader. Through his library, Nariño acquired much of the learning of the eighteenth-century Enlightenment, a critical attitude toward the Spanish empire, a burning desire to speed up the process of reform already under way in the dominions of Spain, and an unbounded admiration for the United States and republican France. The vast number of Nariño's books on the condemned lists of both the Roman *Index* and the Spanish *Indice* increase the mass of evidence for two important facts: (1) Spanish censorship in 1794 was extremely weak; and (2) the books and ideas easily available to Nariño were in the vanguard of every field of learning, ranging from Montesquieu, Voltaire, Diderot, Mably, Raynal, and Destutt de Tracy, to the *Koran,* the *Bible,* Milton, Franklin, Linnaeus, and Buffon, among many others.

The library was truly "catholic" in that it was universal, heterodox, heretical, and hence "damnable" in the very literal sense of the word employed by the Inquisition. It is worthy of consideration for three

---

1. Posada and Ibáñez, *El Precursor,* pp. 164–190. Documents listing properties and books of Nariño confiscated by court action between August 29, 1794, and September 3, 1794.

reasons. First, the ideas contained in his library led Nariño into revolutionary thought and action. Second, when no copies of the translation of the *Rights of Man* could be found, the discovery by the Inquisition of the physical existence of Nariño's library was used to prove his guilt. Third, the ideas contained in his library of books provided the source for Nariño's brilliant defense of himself which became so exasperating to his prosecutors that they not only condemned all printed copies, but ordered them burned by the public hangman along with the book from which Nariño had copied the *Rights of Man*.[2]

Hiding the Traces

When Nariño discovered that his printing of the *Rights of Man* was going to get him into trouble, he proceeded as soon as possible to hide all traces of his boldness. He was completely successful in destroying copies of the *Rights of Man*,[3] but in destroying his immense and valuable library of forbidden books, he was less thorough. His first step was to separate those works most likely to indicate the subversive nature of his republican and revolutionary sympathies. These he placed in trunks and shipped out to his brother's place, "La Serrezuela."[4] In the middle of the night, his brother became frightened and, with the aid of a friendly priest named Gijón, transferred the books to an empty cell in the Capuchin monastery. There the spies of the Inquisition[5] located the books — still damp from having been immersed in water somewhere — and proceeded to identify the real owner, Antonio Nariño.[6]

In spite of missing title pages, the examiners began to identify some of the books, and to trace their provenance. Among the books in French were titles by such condemned authors as Jacques Necker, Montesquieu, William Robertson, Louis de Montalte, Voltaire, Diderot, d'Alembert,

---

2. *Ibid.,* p. 621. Document contained in the November 25, 1799, report to Don Mariano Luis de Urquijo and the Council of the Indies by the *audiencia* of Santa Fé relative to the case of Don Antonio Nariño and Don José Antonio Ricaurte.

3. *Ibid.,* p. 95.

4. *Ibid.,* pp. 152–154. The servant, Ildefonso Rico, on being questioned about the trunks he had helped to move, told his questioners that he had been informed that the trunks were heavy because they contained "unos quesos" — some cheeses!

5. *Ibid.,* pp. 62, 146. See also José Toribio Medina, *Historia del Tribunal del Santo Oficio de Cartagena de las Indias* (Santiago, Chile, 1899), p. 387, (Hereinafter Medina, *Historia del Tribunal*.)

6. Posada and Ibáñez, *El Precursor,* pp. 143–150. Document containing the report of *Oidor* Mosquera on hearings held September 13 and 14, 1794, in the Convent of the Capuchins, Santa Fé de Bogotá, and on September 20, 1794, in the courtroom of the *audiencia* and royal chancellery, Santa Fé de Bogotá.

Raynal, Jean Berruyer,[7] Destutt de Tracy,[8] and Mably.[9] Rousseau was significantly missing, probably destroyed, for Nariño in his defense showed great familiarity with Rousseau and could quote passages verbatim from Foranda's version of the *Social Contract*.[10]

After the government investigators and the Inquisition[11] had listed the seventy-eight[12] volumes of Nariño's choice collection of condemned books, they confiscated all of his properties and proceeded to draw up a list of books found in his home. This tremendous compilation[13] included many anonymous and unknown authors not specifically named either in the Spanish *Indice*[14] or the Roman *Index*.[15] Many of these, however, because of anonymity or heterodoxy, were automatically suspect by reason of title or similarity to some of the most violently condemned works of the Enlightenment.[16]

---

7. *Indice último de los libros prohibidos y mandadoes expurgar* (Madrid, 1790), p. 291. (Hereinafter *Indice último.*)Not all books in the Spanish *Indice* of 1790 are condemned in the Roman *Index* of 1786. Conversely, not all books in the Roman *Index* are condemned in the Spanish *Indice*. It should also be noted that while some authors, Voltaire for instance, were to be condemned for everything they wrote, others were placed on the list for only particular volumes. Many books were condemned "donec corregiatur" and new editions of the expurgated works could be approved. (*Index Librorum Prohibitorum* [Rome, 1786], pp. 185, 233, 219, 279, 88, 133, 134.)

8. *Indice último,* suplemento de 1805, p. 291.

9. *Ibid.*

10. J. R. Spell, *Rousseau in the Spanish World before 1833* (Austin, Texas, 1938), p. 226.

11. An Inquisitorial document from the Inquisition of Cartagena de las Indies, dated November 20, 1794, includes a receipt given to Luis de Mendoza, president of the royal *audiencia* in Santa Fé, for information on "the prohibited books belonging to Don Antonio Nariño." Cf. Posada and Ibáñez, *El Precursor,* pp. 157–158.

12. Seventy-eight was the total named by the Inquisitors, but an actual count of their list indicates a total of eighty-five. (*Ibid.,* pp. 144, 147–150.)

13. The Inquisition listed volumes found, the author (when known), and, in some cases, a few descriptive phrases. (*Ibid.,* pp. 164, 190.) Roland D. Hussey, "Traces of French Enlightenment in Colonial Hispanic America," in A. P. Whitaker, ed., *Latin America and the Enlightenment* [New York, 1942], p. 42.)

E. Taylor Parks and Roberto Liévano claim Nariño had six thousand volumes in his library, but since they give no clue as to their method of obtaining this figure, it seems that the actual list of two thousand is more nearly accurate. (E. Taylor Parks, *Colombia and the United States, 1765–1935* [Durham, N. C., 1935], p. 27. Roberto Liévano, *Viejas estampas* [Bogotá, 1948], p. 8.)

14. *Indice ultimo.*

15. *Index Librorum Prohibitorum.*

16. Anonymous books, called Class III, had been forbidden ever since the edict of 1559 of Paul IV and the Tridentine *Index* of 1564. (*Indice último,* introduction, p. xii.)

Sermons in English by English "padres,"[17] dictionaries of "heresies,"[18] and titles concerning suspect or damnable words and phrases such as "Reason,"[19] "Nature,"[20] "Natural Law,"[21] and "essential order of Nature,"[22] apologies for Spain,[23] paraphrastic manuals, customs of the Israelites, Arabs and Turks,[24] to say nothing of the heretical English — all these were found, in addition to better-known condemned works of Mably, Milton, and Voltaire.[25] They were not of a type which would help Nariño get out of jail.

Last Stand of the Inquisition

The statements of his enemies against him, and the words of Nariño himself,[26] in his fight for Colombian liberty and the rights of man against Spanish monarchy, despotism, and intolerance — all indicate that a last desperate effort was being made after 1789 to use the Inquisition and the *Index* to quell revolution set in motion by the Enlightenment. The *Indice* of 1790 made a hasty gesture to include in its appendices some of the more prominent works assumed to have been instrumental in stirring up revolution in France. In a similar fashion they might generate revolution in Spanish America.[27]

Because Nariño's defense was saturated with quotations from J. Carli,[28] Antonio Capmany,[29] and many enlightened Madrid, Santa Fé,

---

17. Many titles not included in the Madrid *Indice* of 1790 were nevertheless condemned in the New Word by local edict, including English "sermons" as Dr. Dorothy Schons indicates in her *Book Censorship in New Spain* (Austin, Texas, 1950), p. lx, in which she disagrees with J. T. Medina.

18. Posada and Ibáñez, *El Precursor*, p. 167. Liguori was the author.

19. *Ibid.*, p. 172. French title, "Lève de la Raison."

20. *Ibid.*, pp. 186–187. Boyle's *Introduction to Natural History* and Almeida's *Contemplation of Nature*.

21. *Ibid.*, p. 176. *Natural Law* and *Politica Natural*.

22. *Ibid.*, p. 173. By Antonio Pérez y López.

23. *Ibid.*, p. 176. By Juan Pablo Fornet.

24. *Ibid.*, pp. 169, 174. By Padre Ricardo Balsolobre and Felipe de Serf. One of these, Balsolobre's, was a manual of service for the dead, for those who do not believe in the doctrine of Original Sin.

25. In the 1790 *Indice*, Milton is classed "I" (very damnable). See p. 182. All of Voltaire was condemned (p. 279) and even forbidden to Catholic scholars granted dispensation in order to refute heresy.

26. Pérez Sarmiento, *Proceso de Nariño*, pp. 33–153, 89–145.

27. *Ibid.*, p. 77. Nariño quotes Cayetano Filangieri, *Ciencia de legislación*, which was condemned in the *Indice último*, p. 295.

28. Pérez Sarmiento, *Proceso de Nariño*, p. 113.

29. *Ibid.*, pp. 104, 117. Periodicals quoted by Nariño, pp. 100, 101, 113.

and Lima periodicals, there was also a considerable effort made to prevent printed copies from being distributed to restless, inflammable Latin Americans. In fact, Nariño's judges in special secret session of the *audiencia* urged the home government to be on the lookout for printed copies of the defense, which they considered far more perniciously subversive of the empire than the works included in the appendices of the *Indice,* for the Precursor shrewdly quoted non-condemned books to support revolutionary ideas of the rights of man.[30] It was therefore necessary not only to shut up Nariño and his ideas in jail, along with his defense lawyer, Dr. José Ricaurte, but it was also vitally important to get the Inquisition and the *Index* to add their support to the collapsing Spanish empire as quickly as possible. This was accomplished.

In May of 1795, fifteen months after Nariño had burned the last copy of the *Rights of Man,* the Inquisition in Cartagena put his translation under ban by special edict.[31] The Cartagena Inquisition had already damned the original declaration in the year of its issue, 1789.[32] In order to plug other gaps uncovered by the defense, Nariño's prosecutors issued a special plea to condemn specifically, and *in toto,* two books which Nariño had often quoted in his defense: Capmany's *Philosophy of Eloquence* and Carli's *American Letters.* At the time the library had been confiscated, these books had been listed without comment.[33] Needless to say, Nariño's additional references to such well-known condemned works as the *Encyclopedia*[34] confirmed the prosecutors in their belief that his quoting undamned books merely proved the old saying that the Devil himself could quote Scripture. Nariño they considered a devil and very "poisonous."[35]

Nariño's Defense

An analysis of Nariño's shrewd defense makes it clear why his prosecutors considered it a more dangerous doctrine than the *Rights*

---

30. *Ibid.,* pp. 80, 81–89.

31. *Ibid.,* pp. 39, 66.

32. *Ibid.,* pp. 33, 153. Cf. Medina, *Historia del Tribunal,* p. 387. "Since the first ban of 1789 had no effect, Viceroy Ezpeleta sent out on September 5, 1794, a secret *Oficio* to the Cartagena Tribunal stating that the object of this printed work was to seduce simple and incautious persons with pretenses of favoring liberty of religion, and disturbing the good order and government established in the dominion of your majesty ... to which the Inquisitor, Marianna y Zafrilla, heartily agreed in a letter of September 22, 1794, and said he would do all in his power to find and destroy the damned, pernicious book."

33. Pérez Sarmiento, *Proceso de Nariño,* p. 28.

34. *Ibid.,* p. 77.

35. *Ibid.,* p. 81.

of Man[36] and why it was to cost his lawyer, Ricaurte, a slow death by ten years of incarceration.[37] The principal argument throughout was that· the ideas contained in the *Rights of Man* could be found in all sorts of acceptable books and magazines circulating both in Spain and in the colonies.[38] His brief is so shrewdly planned and so clearly indicative of an amazing mastery of the main ideas of the Enlightenment gleaned from his vast library, that it is worthwhile to follow the thread of Nariño's argument in some detail. If proof were needed that the same Enlightenment which bred "Philosopher Princes" also bred "Revolutionary Republicans," one could scarcely find better evidence than in Nariño's defense. For example:

... in *El periódico de Santa Fé,* which circulated widely in the hands of the people, one can read horrible sketches concerning the present French Revolution, and, reasoning as my accusers do ... one could thus become an enthusiastic libertine. . . . Or take the GAZETAS of Spain and do the same. . . . If one can be so easily corrupted by reading about the actions of the National Assembly of France, it would be like saying one could be seduced from the truths of our HOLY RELIGION by the stupid expressions in the Koran. . . . Or take EL ESPIRITU DE LOS MEJORES DIARIOS[39] published in Madrid, found here everywhere in the hands of children and women ... approved by our monarchs who were initial subscribers to it as were also the Chief Ministers of the nation, and in Diary Number 156, Page 615, we find "MAN IS BORN FREE ... as soon as he reaches maturity and reason, he is entitled to choose his country, and entitled to choose the government which best suits him and his ideas. . . . If he has sacrificed a part of his liberty to government, it is to better his lot, and the most important truth to remember is that the rights of prop-

---

36. *Ibid.,* pp. 85, 89. "La censura que merece esta detestable obra se presenta visible en su lectura." The four judges sitting in session on September 19, 1795, indicated their further annoyance with the accused Nariño by stating that he had the temerity to "condemn the cruelty of the conquistadores, calling them assassins. He said they enslaved the natives, oppressed them, tyrannized them, bled them with horrible taxes like the *alcabala* ... whereas it is well known that the proper attitude of loyal subjects is *blind obedience* to our superiors, the only fitting attitude for your majesty's subjects.'"

37. Gonzalo Bulnes, *Nacimiento de las repúblicas americanas* (2 vols., Buenos Aires, 1927), I, 13, misleads the reader by stating that Ricaurte was freed by royal clemency in 1804 after having been jailed at the time of Nariño's return in April, 1797. Technically, this statement is true. However, it is misleading inasmuch as the prisoner died before the order to release him arrived in Cartagena. Ricaurte was not jailed originally because of any crime for which he had been tried and sentenced, but because of the "general principle" that his ideas were subversive. (Pérez Sarmiento, *Proceso de Nariño,* pp. 66–73.)

38. Pérez Sarmiento, *Proceso de Nariño,* p. 99.

39. Spell, *op. cit.,* pp. 115, 144, indicates that Floridablanca, a frightened liberal in 1792, had already reversed himself and quickly suppressed the *Espíritu,* which he had originally so eagerly sponsored a scant three years previously. Nariño was therefore treading on very sore toes.

erty, liberty, and security are the strongest suppors of the well-being of all states. . . . The monarch has no right to disregard the laws in a fit of anger, superstition or tyranny."[40]

Such words must have exasperated the viceroy and Nariño's accusers, for all had been educated in the intellectual climate of the Enlightenment, and all had subscribed with enthusiasm to its revolutionary ideas only a few years or months before Nariño's arrest. To prove this true, and that some of them had committed their ideas to print, Nariño quoted from the 1785 doctoral dissertation of one of his prosecutors, Fiscal Manuel Blaya.[41] This dissertation, entitled "Means of Promoting More Marriages and of Increasing the Population of Europe," had as its main thesis that men would not willingly marry and beget children when they knew their children would inherit a miserable life of slavery in the unreformed, tyrannical, despotic, and irrational monarchies of that day (1785). This shrewd demonstration that his enemies had earlier subscribed to the then liberal, now subversive doctrines of the Enlightment, was hardly calculated to win friends for Nariño, but does not seem to have deterred him from his course.

He went right on embarrassing the erstwhile "liberals." Quoting from number 155 of the *Espíritu de los mejores diarios,* he says:

The creator of the world, having made *all men equal,* it is to their own interests to consult and realize their mutual happiness as individuals of one family, however much they may differ in color and in other things of little import, not essential and founded on whims of chance. Persons who profess to maintain for their own good the Rights of Mankind and of all living persons subject to the obligations of Christianity, must neglect nothing to help all to enjoy the delights of liberty and in particular to aid our fellow beings who have a right to them by the laws and Constitution of the United States, and who now chafe in irons of the most severe slavery. . . . Firmly convinced of the truth of these principles, animated with the desire to spread them to all parts of the world wherever the calamities of oppression reign, and filled with the greatest confidence in the favor and protection of the Universal Father, the subscribers of this society have joined together in Philadelphia to promote the abolition of slavery.[42]

---

40. Pérez Sarmiento, *Proceso de Nariño,* pp. 100, 101.

41. *Ibid.,* pp. 76–80. *Documento* Number 26 in the *Proceso* seems to have called forth an explanation from Blaya who, plaintively hastened to justify his dissertation as the "indiscretions of a young law student at the Academy of Saint Barbara." (p. 76.) He seems to have been alternately angered, annoyed, and worried at his youthful peccadillo, and stated that he thought allowance should be made for the dissertation as the work of a "muchacho que estava entonces aprendiendo." (p. 77.)

42. *Ibid.,* pp. 102–103.

Exasperation of the Judges

No matter that Nariño had found them imbedded in accepted Spanish periodicals, sponsored by the king himself, such subversive ideas as Nariño quoted were scarcely apt to be palatable to a harassed Spanish viceroy, even a reputed liberal such as Ezpeleta. No more acceptable were similar ideas from the expurgated edition of the international legist Heineccius[43] concerning the "Natural Equality of Man," or for that matter, Saint Thomas Aquinas. A partially expurgated work such as Heineccius was automatically suspect, and even in faraway Santa Fé, it must have been common knowledge that the *Encyclopaedia* was almost as damnable and devilish as Voltaire. Such publications were relisted clearly and condemned *in toto* in the new *Indice* of 1790.[44] Since Aquinas was not condemned, it was unforgivable for Nariño to quote passages and phrases reminiscent of Voltaire and Diderot from the Angelic Doctor.

As for Antonio Capmany's *Philosophy of Eloquence,* so subversive it was considered, and so angry did it make Nariño's judges that they secretly requested that the Inquisition issue a special edict condemning both it and Carli.[45] This work also was quoted by Nariño to support his main thesis that revolutionary republican ideas like those of the *Rights of Man* were to be found everywhere in acceptable books read by every educated person. Capmany said: "No man has received from nature the right to command any other; liberty is the gift of heaven and each man has the right to enjoy it starting from the moment when he can use reason." And in a similar vein Nariño quotes, "It seems also according to Heineccius that the power of kings emanates from the people and Heineccius is the legist we are ordered to follow in our schools."[46]

In order to estimate the full exasperation of Nariño's judges, when, like Blaya, they found their own words quoted to show that they had once thought and written like the accused, it is well to remember that events in France, from 1789 to 1794, had aroused fear, and a rapid

---

43. *Indice último,* p. 120. Hugo Grotius, the "Father of International Law," was condemned by name and all his works were condemned specifically by title. It is therefore not surprising to find that some lesser known commentator like Heineccius was similarly suspect. The Roman *Index* of 1786 lists and condemns by title seven works of Grotius (p. 127) and all of the works of Pufendorf (p. 235).

44. *Indice último,* pp. 9, 248. (Aeneas Seneca was also condemned by name and *in toto.*)

45. Pérez Sarmiento, *Proceso de Nariño,* p. 28.

46. *Ibid.,* pp. 104–105.

retreat from liberalism and reform in Spain. The small but influential clique of liberals (who had joined Aranda after 1765 in the formation of the Royal Basque Society of Friends of the Country) [47] found themselves in disagreement as to how far they should retreat from their old liberalism and reformist plans in these hectic years. The Basque reformers who had so recently (1767), succeeded in ousting the powerful organization of their famous antecedent, Ignatius Loyola, now felt called upon to revive the Inquisition, although Aranda had once boasted that, except for his indiscretion in mentioning his hopes to Voltaire,[48] he would have ousted it, along with the Jesuits. By the time Nariño was quoting from books and periodicals (sponsored by the crown itself for a third of a century), the Basque Society clique had been replaced by Godoy.[49] Aranda's brief return to power, in 1792, lasted less than a year, and was followed by such a complete overthrow of the reformers that Aranda himself was persecuted by the revived Inquisition whose plans for thorough revenge were foiled only by the victim's sudden death.[50] Nariño's defense, therefore, fell on the unsympathetic ears of the new Godoy ministry. Almost every book and periodical used by Nariño was condemned in the new wave of censorship, and this was especially true of the *Espíritu de los mejores diarios,*[51] quoted so often in the *defensa.*

Nariño's possession of books [52] on how to organize a Basque model reform society would therefore constitute *prima facie* evidence of his interest in the newly unseated, dispossessed, and suspect liberals. Though only recently and briefly reseated in the person of Aranda, by mid-1794

---

47. José Torre Revello, *El Periodismo en América durante la dominación española* (Buenos Aires, 1940), p. 172. This work gives some valuable information on the Basque Society which bears directly on Nariño. He states that the first one, founded by Aranda and his friends in Madrid, was modeled on a similar British Economic Society. There were soon seventy branches in Spain and the colonies, that the first one in Colombia met at Mompós from September 12, 1784, to December 19, 1784. Their proceedings were printed by the royal printer Espinosa de Monteros, who was Nariño's printer of the *Rights of Man.*

48. Spell, *op. cit.,* p. 49.

49. *Ibid.,* p. 144. Spell quotes Godoy's own admission that the reformers were forced into hiding and all periodicals except the *Gazeta* eliminated. The *Gazeta* was allowed to speak "less of France than if it had been China." (C. E. Chapman, *History of Spain* [New York, 1927], pp. 228, 432.)

50. Spell, *op. cit.,* pp. 51, 144.

51. Posada and Ibáñez, *El Precursor,* p. 632.

52. *Ibid.,* pp. 174, 176. The titles of the books were *Ensayo de la Sociedad Vascongada de los Amigos del País* and *Estatuto para gobierno de la Real Sociedad Vascongada.*

the liberals' popularity[53] and power had been rapidly reversed. Following Aranda's fall they were immediately persecuted as subversives, traitors, and· revolutionaries.[54] Menéndez y Pelayo probably represented rather accurately the spirit of reaction when he damned the Aranda liberals for favoring such accursed heretical ideas as civil marriage, public education, and religious toleration, and of course, for weakness and treason in the face of the French advance of 1794.[55] There is probably a certain amount of truth in his charge that sympathy with French ideas weakened Spanish resistance to French armies. There also appear to be reasonable grounds for his claim that the economic societies, hastily abolished by the ex-liberal, Floridablanca, in 1791–1793, had gone underground and at once converted themselves into "Patriotic Societies of French Style."[56] Like Aranda, Nariño was caught in the backlash of reaction generated by the French Revolution, hence the claim that the excesses of the French Revolution set back the cause of moderate reform and progress not half a century, as in England,[57] but until modern times.[58]

Empire Ripe for Picking

Although the events of 1789–1794 threw Spain into a nightmare of revolution and counterrevolution, they were not likely to prove annoying or threatening to her greedy neighbors. The greatest empire in the world was now a plum ripe for the picking. As long as anything was to be gained by keeping Spain weak, neither England, France, nor the United States would be eager to end the chaos of revolutions in the Americas, or in Spain. If Spain became another Poland, no one but Spain would

53. Rafael Altamira, *A History of Spain from the Beginnings to the Present Day,* trans. by Muna Lee (New York, 1949), pp. 513–514, attributes the meteoric rise and fall of Aranda in 1793 to the queen who put him in only long enough to force Godoy to pay less attention to another woman and more to her. French pressure was a secondary influence.

54. Antonio Ballesteros y Beretta, *Historia de España y su influencia en la historia universal* (9 vols., Barcelona, 1918–1941), V, 251–253, 257. This work states that Aranda was removed for vacillating and for failing to adopt a tough policy toward France, that he was exiled to Jaen and finally jailed in the Granadine prison of the Alhambra for urging Godoy to make peace with France and for criticizing Godoy's failure in foreign affairs.

55. Marcelino Menéndez y Pelayo, *Historia de los heterodoxos españoles* (2nd ed., 7 vols., Madrid, 1911–1932), VI (1930), 270.

56. *Ibid.,* p. 296.

57. W. T. Laprade, *England and the French Revolution, 1789–1797* (Baltimore, 1909), *passim.*

58. Joseph McCabe, *Spain in Revolt, 1814–1931* (New York, 1932). This author was overly optimistic when he thought this period of violent revolution and counter-revolution had ended in 1931 with a moderate constitutional republic.

care — least of all such American Spaniards as Nariño who dreamed of independence. England, France, and the United States all offered to aid the cause of Colombian independence for selfish and often conflicting reasons. From each, Nariño hoped to borrow aims and ideas, but always it was independence he sought.

The model or hero whom Nariño admired more than any other was not a Frenchman, but an American, Benjamin Franklin. Before we consider the failure of Nariño's *defensa,* his escape from the prison ship in Cádiz harbor, and his amazing Odyssey back to Santa Fé via Madrid, Paris, London, Bordeaux, and Venezuela, it might be of value to summarize the influence of Franklin on him. Besides knowledge of the new scientists — Condillac, Linnaeus, Buffon, and those who established the scientific spirit and method: Galileo, Newton and Descartes — Nariño had a library,[59] and a laboratory equipped à la Franklin for experiments in electricity. In his "Santuario" he had a bust of Franklin and a motto on a scroll which read, "He snatched the lightning from the skies and the sceptre from the tyrant's hand." In his defense peroration, Nariño closed with the fervid hope that the land of reason, liberty, and toleration, the land of Franklin, Washington, Hancock, and the Adamses would never die.[60]

The *audienca* in Santa Fé found him guilty on November 28, 1795, of sedition, treason, and attempted overthrow of the government. It ordered the *Rights of Man,* from which he copied, to be burned by the hangman in the principal square of Santa Fé and Nariño's property confiscated; and the *audiencia* sentenced Nariño himself to exile and confinement, preferably to the rockpile of a North African *presidio.*[61]

---

59. Posada and Ibáñez, *El Precursor,* pp. 164–186. Over a hundred volumes in Nariño's libraries are recognizable as scientific, and include such fields as medicine, botany, chemistry, physics, surgery, mathematics, and electricity.

60. *Ibid.,* p. 80.

61. *Ibid.,* p. 620.

CHAPTER III

A REVOLUTIONARY IN EXILE

Travels In Europe

Antonio Nariño, onetime friend and official of the viceroyalty, had greatly offended the viceroy, more than he at first realized, by the rash act of printing *The Rights of Man*. Having previously won the viceroy's friendship by his congeniality and vast culture, now by one foolhardy move, Nariño had apparently sacrificed career, family, and possibly even his own life.

There seemed to be little room for hope as he surveyed his situation. The *audiencia,* applying all the rigor of the *Leyes de la Partida*[1] had sentenced him to perpetual exile, loss of all properties, and ten years imprisonment in Africa in whatever *presidio* the king selected. At first thought, there appeared to be no escape from so specific a sentence. There were, however, some procedures that knowledge of Spanish justice and the Spanish court might uncover. Spanish administration of law in 1795, was infamous for tempering justice with mercy — provided one had money and well-placed friends. Known collectively as the "Unholy Trinity," the king, Charles IV, his wife, María Luisa, and especially the chief minister, Manuel Godoy, Duke of Alcudia and "Prince of the Peace," were reputed eager to do favors for a price. Godoy loved the titles which the Queen piled on her young lover in quick succession, but even more he loved the money which came pouring in with them.[2] To

---

1. Guillermo Hernández de Alba, letter from Bogotá to this writer, dated December 10, 1963. The sentence in full, dated November 28, 1795, is printed in full, from the documents in Madrid, in Dr. Hernández de Alba's *El Proceso de Nariño, a la luz de documentos inéditos,* Bogotá ,1958, pp. 271 and 272.

2. Ballesteros y Beretta, *Historia de España,* V, 250–290 and Jacques Chastenet, *Godoy, Master of Spain, 1792–1808,* translated by J. F. Huntington, London, 1953, p. 56 states that forty million francs went with the title Duke of La Alcudia, granted to Godoy in November, 1792. Along with the granting of the title "Prince of the Peace" to Godoy on September 4, 1795, Godoy was given as a reward for making peace with France a shower of rewards for his friends and relations: four grandee-ships of Spain, one golden fleece, seven Grand Crosses of Charles III, ten Grand Cordons of Maria Luisa, thirty-seven Chamberlains' Keys, four Councillorships of State, three Captain-Generalships, twenty-seven Lieutenant-Generalships, forty-six Major-Generalships and seventy-nine Brigadier-Generalships. (p. 68)

reach Godoy and the court, however, Nariño must somehow get to Madrid. At first this seemed improbable and very nearly impossible, but most unexpectedly, the viceroy decided to send Nariño to Spain.

Enemy of the Viceroy

The fact that Nariño asked to be sent to Spain, and that the viceroy, after some delay, sent him, is not to be misconstrued as indication that the viceroy was trying to help his former friend. The contrary is true. The viceroy now considered Nariño a dangerous enemy who could ruin his career. He wanted Nariño eliminated forever — from New Granada, from life, even from history. Because he feared the influence of Nariño's friends, the power and prestige of his high birth, and the creole's very presence in the capital, even though locked up in a jail, the viceroy felt obliged to operate within the law: this required the formalities of a trial, a sentence, and a committment to jail. Hence the viceroy wanted to send Nariño to Africa by way of the Cádiz jail. Now Nariño also wanted to get to Spain. If the road to Madrid led through Cádiz, this was well enough. Nariño's aim was to attend in person to his defense at Madrid before the tribunal of the Supreme Council of the Indies.[3] Therefore, as far as the harbor of Cádiz, Nariño's wishes coincided with the viceroy's — but no further — not to Africa, and definitely not to the Cádiz jail. Thus when the prison ship arrived in Cádiz harbor, Nariño was to be forced to act to save his life. His daring plan for this evolved during the crossing to Havana[4] after he discovered that somehow his own name had been omitted from the list of captive prisoners.

During the fifteen months of Nariño's questionings, trial, and jailing in Santa Fé, the viceroy had become increasingly convinced that Nariño constituted a grave danger to his career. After all, Nariño had said, not just once but repeatedly, that the book from which he copied *The Rights of Man* belonged to the viceroy, and that it had been loaned to him by the viceroy's nephew, Don Cayetano Ramírez.[5] Under further questioning Nariño not only refused to recant or modify this statement but more fully and more specifically emphasized the original ownership of the

---

3. Letter of Dr. Guillermo Hernández de Alba of December 10, 1963, to this writer, cited above. See also, *El Precursor, op. cit.,* p. 246, in which Nariño stated that he had escaped in a falucho during the confusion normal to ships entering port, "having learned previously that I was not listed in the partida de registro....This information I acquired by accident having observed the report of the Maestre de registro while he was making a smooth copy from the log."

4. *Ibid.*

5. Guillermo Hernández de Alba, *El Proceso de Nariño, op. cit.,* pp. 101, 118 and 224, 275.

book by the viceroy.[6] He thus pointedly rejected a chance to clear Ezpeleta by blaming someone else, or by being vague about the origin of the subversive book.

In a "Protest and Exclamation," dated July 15, 1795, Nariño said:

> . . . You took confession from me in a procedure full of defects, when I was more or less in a dying condition. Knowing the violence with which I was treated, you tried to deny me all recourse to defense which is permitted me by natural, divine and human law. . . . I requested for my defense that a copy be made of the paper *(The Rights of Man)* which is located in his Excellency's book . . . and in the use of my rights of defense which belong to me and which I should set forth, I was obliged to object for my part, to various defects in procedure and to present important facts, especially since his Excellency, the viceroy himself introduced *The History of the French Revolution.*[7]

Writing from Cartagena de Indias on December 30, 1795, in a letter of supplication to the Duke of Alcudia, "Prince of the Peace," i.e., Manuel Godoy, Nariño reiterated his charges that the book from which he had copied *The Rights of Man* came from "a small history of France belonging to your own viceroy who had loaned it, to be read, to his nephew, the Captain of the Guards, Don Cayetano Ramírez."[8]

Viceroy Ezpeleta reacted to Nariño's accusation with consultations and explanations. He consulted with the *audiencia,* and he explained to Spain. He told the court in Spain, and more specifically Godoy, that he had finally decided that the best and safest course of action to maintain the security and quiet of New Granada required sending Nariño to Spain.[9] The presence of Nariño's powerful friends in Santa Fé made it dangerous to keep him there in jail any longer. Nariño was, therefore being sent under heavy guard, first to the coast, down the Magdalena River, then on a Spanish warship to Cádiz, with a provision stopover en route at Havana. In Spain, he would be interred pending final disposition of his case by the king. The viceroy expected that Nariño would depart from the Cádiz jail — if ever — to his demise in the blazing heat of an African Presidio. Exile to Africa would put a quick end to him, as both Nariño and the viceroy knew full well.

---

6. *Ibid.,* pp. 224, 274 and 275.

7. *Ibid.,* pp. 223 and 224. This excellent set of documents from Madrid of Dr. Hernández de Alba also settles the year of Nariño's birth and the reason and date of his arrest. Nariño stated that he was twenty-nine years old in 1794 (pp. 76 and 99) and that he was arrested on August 29, 1794, for printing *The Rights of Man* (not because of any shortage in his accounts as Treasurer of Tithes). (Pp. 30, 31, 40, and 41.)

8. *Ibid.,* p. 275.

9. Pedro Torres Lanzas, *Independencia de América, Fuentes Para su Estudio,* 6 vols., Madrid, 1912, I, 133.

A Desperate Situation

Death could as well end Nariño's career in the Cádiz jail, as in the case (1816), of the Venezuelan Precursor, Francisco de Miranda.[10] Either way, Nariño's situation was desperate, clearly recognizable in the tone of the impassioned pleas which both he and his wife wrote at this time. His life was hanging by a thread, and only a strong appeal would have a chance — strong enough to cause the king or his minister to reverse the decision of the Santa Fé viceroy and the *audiencia*. The argument which Nariño chose to use was that the *oidores* (judges) of the *audiencia* had created an imaginary conspiracy, and that by making threats and by offering rewards of money they had stirred up informers and low characters to inform on him and on other victims of the vindictive *audiencia*.[11]

Significantly, the *audiencia* felt it necessary to reply to Nariño's accusations and to explain their actions. They felt compelled to cancel out any acceptance of Nariño's charges in Spain, and in addition to forestall and answer in advance any charges which Nariño's influential friends might make. This would not be an easy task. One *oidor*, Ezterripa, did not even agree with the majority, and objected to their procedures, their findings, and their verdict.[12]

The *cabildo*, or city government, further weakened the viceroy's stand by insisting that its voice should be heard in Nariño's case, and that the *audiencia* had exceeded its powers by disregarding the *cabildo's* jurisdictional claims.[13]

Nariño was getting strong support from the creole *cabildo* of Santa Fé, which was to be expected, and some support from the Spanish dominated *audiencia*, which was an unexpected source of great help to Nariño and harm to the viceroy. Nariño and his wife appealed to save his life, his honor and his family, urging for consideration the long and respected career of his father as a well-known royal official (treasurer)

---

10. William S. Robertson, *The Life of Miranda,* 2 vols., Chapel Hill, N. C., 1929, II, 213.

11. Hernández de Alba, *El Proceso de Nariño, op. cit.,* p. 274.

12. José Manuel Pérez Sarmiento. *Causas célebres a los Precursores,* 2 vols., Bogotá, 1939, II, pp. 53–58.

13. *Ibid.,* vol. I, pp. 272–290 and 348–356, 363, 375 and especially pp. 430–485. In Madrid, on June 4, 1799, The Council of the Indies reviewed the case of Nariño and found it full of irregularities. Torture was specifically condemned. However, the Council decided they should publicly support the acts of the viceroy and *audiencia* while simultaneously reprimanding them in private for their irregularities. They shall be "advised to observe punctually the Laws of the Realm in the future." (p. 515.)

in Santa Fé, as well as Nariño's own career. Furthermore, it was claimed that there had been outrageous irregularities which should void the case. Viceroy Ezpeleta, for his part, defended his methods of extracting confessions and buying informers on the grounds of urgent need to maintain the security of the realm against subversive revolutionary plotters.

Finally, on December 19, 1795, the viceroy mailed an urgent special dispatch to Godoy, "The Prince of the Peace," in which he said that he had decided to order Nariño to Spain, under special guard, in response to the urgent official request for such action made to him by his *audiencia*.[14]

The viceroy appeared to have finally shed his troublesome thorn and former friend, Nariño. All that now remained was for the king to name Nariño's *presidio* in Africa and thus end the case. In fact the king did name Nariño's place of punishment. In his sentence handed down on October 25, 1796, it was to be the Presidio of Peñon in Africa, where he was to have served ten years. The remainder of the king's sentence included perpetual banishment from the American Dominions, confiscation of all goods and of his printing press, burning by the public hangman, on the principal square, of the book from which he had copied the references to *The Rights of Man*, along with the copies of his defense answering the new accusations of the Fiscal, and finally the transfer of Nariño to Spain under guard.[15] The sentence would have been carried out in full if Nariño had not made and successfully carried out his plan to escape from the warship San Gabriel upon arrival in the port of Cádiz. This dispatch of December 19, 1795, initiated a journey of more than a year for Nariño, first as prisoner, then as fugitive.

A Strenuous Trip

The year of travel carried the Precursor from Santa Fé to Europe and back again, a strenuous trip even with modern steamships, a tremendous feat and a veritable saga with the eighteenth-century modes of travel — by horse, by carriage, and by sailing vessel. From Santa Fé, Nariño went down the Magdalena River to Cartagena in about two weeks.[16] From Cartagena, he sailed to Cádiz, Spain, by way of Havana,

---

14. Torres Lanzas, *Independencia de América, op. cit.*, I, 143, Document No. 472, Dec. 19, 1795, and in full in *Causas célebres, op. cit.*, I, 153.

15. Hernández de Alba, *El Proceso de Nariño, op. cit.*, pp. 289, 290.

16. Torres Lanzas, *op. cit.*, p. 145. José Manuel Pérez Sarmiento, ed., *Causas célebres a los precursores: "Derechos del hombre," pesquisa de sublevación, pasquines sediciosos; copias fieles y exactas de los originales que se guardan en el Archivo General de Indias* (2 vols., Bogotá, 1939), I, 157.

Cuba.[17] Between March 17 and December 12, 1796, his itinerary criss-crossed Europe, carrying him from Cádiz to Madrid, from Madrid to Paris, from Paris to London, and from London to Bordeaux by way of Paris again.[18] From Bordeaux, Nariño went to Santa Fé by way of the islands and Coro, Venezuela,[19] arriving back home in a little over a year on April 5 or 6, 1797.[20]

The trip down the Magdalena River was carried out with all possible haste. By January 16, 1796, he was reported aboard the mail packet *Floridablanca,* which had just arrived in Havana from Cartagena.[21] The governor of Cuba complied with Ezpeleta's instructions by lodging Nariño in the fortress of El Príncipe, for safekeeping. After six days, Governor Las Casas put Nariño, and the others implicated, under special-departure registry aboard the warships *San Juan* and *San Gabriel,* bound for Cádiz. On January 22, 1796, the *San Gabriel,* with Nariño aboard, sailed from Havana.[22]

Nariño and his friends received special care in their seventy-day voyage from Cartagena to Cádiz. Originally they were allowed three *reales* each per day. Because of inflation in Havana their two daily rations there and for the rest of the trip were increased to five *reales* per day.[23] At sea Nariño was not very strictly confined. He probably visited often with his four old friends, as well as with the captain. These four friends included: Joseph de Ayala, militia lieutenant of Santa Fé, Ignacio Sandino, lawyer of the royal *audiencia* of Santa Fé; Manuel Antonio Froes, medical doctor, and Bernardo Cifuentes. Nariño was listed as "Treasurer of Tithes."[24]

About the same time that Nariño sailed from Cartagena for Cádiz, his wife, Magdalena Ortega, mailed the King an urgent letter, dated

---

17. Posada and Ibáñez, *El Precursor,* pp. 212–246. Torres Lanzas, *Independencia de América,* I, 145, 150, 151. Pérez Sarmiento, *Causas célebres,* I, 156, 157 (Documents 34–36).

18. Posada and Ibáñez, *El Precursor,* p. 259. Deposition of Nariño to the viceroy, dated August 13, 1797.

19. *Ibid.*

20. *Ibid.,* pp. 228, 238, 259. Torres Lanzas, *Independencia de América,* I, 173. Pérez Sarmiento, *Causas célebres,* I, 187.

21. Torres Lanzas, *Independencia de América,* I, 145; Vejarano, p. 52.

22. *Ibid.,* I, 151. Pérez Sarmiento, *Causas célebres,* I, 157.

23. Posada and Ibáñez, *El Precursor,* p. 212. Pérez Sarmiento, *Causas célebres,* I, 487.

24. Torres Lanzas, *Independencia de América,* I, 150–151.

January 19, begging clemency for her husband.[25] The prisoner himself became very worried as his ship neared its final destination. In Havana, he had kept his word to make no effort to escape. Here it was different. His future depended on success in getting to Madrid to plead his case in person. A long delay could be disastrous. Ten years in the *presidio* of the Peñon in Africa would probably be fatal. He also knew both the viceroy and the *audiencia* were solidly against him. There seemed to be only one solution. Upon arrival in Cádiz, he jumped ship and headed for Madrid.[26] (See article by Leopoldo Uprimny, Oct., 1958, *Revista de Rosario,* pp. 125–127.)

Cádiz at this time was a busy international port, full of French, English, and Italian merchants.[27] Rowboats, the "bumboats" so familiar to all Mediterranean travelers, crowded around ships as they entered the harbor. The hubbub and confusion of entering port was ideally suited for escape. It was no time for a captain to be watching prisoners. Safety of the ship was his first concern.

Two Versions of Escape

There are two official versions explaining how Nariño escaped. Since they agree rather closely, they bear the appearance of truth, but not the whole truth. According to the port official checking arrivals (the *juez de arribadas*), Manuel González Guiral, Nariño escaped while the *San Gabriel* was moving from its anchorage to the docks.[28] The captain, Manuel de Pando, gave a different version. He stated that there were three reasons for his failure to prevent the escape: first, Nariño had kept his word of honor not to escape in Havana which would have been easy; second, it was a dark night on March 17 at the time of the escape, and

25. Torres Lanzas, *Independencia de América,* I, 145. Pérez Sarmiento, *Causas célebres,* I, 153–156. Magdalena Ortega's letter claimed that her husband was the victim of a great injustice. Leopoldo Uprimny and the Concejo agreed! She stated the trial had been most irregular, that confession had been extorted from her husband while he had been sick and delirious and that there were many other irregularities. Furthermore, she claimed that great hardships had resulted to her and her small children as a result of the confiscation of all of his property, and that of his wife and of all close relatives upon whom she might depend for help in raising her large family. To all practical purposes, she had been left a widow and a pauper. To right this wrong, and to clear an ancient and honorable family of infamous accusations, she asked that her husband be allowed to plead his case in person before the court in Spain.

26. Pérez Sarmiento, *Causas célebres,* I, 157. Official report of Captain Manuel de Pando to the Prince of the Peace via Don Manuel Guiral, Cádiz, April 6, 1796.

27. C. E. Chapman, *A History of Spain* (New York, 1927), p. 470.

28. Torres Lanzas, *Independencia de América,* I, 150, 151. Documents 498 and 500, Estado, Santa Fé.

third, he was busy taking soundings off the point of Cádiz, as required by law.[29] The captain's excuses are very plausible but omit some significant details. On March 18, an official list of passengers was sent ashore which included Nariño. Then four more crucial days elapsed before the official report of March 22 warned the Madrid authorities of Nariño's absence and flight. No excuse was offered to explain this gross negligence.[30] Nariño or his friends may have bribed the captain. By the time the Cádiz authorities had mailed an amplifying report, on April 8, their escaped prisoner had already been in Madrid for two weeks.[31]

In his confession of 1797 in Santa Fé, extorted under threats of torture and reprisals, the Precursor largely corroborated the captain's story, but added some illuminating supplements. In Cádiz, he still had money on deposit, and wealthy business friends who had helped him market his quinine, sugar, and cacao in the days when he had been treasurer of tithes. One of these wealthy friends, Esteban de Amador, had helped him to escape and to get to Madrid, giving him money and a license to ride the mail-coach. Amador had accepted a draft from his friend, probably drawn on the quinine account.[32] If this draft was on Nariño's person unobserved in the crossing from Cartagena, then certainly there had been laxness or collusion or both, on the part of the captain and his officers. The fact that Nariño was able to observe that the ship's officers omitted his name in transferring the list of passengers from the rough log to the smooth log[33] adds further evidence that he had the run of the ship, was often not confined, and was on friendly terms with the captain.

About the time word of his escape reached Madrid, on March 29, 1796, the king was presented with a petition signed by this escaped convict — for such he was at this moment in the eyes of Spanish officialdom. In the petition Nariño asked His Majesty's permission to be put at liberty in order to plead his case in person before the Council of the Indies.[34] Even for Charles IV and Godoy, vacillating, weak, and corrupt as they were, this was too much. From the summer palace south of Madrid at Aranjuez they issued a blistering royal order to the president

29. Pérez Sarmiento, *Causas célebres,* I, 157.

30. *Ibid.,* I, 156. Torres Lanzas, *Independencia de América,* I, 151.

31. Pérez Sarmiento, *Causas célebres,* I, 157. Torres Lanzas, *Independencia de América,* I, 151–152.

32. Posada and Ibáñez, *El Precursor,* pp. 16–23, 246.

33. *Ibid.*

34. Torres Lanzas, *Independencia de América,* I, 151–152.

of the Council of the Indies telling him to capture Nariño immediately, to put him in jail in Madrid, and to waste no time in reporting back to the king when the mission was accomplished.[35]

What followed this order is best told in the words of Nariño and shows the low level to which Charles IV and the "Unholy Trinity" had brought the once great Spain of his father, Charles III. Nariño says that while he was taking his afternoon stroll in the Prado, D. José María Vagoaga called him aside to tell him that everything was just about fixed, for the minister of state (Godoy) had his pen in hand poised to sign his pardon.

At that very moment Nariño's lawyer, Don Sebastian Martín de Rojas, rushed up to report bad news. Some minor clerk in Godoy's office had exclaimed that he was vexed with Nariño's extravagant demands and that Nariño ought to give thanks to God that he was still free to take his afternoon stroll. The very next day Nariño noticed that some of his warm Madrid friends began to act very cool toward him. Count Piñal of the Council of the Indies and his wife, who had been most cordial, stopped exchanging visits with him. Don Lucas Palacio, retired officer of the guard and retired minister of war, suddenly stopped seeing him. Two lawyers, Don Francisco Silvestre and Don Joaquín de Urrutia, began to act very strangely. Viceroy Ezpeleta's friends in Madrid may have brought about this sudden shift of attitude against Nariño. Finally, he asked Silvestre to help him get a passport to France whence he would follow the fate of his case at a healthier distance from the suddenly unfriendly court.[36]

Departure for Paris

On June 13, 1796, Nariño left Madrid for Paris, traveling on a forged passport obtained by "friends," who helped him pass the frontier and arrive successfully in Paris on July 29, 1796.[37]

That a member of the Council of the Indies, Silvestre, a recent minister of war, Isidor Vincente, and many other high officials snubbed Nariño once they learned the king's displeasure seems fairly natural. That they not only befriended this escaped revolutionary in Madrid, but also helped him to escape on a forged passport seems to prove even more than his escape from Cádiz the existence of a wide support for Nariño and very extensive opposition to Charles IV, Godoy, and the Spanish

---

35. *Ibid.,* I, 152.
36. Posada and Ibáñez, *El Precursor,* pp. 246–248.
37. *Ibid.,* pp. 259–261.

government of 1796.[38] Chastenet describes rising resentment especially against Godoy.

Apart from the fact that Madrid was no longer safe for Nariño, there were other reasons for the trip to Paris. The French capital was the center of revolutionary Europe. As such, it had already attracted many other revolutionary and republican-minded plotters of Latin-American independence headed by the chief plotter of all, the "Precursor" Francisco de Miranda. In the spring of 1796, though technically under arrest and observation by the Directory, Miranda was in constant communication with such varied enemies of Spain as Hamilton, Knox, Tom Paine, Monroe, and Pitt. His house had become a rendezvous for a variety of English, French, and North and South Americans, united mainly by the one desire they had in common: to strip Spain of her empire in America.[39]

Also in Paris from New Granada at this time was another leader in the independence movement, a close friend of Nariño — the elusive Pedro Fermín de Vargas — whose name had been found on the flyleaf of some of Nariño's condemned books.[40] This was the Vargas still wanted for agitating the Santa Fé de Bogotá revolt against Spain in July, 1794, and the same who admitted to Miranda in 1799 that he had finally fled from Santa Fé at the time of Nariño's arrest because some of his most incriminating papers had been found in Nariño's confiscated library.[41] Vargas was not only very elusive, but those with whom he was in contact in Havana, considered him quite a picaresque figure. There he was primarily known to Spanish spies for having carried off a married woman, Barbara Forero, in his flight from Santa Fé de Bogotá.[42]

In Paris, Nariño admittedly communicated with one of the important members of the Council of Five Hundred, Tallien.[43] Their meeting was undoubtedly arranged through Tallien's Franco-Spanish mistress, the reigning toast of Paris, Teresa Cabarrús, known as "Our Lady of

---

38. Palacios, a native of Caracas, provided the passport. (*Ibid.,* p. 641.)

39. William Spence Robertson, *Francisco de Miranda and the Revolutionizing of Spanish America* (Annual *Report* of the American Historical Association for the year 1907, vol. I), Washington, 1908.

40. Posada and Ibáñez, *El Precursor,* pp. 148–149; Montesquieu's *Esprit des lois* and *Essai sur le despotisme; Necker's Importance des opinions religieuses; Collection of Laws of the United States* dedicated to Dr. Franklin.

41. Robertson, *Francisco de Miranda,* p. 338. Also see the documents from Madrid printed by Guillermo Hernández de Alba in Bogotá in 1958 in *El Proceso de Nariño a la luz de documentos inéditos: "Socrates y Rousseau,"* p. 160.

42. Torres Lanzas, *Independencia de América,* I, 198, 239. Fuentes' Havana report.

43. Posada and Ibáñez, *El Precursor,* p. 238. Questions put to Nariño by Viceroy Pedro Mendinueta, Santa Fé, August 4, 1797.

Thermidor." Teresa had connections both in France and Spain. Her father, Francisco de Cabarrús, a wizard of high finance, was being pushed at this time as Spain's candidate for ambassador to Paris.[44]

Teresa's lover, Tallien, was interested in plans to expand French power at the expense of Spain, especially in the New World where Spain had already yielded Santo Domingo in July, 1795, and in 1796 was under constant pressure from General Perpignan in Madrid to hand over Louisiana also. Spain was likewise being urged to attack England — which she did in October, 1796 — possibly because Charles IV was näive enough to believe that the Directory was about to re-establish monarchy by putting the Spanish Bourbons on the vacant French throne.[45]

But Teresa, with an eye to her own future, was making other and different plans. Ominous signs of discontent with the government of the Directory had caused her to extend her intimate favors to possible future leaders who might come to the top through coups or revolts. Two of the possible future leaders, the director Barras and the banker Ouvrard, were soon occupying much of her time. When a third appeared, a swarthy young general from Corsica named Bonaparte, she passed him along to her good friend the Franco-American creole from Martinique, Josephine de Beauharnais. At the moment Teresa's choice undoubtedly seemed sound since Barras and Ouvrard were famous, powerful millionaires who could expect to remain in Paris as civilians and take care of their political and financial futures. Bonaparte, on the other hand, was a poor, comparatively unknown general, apt to be killed any day on some foreign battlefield.[46]

While Charles IV was still smarting from Nariño's two escapes — from Cádiz and Madrid — another letter arrived in Madrid from Nariño's lawyer, Ricaurte, beseeching the king once more to restore to the former royal fiscal agent, Ricaurte, his position on the *audiencia,* his honor, his liberty, and his property, of which the *audiencia* had despoiled him. The letter included a justification of the defense presentation which he had made on behalf of his brother-in-law, Antonio Nariño.[47] Meantime, on July 29, 1796, after conferences with Tallien and special briefing by Miranda, Nariño left Paris for England.[48]

---

44. *Enciclopedia universal ilustrada* (72 vols., Madrid, n.d.) X, 96–97.

45. Chapman, *op. cit.,* pp. 403–405.

46. *Enciclopedia universal ilustrada, LIX, 161.

47. Torres Lanzas, *Independencia de América,* I, 161.

48. Posada and Ibáñez, *El Precursor,* p. 259. Nariño's testimony of August 13, 1797. Robertson, *Francisco de Miranda,* p. 316.

In order to follow Nariño at this point it is important to know that during his stay in London he changed his name and became "alias Don Palacio Ortíz," one of the "Commissioners of South America in Europe." Along with men like Pedro J. Caro, Canon Victoria, or "Olavide" from Peru, Manuel Gual from Caracas, and Pedro Fermín de Vargas from Socorro, Nariño was an important part of Miranda's plot against Spain.[49] On October 4, 1796, nine weeks after leaving Paris for London, Nariño left London for Paris.[50] Since the date of his arrival in London is not available, we can only estimate several weeks for traveling both ways and estimate that about four weeks was spent en route and about five weeks plotting in London.

Meeting of Plotters

Back in Paris, Nariño conferred with Miranda and met Pedro J. Caro. In 1796, Caro was a trusted agent of Miranda, although he may already have been planning the betrayal which followed in 1800, when he transferred to Spanish hands a large number of secret documents, letters, and maps. It may be that his treachery was a result of Nariño's confessions about Caro and other conspirators, made to the Spanish in 1797. However, it is more likely that Governor Thomas Picton of Trinidad had him accurately spotted, in 1797, as a Spanish spy carefully planted in Miranda's plot.[51]

Further study of the career of Pedro J. Caro opens up all sorts of intriguing and confusing possibilities. The Archives of the Indies contains many letters of Miranda which Caro began to feed to the Spanish government on May 31, 1800, from Hamburg. Between that date and April 20, 1801, when Caro was in Paris, he turned over twenty letters concerning Miranda's plots to the Spanish government. But in spite of the insistence of Consul José de Ocariz and others who tried to send him back to London for three years beginning on July 3, 1800, Caro refused to re-enter the plot in England.[52]

In Paris, he complained that he was sick and without sufficient funds. He argued that Caracas, Santa Fé, or Madrid would be a better place to re-enter the plot. He claimed that he had again met briefly with

---

49. *Archivo Miranda, Ernesto Restrepo Tirado,* ed. (24 vols., Caracas, 1929–1950), XV.

50. Posada and Ibáñez, *El Precursor,* p. 259.

51. William Spence Robertson, *The Life of Miranda* (2 vols., Chapel Hill, N. C., 1929), I, 191–192. Pérez Sarmiento, *Causas célebres,* I, 187. Posada and Ibáñez, *El Precursor,* pp. 263–259 ,641.

52. Torres Lanzas, *Independencia de América,* I, 276. See also *Ibid., passim,* pp. 54–320 and typescript copies of these documents in possession of the author.

Miranda in Paris, after which he was granted his urgent request to be sent to Madrid.[53] In Madrid he continued his querulous complaints about poverty and unfair treatment by the Spanish government. He said that he had not been given the absolute pardon promised him even though he had fully kept his part of the bargain in getting originals and copies of many of Miranda's letters.[54]

Caro was finally granted the requested letter of complete pardon on February 2, 1802. But the king stated that all persons dealing with Caro must have top-secret clearance and that he was to be carefully watched as the most valuable source of information on the Miranda plots against Spain — a warning which was reiterated too late on July 22, 1802.[55]

On July 23, 1802, the court was in an uproar. Caro had disappeared from Madrid! The mysterious spy had vanished from Spain. Continuous searches to discover his hiding place in Madrid, begun on July 23, 1802, and still continuing on August 28, 1802, brought the same laconic comment from the police: "No result." On August 3, 1802, Don Ignacio Martínez de Villela ended his special report to the Council of the Indies with the same words, "No result." [56]

Suddenly, in the spring of 1803, the Spanish court received a letter from Caro in Lisbon, dated April 8. Once again he begged for forgiveness and understanding. He explained that he had been poor, sick, and friendless in Madrid and in danger from his enemies. For those reasons he had been obliged to leave.

Frantic searches by the Spanish ambassador in Lisbon during May and June of 1803 turned up nothing but conflicting rumors. Some said he was sick, some said he was dead, some that he had gone to England, or Mexico — who knows? On April 24, 1803, the King wrote a peremptory order for him to return to Spain immediately. That order — still unanswered — now rests in the Archives of the Indies in Seville.[57]

After co-plotter Nariño had left Caro in Paris, he headed for Bordeaux, onetime home of the Cabarrús family. There "friends," possibly the lovely Teresa herself, provided money, passage on a neutral

---

53. *Ibid.,* I, 295, 296, 297, 304.

54. *Ibid.,* I, 310. Document 1,021, dated Madrid, July 5, 1802, from Don Pedro Josef Caro to the Minister of State, Estado, Caracas, Legajo 4, item 125.

55. Torres Lanzas, *Independencia de América,* I, 307, 310, 311.

56. *Ibid.,* I, 312, 313. Reports contained in Estado, Caracas, Legajo 4.

57. *Ibid.,* I, 311, 320, 321, 326. Also microfilm and typescript copies in the possession of the author.

vessel, and a new identity. Don Palacio Ortíz was replaced with a somewhat similar alias, "Don Francisco Simón Alvarez de Ortú," a rather thinly disguised combination of his mother's family name combined with that of his wife, Magdalena Ortega. He was now headed for home on December 12, 1796, ready to carry out the bold plans he had carefully worked out with Caro, Miranda, Vargas, and others, in Madrid, Paris, London, and America.[58]

Shifting Alliances

The new Spanish orientation away from the English alliance of 1795 toward the French allegiance of 1796, made the existence of a Hispanic "traitor" in London or Paris about as secure as that of a tight-rope walker. Rapid shifts were especially hard to predict because of the uncertain rises and falls of the court favorite, Godoy. Somehow these fluctuations, determined largely by Godoy's popularity at the moment with the queen, had to be averaged into the normal shifting of European alliances caused by mutual European distrusts. Even then, diplomacy was largely a matter of making guesses, especially where Spain was concerned. In 1796 and 1797, Spain and France were technically allied in a war against England. But Spain and France completely distrusted each other as allies. The difficulty caused by too many variables was further confused by the complex pattern of jealousies involved in government by multiple executives. The Directory of France consisted of a five-man executive. The executive power in Spain was split four ways, if we count Ferdinand. At any moment these multiple executives threatened to explode into chaos, civil war, and the threat of eventual dictatorship in either or both countries.[59]

In such a quicksand, an unwary exile could easily be trapped. It was possible for Nariño to be well received in Paris, and then soon find London more hospitable to his plans of independence. It was also possible to be caught in either place on short notice or none at all. Nariño was truly a man without a country at this point. Moving rapidly in a treacherous morass, he ignored the risks and pushed new contacts to help the plot. Thus, in Paris, he met two friendly merchants named Aldarían and De la Serre. In London he met two merchants close to Pitt, named Campbell and Short. While living in London with an exile named Palacio, he had also had the temerity, or possibly the curiosity, to pay his respects to the Spanish ambassador and the Spanish consul,

---

58. Posada and Ibáñez, *El Precursor,* pp. 227, 238, 259, 260.

59. Chapman, *op. cit.,* p. 404. Martin Hume, *Modern Spain* (London, 1923), pp. 30–34.

informing their excellencies that he was a traveling merchant from Madrid.[60] During his travels in exile he had also made the acquaintance of two lesser known merchants named Seironaburscher and Gramont who were interested in financing the plot. They both had interests in British America and saw an opportunity to increase their business and profits by supporting Nariño's plans.[61]

Between the time he left London on October 4, 1796, and the time he left Bordeaux on December 12, 1796, Nariño wrote several letters to Madrid and America. In spite of much prodding by his inquisitors after his capture in 1797, he insisted that these letters were primarily personal missives to his wife, and inquiries to José Caicedo in Santa Fé, and Francisco Silvestre and Andrés Otero in Madrid, concerning the status of his pending case.[62]

The arrival of Nariño and Vargas in the New World coincided with the British capture of Trinidad, and the revolts in Caracas and La Guayra. All of these attacks proved upsetting to the Spanish empire in America. Since Spain could not move in all places at once, some of these attacks were bound to be successful. Their timing was excellent and obviously well planned. The simultaneous nature of these outbreaks was no accident. It was part of British grand strategy which called for close cooperation between England, the United States, and the independence movements in Spanish America, with the possible collusion or neutrality of France. The primary objective was the creation of new markets free of Spanish control.[63]

The British Master Plan

The British master plan, to destroy the Spanish empire in America during 1797 and 1798, was originally made in August, 1796. A prominent supporter of the plan was Nicholas Vansittart, barrister, politician, and merchant. Closely associated with Vansittart was another merchant, Henry Dundas, Lord Melville, Secretary of State for War, who was to present the plan to his close friend, Pitt. This was a fusion

---

60. Posada and Ibáñez, *El Precursor,* p. 228. Report forwarded via the archbishop to Viceroy Mendinueta containing Nariño's July 30, 1797, testimony.

61. *Ibid.,* pp. 228, 238, 259. Nariño's report of July 30, 1797, and his amplifying testimony given in response to additional viceregal questioning on August 4, 1797.

62. *Ibid.* En route from Bordeaux, a Philadelphia merchant of 64 North Front St., as well as a merchant from Basseterre, Guadalupe, Mr. du Peyrou, offered to help finance his plans. The Philadelphia merchant was named Coulon or Conlon. See *ibid.,* 6. 229.

63. *Ibid.,* p. 252. Torres Lanzas, *Independencia de América,* I, 173–184. Robertson, *Life of Miranda,* I, 160.

of plans suggested by Miranda, Vargas, Caro, and Nariño, modified to suit British plans for new markets in America. The first step in the plan, the conquest of Trinidad as a staging area for the attack on Venezuela, encountered little opposition. Trinidad was captured by the British in February, 1797. By April, 1797, Dundas was already urging Governor Picton, the new British governor of Trinidad, to do everything possible to promote commerce with the creole merchants of the mainland. If they showed any interest in revolt and independence, Picton was to promise English aid. This he promptly and enthusiastically did by distributing through his agents in Venezuela a pamphlet including the promise of aid along with a glowing summary of the business profits to be gained by revolt and independence.[64]

Developments following the capture of Trinidad indicate the speed with which England threatened to carry out the Vansittart plan. Trinidad capitulated on February 18, 1797.[65] On March 4, Nariño landed at Coro, Venezuela. An abortive revolt broke out in Coro and on March 6 was suppressed temporarily by the execution of its leader, José Leonardo Chirinos. Eight days later, March 14, Captain General Carbonell yielded to urgent British pressures, and signed the final surrender papers for Trinidad. On April 18, he then passed two orders: one excluding Trinidad refugees from Venezuela, the other pronouncing the death sentence upon anyone trading with the British, *especially* the British on Trinidad. On May 29, a new revolt was suppressed in Coro, but June 4, the governor angrily reported that four of the leaders had escaped from the jail in La Guayra. On July 13 and 14, the independence leaders, Manuel Gual and Joseph Maria España, celebrated the French Revolutionary holiday by escaping from the Caracas prison.[66]

Additional Plans

Meanwhile Vargas and the governor of Jamaica were making an additional plan to keep the Spaniards off balance. There was to be an attack up the Orinoco River, and then a movement northward to Caracas, to be synchronized with local uprisings led by creole leaders in Venezuela. Unfortunately for Vargas, the plan was intercepted by vice-regal agents in New Granada. Vargas, however, did not give up but went to New York for help (see Torres Lanzas, vol. I, p. 213). Viceroy

64. Robertson, *Life of Miranda,* I, 160–162.
65. Torres Lanzas, *Independencia de América,* I, 173.
66. Posada and Ibáñez, *El Precursor,* p. 259. Torres Lanzas, *Independencia de América,* I, 173–182.

Mendinueta forwarded the information on the Vargas plans to the officials in Spain on January 19, 1799.[67]

Pedro J. Caro was also planning to coordinate British naval attacks with local uprisings in Venezuela, and might have succeeded except for two unexpected events. Just before sailing time, there was a mutiny in the British navy. The Spanish ambassador in Paris, Nicolas de Azara, got wind of the plans, and wrote in alarm to Madrid: "Be on the lookout for the arrival of Caro, most ingeniously disguised as a negro, with a negro wig that so perfectly imitates the wooly hair of a negro that it appears natural, and his whole body so skillfully dyed that neither sweat nor rain will alter it." [68] This was the precarious situation of beleaguered Spain on the morning of Bastille day, July 14, 1797.

---

67. Pérez Sarmiento. *Causas célebres,* L, 187. Confidential report to Pedro Mendinueta of *Oidor* Alba, dated Santa Fé, January 19, 1799, forwarded for action to the minister of war, Don Manuel Alvarez (Document number 52).

68. *Ibid.,* I, 174–175. Confidential letter from Don Nicolas de Azara, Spanish ambassador in Paris, to Don Francisco Saavedra, dated Paris, July 25, 1798 (Document number 47), also: Gill, Conrad, *The Naval Mutinies of 1797,* Manchester, England, 1913. (Mutinies at the Nore and Spithead)

CHAPTER IV

RETURN AND REPENTANCE

Success was almost in Nariño's grasp on the morning of Bastille day. While Caro had gone to America disguised as a Negro, and Miranda was shortly to arrive in England disguised as a Russian,[1] Nariño had arrived in his native Santa Fé April 5 or 6, 1797, disguised as a priest.[2] Nariño's motives for thus risking his life were mixed. He appeared to be putting his head back in the jaws of the lion. But at this point in his life, he was not safe anywhere, and undoubtedly he was eager to see his family and his homeland. His move was also part of a plan developed by Miranda in Paris, Vansittart and Dundas in London, Vargas in Jamaica, Picton in Trinidad, Senator Blount in West Tennessee, and Governor Simcoe in Canada.[3] It tied in closely with the British plan for using recently captured Trinidad as a staging area for attack on the Spanish mainland — this to occur simultaneously with the movement of creole fifth columnists, under cover of British attack, to overthrow Spanish rule and declare for independence. Miranda's own words corroborate what the "educated guesses" of Ambassador Azara in Paris and Irujo in Philadelphia were transmitting to the home government in Spain.[4]

---

1. Robertson, *Life of Miranda,* I, 164.

2. Posada and Ibáñez, *El Precursor,* pp. 213–215, 259. Report to *Oidor* Hernández de Alba of witness Manuel de Mendoza, Santa Fé, July 3, 1797; Nariño's confession, August 13, 1797.

3. Robertson, *Francisco de Miranda,* pp. 310–316 . *Dictionary of American Biography* (21 vols., New York, 1928–1937), II, 390–391. Frederick J. Turner, "Documents on the Blount Conspiracy, 1795–1797," *American Historical Review,* X (April, 1905), 574–606. Also see Turner's "The Policy of France Toward the Mississippi Valley in the Period of Washington and Adams," *American Historical Review,* X (January, 1905), 274.

4. Pérez Sarmiento, *Causas célebres,* I, 174–175. Turner, "Documents on the Blount Conspiracy," p. 591. Robertson, *Francisco de Miranda,* p. 313. Torres Lanzas, *Independencia de América,* I, 179.

Miranda wrote as follows:

In the month of January, 1797, in view of the ratification of the offensive and
defensive treaty of Spain with the French Republic I wrote to Mr. Turnbull in
London by means of a trusty person whom I charged with the commission of
presenting himself to Mr. Pitt. . . . My original object was nothing less than
the liberty and independence of my native land . . . now the conditions were
more suitable for the beginning of the enterprise, namely a war between Spain
and England . . . besides there was a probability that hostilities would soon
break out between France and the United States and between the United States
and Spain. . . .[5]

That Nariño was one of Miranda's agents (called Palacio Ortíz
in England), has been established, but the events leading to his reappear-
ance in Santa Fé on July 14, 1797, need some recapitulation. While en
route from Bordeaux to San Bartolomé aboard the *Sicilia de Bastón,*
Nariño met a Philadelphia merchant named P. Coulon or Conlon of
64 Front Street, who offered to assist the revolt by equipping and arming
two thousand men. He also suggested other merchants in the polyglot
islands of the Caribbean who would do anything for money. Among
those eager to assist were: Mr. du Peyron, Basse Terre Guadalupe,
agents of Campbell and Short in Saint Bartholomew and Mr. Toulousan
(Tomlinson?) and Mr. Petiton of St. Thomas, who voluntarily offered
news of Vargas en route to Jamaica. Others were Mr. Cipriani and Mr.
Isaac Lopez, St. Thomas, Mr. Levy and Mr. Gómez, friends of Mr.
Tomlinson in St. Thomas, and finally, in Curaçao, the notorious corsair
Pedrote and his friend D. Pedro Rico who, for a price, so kindly helped
Nariño to get passage to Coro, Venezuela.[6]

Prelude to Surrender

In one month, Nariño traveled from Coro to Santa Fé. Along the
way he stopped to search out the land and test the temper of the people,
appraising support for an independence movement and how much
opposition he might expect. As an optimist he was encouraged, but as a
realist he felt the time was not quite ripe to take his calculated risk until
public opinion had been further swayed in favor of his plan — a correct
estimate of the situation, as later events showed. Passing over Lake
Maracaibo, he went to Santa Rosa, from there to the ponds of
Chiriguana where he again found traces of Vargas, thence to Bailadores,
La Grita, Cúcuta, Pamplona, Tequía, Cerinza, Tunja, Chocontá and

---

5. Robertson, *Life of Miranda,* I, 163.

6. Posada and Ibáñez, *El Precursor,* pp. 228–230. Nariño's confessions of July
30, 1797.

Santa Fé de Bogotá, where he rested in hiding six days, from April 6 to April 12.[7]

On April 13, Nariño took another exploratory trip of two months duration,[8] north to Tunja, Vélez, and Girón, and back to Santa Fé for further reconnoitering and meeting with leaders. He also headed into trouble, for on this trip he was recognized and denounced to the authorities by a former acquaintance, Manuel de Mendoza. Mendoza hastened to inform one of Nariño's old adversaries, the *Oidor* Juan Hernández de Alba, who started the search that finally ended in Nariño's capture.[9] Hernández recognized Nariño in spite of a broadbrimmed hat, a shawl over his face, and an attempt to disguise his voice. Just to be sure, he followed Nariño into a *chicha* store where for lack of *chicha*, Nariño drank brandy. Hernández quizzed Nariño's guide who admitted that his patron avoided towns, as at Vela, by swimming his horse at fords above the bridges.[10]

While Hernández de Alba, Carrasco — who denounced him — and other ancient enemies spent two frantic and fruitless weeks trying to locate Nariño by watching his wife, his friends, his relatives, and his house, Nariño remained hidden. He stayed with his brother José one day, the thirteenth of June, where he arrived at five in the morning. His sisters, Luisa and Dolores, and his wife visited him there. Dolores suggested that he move that night to her house, where he would less likely to be discovered, since her husband was away and the house was empty. Until July 8 Nariño was visited in this hiding place at Dolores's house by only two friends, Dr. Gómez and Don Jorge Lozano. During the night of July 8, fearing spies had followed his friends, he moved with Dolores to the house of her friend Doña Magdalena Cabrera. During the next eight days, Dr. Gómez again made a short visit and Don José Caicedo called. Fearing that Caicedo had been trailed, Nariño moved again, this time to the house of his sister Benedicta, where he stayed from July 17 until he surrendered himself, through the archbishop, to the viceroy on July 19.[11]

---

7. *Ibid.*, pp. 230–259. See map in Henao and Arrubla, *History of Colombia*, p. 506. Also see maps in J. M. Restrepo, *Historia de la revolución de Colombia, Atlas* (Paris, 1827).

8. Posada and Ibáñez, *El Precursor*, p. 230.

9. *Ibid.*, pp. 213, 214, 215–231.

10. *Ibid.*, p. 214. Testimony given to *Oidor* Don Juan Hernández de Alba by Manuel de Mendoza in Santa Fé, July 3, 1797, relative to his recognition of Nariño on June 7, 1797, near San Gil.

11. *Ibid.*, pp. 215–218, 231, 258. Reports of Mendinueta and Hernández de Alba and confession of Nariño.

July 4 was the day of revolution in America, as July 14 was in France. Nariño might have planned for revolution on either date with good psychological effect, but he seems to have preferred July 14. Why, then, did he fail to revolt on the fourteenth, and surrender instead, on the nineteenth of July, 1797? He has been accused of "weakness, loss of nerve, and lack of courage for this last minute surrender."[12] He has also been accused by Madariaga of revealing the other plotters, and at first sight, his three successive confessions appear to indicate that Nariño did supply the Spanish authorities with names, places, and plans in such a way as to harm the cause of rebellion and independence.[13]

Reasons for Surrender

Nariño seems to have felt that he was being watched and would soon be caught. He also felt he could trust the archbishop's word of honor to get him a safe conduct. The major reason for surrender seems to have been a conviction, based on his trip north, that he lacked sufficient support, a condition which would lead only to another bloody betrayal and defeat as in the *Comunero* revolt of 1781. He had no desire to see his family, friends, and neghbors crushed in a premature and therefore hopeless and abortive revolt. In this uncertain frame of mind, and with his wife, Magdalena Ortega, as intermediary, Nariño bargained with the archbishop, who extracted a solemn promise from the viceroy to grant clemency, *salvo-conducto,* and guarantees that Nariño's surrender would not result in any punishment involving torture of body, loss of life, or loss of blood to him or his family.[14]

The reasons the viceroy and the *audiencia* were willing to accept this compromise were many and cogent, as they stated to the king. They were willing to accept a partial victory over the revolutionary because they knew their own weaknesses and feared Nariño's strength. They

12. Salvador de Madariaga, *Fall of the Spanish Empire* (London, 1948), p. 339.

13. Posada and Ibáñez, *El Precursor,* pp. 226–238, 246–253, 261–262. Confessions and testimony of Nariño to Viceroy Mendinueta in Santa Fé on July 30, 1797, August 13, 1797, and August 19, 1797, extended by additional remarks on September 3, 1797. Guillermo Hernández de Alba, *El Proceso de Nariño,* Bogotá, 1958, p. 160, contains a sketch of Nariño's study in which Rousseau's name, paired with Socrates, heads the list.

14. Pérez Sarmiento, *Causas célebres,* I, 162–164. *Acuerdo* in full. Torres Lanzas, *Independencia de América,* I, 180–181. Document number 603, Santa Fé, July 13, 1797, copy of royal *acuerdo* submitted as a result of special session of the *audiencia* called to consider the threat created by the plans of Nariño and Vargas to revolutionize Santa Fé. Estado, Santa Fé, Legajo 4 (40). This document is numbered 40 in *Causas célebres* and indicates that in addition to the viceroy, the president, regent, *oidores,* and fiscal of the criminal court were all present. Count Torre de Velarde was the addressee and signed a certified copy of the report.

lacked troops, and they lacked popular support, which Nariño was known to have, and he might have troops, also, ready to throw aside their peaceful guise and rush to arms. Short of direct aid from Spain, the best hope of protection for the viceroy was to accept Nariño's qualified surrender.

Nariño did indeed have supporters ready to spring. The plan destroyed by his surrender, was as follows: a small British naval squadron from Trindad would make a feigned attack on Cartagena to draw in Spanish troops there, thus stripping other thinly garrisoned areas. Meanwhile, the real attack would be made up the Orinoco River through Guiana, and up the Meta River to join forces with natives in revolt. Much assistance would come from creole parish priests favoring revolt whom Nariño had met on his trip from Coro and the coast. Pedro Fermín de Vargas was cooperating with the plan. The action was to begin outside the capital in the small town of Palogordo, between Barichara and Simacotá. The men would gather there during the confusion of a fiesta day. Escorted by armed followers, Nariño would make a speech in the plaza of Palogordo. Success at this point would mean the triumph of the plan as a whole. Around Palogordo were tough, disaffected mountaineers who had already indicated their willingness to join Nariño. Moving with their aid, Nariño next planned to take possession of the narrows and bridge crossings which, entrenched, would give him control of all villages within half-a-day's ride, or seventy thousand people. Then he planned to send messages to the towns, the *cabildos,* the priests, and the militia urging them to join, thus bringing out in the open on his side the supporters yet undiscovered as well as known friends. Weapons would consist principally of muskets, whatever iron could be improvised into lances, and the slings with which the local population were so adept. Money was no immediate problem. These frugal mountaineers would provide their own clothes and shoes. An intimate knowledge of the roads and locations of thinly staffed garrisons favored Nariño against the defenders. Precipitous mountain roads, narrow bridges where one man could block passage, impassable river gorges, and shallow rapids where natives knew how to swim their mounts, all gave Nariño an advantage over Spanish troops not accustomed to such rigorous mountain travel and probably unable to transport the artillery — their only advantage — into such rocky terrain. Heavy artillery would never reach the area, and no light artillery was available in Santa Fé. All guides who might lead royal troops would be likely to lead them into a trap and were therefore worse than useless to the viceroy.

The parish priests of the towns were usually with Nariño; two in the towns of Cácota and Barichara had indicated they would support whichever side won control of their parishes. Nariño counted heavily on popular discontent over excessive taxation to favor his cause, as well as on conditions abroad, the near collapse of the exchequer, and the lack of sufficient force to collect taxes, enforce laws, or suppress rebellion. Having won the countryside, Nariño expected the beleaguered Spanish forces in the Santa Fé area of Cundinamarca to surrender just as rapidly as they had to the *Comuneros* of 1781. The mere mention of Salvador Plata, P. Finistrada, and the revolt of 1781, would be enough to start the revolution in some towns.[15]

Nariño's surrender represented the culmination of several weeks' detective work on the part of his enemies. Their first proof that trouble was brewing came from the July 2 revolutionary sermon of Father Lorenzo Ferreira in Anolayma.[16] Ferreira's was the voice, but the words sounded like Nariño. He said the Spaniards claimed to have come to America to implant Christianity but instead they had tyrannized over the natives, persecuting them so harshly that they would attempt to escape their cruel masters by flinging themselves from high cliffs, as the only way out of their troubles. In their greed, the Spaniards had taken not only gold and land but women and children; the native men had been loaded with work, hunger, and diseases, which were the underlying causes of both past and present colonial misfortunes and dissatisfactions. Some day those who showed forgiveness, charity and love would be pardoned in heaven and those who did not would be punished on earth as well as in heaven.

"Excellency, you know this kind of subversive talk could be very destructive of both church and state," said the informers Francisco Xavier Galán and Benito San Luís in their urgent special report of July 4, from Anolayma.[17]

Nariño had been reported seen near Santa Fé the day before receipt of the sermon. The very next day the viceroy told *Oidor* Hernández to get busy and find Nariño. On July 5, orders went out to Tunja to find the woman, Barbara, near Tunja, who had sold brandy to Nariño and to find the peon who acted as Nariño's guide. Barros and Carrasco reported no luck in their search by July 7, as did unnamed spies reporting to the viceroy on July 9.

The same day, José Caicedo approached the archbishop who requested a compromise for Nariño from the viceroy in return for

---

15. Posada and Ibáñez, *El Precursor*, pp. 25, 253–255, 259–262.

16. Torres Lanzas, *Independencia de América,* I, 180. Pérez Sarmiento, *Causas célebres,* I, 164.

17. *Ibid.,* I, 165.

information. Without committing himself, the viceroy redoubled his search but to no avail. In desperation on the eve of Bastille day, July 13, 1797, the viceroy held a special meeting with the *audiencia* in the palace to decide what to do about the crisis. The *audiencia* was particularly disturbed about the rumor that Tallien had told Nariño there would be secret help from French naval forces in spite of the public appearances of an alliance between France and Spain. Similarly disturbing was the archbishop's report that Nariño had received encouragement from Lord Liverpool and others in England in spite of the outward official coolness of Pitt himself. The feint on Cartagena, the attack up the Orinoco and Meta Rivers, the joint planning of Nariño and Vargas, the disaffection of local priests, and the possibilities of local risings caused the viceroy to send out special alerts including an order to rejail Ricaurte. But for the moment the viceroy refused again to make a deal with the archbishop. The viceregal officials were ordered to find Nariño and Vargas, and to jail them.[18]

The First Confession

July 14, 1797, came and went with no explosion, no revolt led by Nariño, no concessions by the viceroy but an atmosphere of tense, impending violence which seems to have corroded nerves on both sides. On the seventeenth, the viceroy held another long conference with the sick and aging archbishop. In return for the viceregal promise that no information given at this meeting would be used to originate against Nariño a suit involving torture, corporal or sanguinary punishment, or cast any reflections on the archbishop, the latter presented the viceroy with Nariño's first confession and recantation.

It was a very brief confession, confirming, but not adding much to what the viceroy already knew about Nariño's travels and plans. The Precursor admitted planning revolution in London, in Paris, and in New Granada. He admitted trying to avoid the impending imprisonment in Africa, changing his name on returning from London to Paris, accepting a neutral passport in Bordeaux, and, at times while en route to Santa Fé, covering his face with a shawl. He claimed, however, that he did not adopt any special disguise, nor leave the king's highway while on the way from Coro to Santa Fé. He further stated that he remained hidden only in order to spend a little time with his wife and children while waiting for a final word on his case, and that he fully intended to surrender himself if favorable adjustment were made to his sentence. He claimed to have communicated with no one but Spaniards in London.

He did admit knowing of English offers to prevent Spanish

---

18. Posada and Ibáñez, *El Precursor,* pp. 216–218. *Acuerdo extraordinario* of July 13, 1797, held in the viceregal palace, Viceroy Pedro Mendinueta presiding.

reinforcements from arriving in case of revolts in New Granada, but to count this as a firm promise was to indicate one's ignorance of the government of English cabinets, especially the cabinet of 1796.

All this the archbishop said he would have presented two days sooner had it not been for pains in the heart, stomach, and head; furthermore, he wanted the viceroy to swear again to keep the sacred promise given to Nariño relative to the conditions attached to his final surrender. Having once again extracted the viceroy's promise to keep his word as a man of honor, the archbishop produced Nariño and his confession.[19]

July 19, 1797, must have been a particularly hectic day in the life of the viceroy, to judge from the quantity of official correspondence for that day. No less than five confidential letters were sent to Godoy in Spain — two from Viceroy Mendinueta, two from the *audiencia,* and one from a member of the *audiencia, Oidor* Count de Torre Velarde.[20]

The count reported on the planned outbreak of revolution on July 14, and the tentative arrangements of the viceroy to gain information through the archbishop, provided no blood penalties should result from the archbishop's efforts to arrange compromise with Nariño.[21] Viceroy Mendinueta, in a very secret letter, described the excitement over the return of Nariño and Vargas, and the military preparations being made to concentrate troops in areas most likely to revolt or be attacked by England. He also begged for more troops to supplement his very scanty forces. In another letter on July 19, Viceroy Mendinueta hastened to inform Godoy of the surrender of Nariño through the intermediation of the archbishop, of the conditions required and signed by all parties prior to Nariño's surrender, and of the danger existing in the probable presence of Nariño's co-plotter, Vargas. The same mail of July 19, 1797, carried a letter from the *audiencia* promising to lock up Ricaurte incommunicado in the Cartagena *castillo,* as required by royal order dated October 26, 1796, and a second letter telling of the return and surrender of Nariño and a statement to the effect that "Vargas is much the more dangerous,"[22] which could be considered factual for the simple reason that Vargas was still free while Nariño had given himself up!

19. *Ibid.,* pp. 218–222. Pérez Sarmiento, *Causas célebres,* I, 166–168. Document number 43, from Baltasar Jaime, archbishop of Santa Fé, to Viceroy Pedro Mendinueta, Santa Fé, July 17, 1797, countersigned as a certified copy by the Count of Torre Velarde.

20. Torres Lanzas, *Independencia de América,* I, 182–183.

21. *Ibid.,* I, 182, Pérez Sarmiento, *Causas célebres,* I, 166–170.

22. Torres Lanzas, *Independencia de América,* I, 183. Pérez Sarmiento, *Causas célebres,* I, 37, 170, 173, 159.

CHAPTER V

UNDER SURVEILLANCE

The Reconstruction Of Respectability

Eleven crucial days elapsed between Nariño's surrender July 19, 1797, and his confession of July 30.[1] During that period, the viceroy was busily gathering evidence and making plans to crush any revolts that might break out in conjunction with English attacks from the sea, or up the Orinoco River. Nariño, meanwhile, had begun to play what was to become one of his most sustained and difficult roles — that of repentant sinner. This pose was part of a great effort to reconstruct himself in the character and reputation of a reliable royalist. He must have gagged a little at his new lines, but the stakes were high. With his life and those of his family and friends in the balance, stubborn pride could prove too costly; he must swallow pride for the time being, eat his old words, and mouth new ones. He spent more than a decade trying to convince royal authorities in Spain and America that he was truly repentant, a loyal vassal, and a completely frank and sincere informer against his former revolutionary associates. Beginning with surrender, he exerted all his tremendous energy and talent to reconstructing both reputation and fortune. But he found himself continuously under sur-veillance, never quite trusted, never quite restored to his former position, politically, socially, or economically. His life until his rearrest on October 15, 1809,[2] was the life of a prisoner, and later that of a parolee, with all of the heartbreaks that can make an ex-convict's life so bitterly frus-trating. Not once but three times, Nariño was questioned to see whether he might be led to trap himself with contradictions, and made to uncover more and more of his associates in the republican independence plot.

Indications from elsewhere in South America show that the inde-pendence movement was still very much alive. Picornell, Cortez Gual, and España had escaped from jail in Caracas after the abortive July revolution of 1797, and were threatening to return and overthrow

---

1. Hernández de Alba, *El Proceso de Nariño, op. cit.,* p. 74, gives a fuller confession of Nariño, dated September 5, 1794.

2. Posada and Ibáñez, *El Precursor,* pp. 233, 278.

Governor General Carbonell. Their presence on the nearby islands of Curaçao and Trinidad was an ever-present danger to Spanish rulers in Caracas and Santa Fé.[3]

Aftermath of Surrender

This was the atmosphere of continual revolt, alarm, and uprising in which Nariño was trying desperately to convince authorities that he was truly penitent and reformed, and would do just about anything necessary to convince his captors of his full repentance and cooperation. Through continual questioning and comparing of answers, the authorities were trying to get Nariño to tell much more than he was prepared to tell. His basic approach was to tell a part of the truth always, to be steadily consistent, but never to tell the whole truth. After three additional confessions, made on September 5, 1797,[4] July 30, 1797, and August 13, 1797, Nariño was able to convince the viceroy of his "probity and fidelity."[5] In his letter of September 11, 1797, to Spain, Viceroy Mendinueta added that he hoped the new administration would help him to keep his realm in its new state of apparent calm and peace by reforming some of the abuses which had caused revolts. In order to test Nariño's sincerity further, the viceroy informed the court that Nariño would be required to analyze in writing the abuses most in need of reform and summarize the best methods for carrying out the reforms in order to prevent future revolts.[6]

Nariño replied on September 13, 1797, that the viceroy could calm the people by keeping his word to give his prisoner better treatment. Furthermore, he said, it would be much easier for him to write a good analysis of the reform out of jail where materials would be available, than in jail with no reference works, no place to write, and not enough food and exercise to keep healthy.[7]

This appeal failed to free Nariño. Two years later, in 1799, Nariño was still in the cavalry barracks jail in Santa Fé, still complaining that the viceroy had not kept his word even though he, Nariño, had complied in full with every request made by the viceroy.[8] Why then was Nariño still in jail? Had the viceroy not intended to keep his word to the revolutionary leader or were there other reasons?

---

3. Torres Lanzas, *Independencia de América,* I, 182–202.

4. Hernández de Alba, *El Proceso de Nariño, op. cit.,* p. 74.

5. Posada and Ibáñez, *El Precursor,* pp. 246–263, 265–267, 271.

6. *Ibid.,* p. 271.

7. *Ibid.,* pp. 271–273.

8. *Ibid.,* pp. 274–275.

There were other reasons. Spanish law courts moved slowly. Prisoners in jail were easier to watch than parolees. Viceroys in Santa Fé could not expect answers to requests for advice in much less than a year at the earliest. There is also evidence that the viceroy was hoping to catch Vargas, Caro, and perhaps Miranda, and to find out more about Nariño's contacts in Santa Fé. For instance, a secret letter dated July 18[9] was issued by the viceroy in Santa Fé on procedure to be followed after the capture of Nariño and Vargas. All correspondence was to use the code name, Monsieur Lebruc, in referring to either Vargas or Nariño, who were to be moved only at night after capture to avoid mob risings. The viceroy was to be kept informed of all routes and stopping places en route to Santa Fé. All possible precautions were to be taken to capture their papers and books and to make an exact record of these, as well as memoranda of appearance and clothing of the men at the time of capture.

Hunting the Conspirators

A careful description of both men was included. Nariño was thirty-four, Vargas between thirty-four and thirty-eight. Both men were well built but Vargas was much taller, about six feet, and slightly bowlegged. Both had dark eyes and large noses, Vargas' somewhat beak-like, and Nariño's freckled. Nariño had piercing popeyes. Vargas had noticeably negroid skin and large, protuberant ankle- and toe-bones.

A day before entering the city with either or both "Mr. Lebrucs," the captors were to warn the viceroy and await orders for final disposition of their prisoners.[10] Due to Nariño's surrender on the following day, July 19, and Vargas' total disappearance, these elaborate precautions were not carried out. But the attempt to locate Vargas through intensive questioning of Nariño began and achieved some success.

What did Nariño tell about Vargas? In his August 13 amplifying confession, Nariño told very little. He claimed not to have told Vargas the state or plan of his projects. He had heard a little about Vargas from a priest and the *alcaldes* of Pamplona, but he had received no letters from him and was not even sure the man described to him in Pamplona was Vargas.[11]

Six days later, August 19, 1797, the viceroy sought the help of the governor of Havana in an effort to locate Vargas whom he described in his letter as "Corregidor of Zipaquirá in 1791, who fled this kingdom carrying off with him Barbara Forero . . . whom we have now captured

9. *Ibid.,* pp. 233–238.
10. *Ibid.,* pp. 237–329.
11. *Ibid.,* p. 253.

here."[12] Barbara stated that Pedro Vargas had left her in Jamaica when he sailed for Madrid to try for a pardon. Since the postmaster general in Santa Fé had received an 800 *reales* money order from D. Fermín Sarmiento in Havana for Barbara Forero on May 31, 1797, and Vargas had used that alias after his disappearance during the abortive revolt of 1794, and was known to have been friendly with José Fuertes, administrator of the post office in Havana, the viceroy hoped the governor of Cuba could pick up Vargas' trail in Havana.[13]

Fuertes was a notorious informer against Vargas.[14] Vargas' reliance on the postal administrator as a confidant would seem incomprehensible, were it not for the possibility that Vargas was trying once more to misinform Spanish officials through a medium who was either gullible or cooperative.[15]

According to Fuertes' first offer to spy on Vargas, dated October 18, 1794, Vargas and Miranda were both associated not only with Nariño but with a Frenchman named Vidal, a former captain of grenadiers, who, after marrying a wealthy and influential woman in Cayenne and learning Spanish rapidly, had become a big slave trader in Cartagena in 1785 and 1786. After going bankrupt several times, Don Antonio Vidal, as he now styled himself, was firmly planted at the mouth of the Orinoco at Guarico as a local despot and he was reputed ready to open the river for Miranda's invasion up the Orinoco and Meta toward Santa Fé de Bogotá.[16]

The viceroy's efforts to get Nariño to mention Miranda were never successful. This omission was very noticeable and may have caused the viceroy to be suspicious that Nariño was not telling the whole truth. Significantly, Nariño was also quite vague about Caro when first questioned: "A native of Havana I met in Paris, dark-skinned, about fifty trying to get help to free Peru ... I don't remember his name."[17] However, under further questioning the same day, Nariño was able to remember the man was José Caro. On August 13, 1797, Nariño described Caro as a man he met in a restaurant in Paris, a place fre-

---

12. *Ibid.*, p. 268.

13. *Ibid.*, pp. 268–269.

14. Torres Lanzas, *Independencia de América,* I, 97, 153, 178, 197, 198, 202, 204, 205, 209, 213, 217, 219, 265, 275, 298, 304, 306. Pérez Sarmiento, *Causas célebres,* I, 232.

15. Between October 18, 1794, and January 2, 1802, Fuertes informed on Vargas no less than eighteen times; on three of these occasions he withheld Vargas' money left on account in Havana.

16. Pérez Sarmiento, *Causas célebres,* I, 234.

17. Posada and Ibáñez, *El Precursor,* p. 227.

quented by Spanish Americans. They ate together, visited with each other, compared notes and found they both had plans to free South America from Spanish rule with English or French help. His friends were in Lima — Nariño couldn't remember their names, didn't have the least idea! The man "spoke little, seemed very intelligent•but not very well acquainted with politics and I am ignorant of his connections and other circumstances."[18]

On August 5, 1797, Viceroy Mendinueta wrote the viceroy of Peru in Lima to be on the lookout for Pedro J. Caro and for any letters Caro might address to his old Paris friend, Don Francisco.[19]

All efforts to incriminate Nariño's friends and relations in Santa Fé proved vain, and his naming of parish priests as revolutionaries was probably recognized for the trick it was, to implicate royalists and cover up republicans. At least the viceroy took no action except against the one priest who had shown genuine revolutionary fervor, Dr. Lorenzo Ferreira of Anolayma, the preacher of the violent anti-Spanish sermon of July 2, 1797.[20] In an effort to convince the viceroy that he had truly betrayed the revolution, Nariño could have implicated many leading creoles of Santa Fé, but he did not do so.

Delays in Justice

The long judicial dispute engaged in by the previous viceroy over whether or not the case against Nariño should originate in the *audiencia* or the *cabildo* was won by the *audiencia*. However, the *cabildo's* complaints to Spain against improper procedure and interference with the elections of *cabildo* officials may have done much to delay, confuse, and weaken the case against Nariño.[21]

On September 11, 1797, Viceroy Mendinueta seemed to be fairly well satisfied with the completeness, sincerity, and accuracy of Nariño's confession. He apparently wished to make favorable reply to the appealing letter of Nariño dated September 3, 1797, in which Nariño said, "I have put my fate and my heart in your hands but apparently you have forgotten your word of honor even though I have complied with your every request."[22] In his sentence of September 11, Viceroy Mendinueta called attention to the improved public tranquility, and to Nariño's

---

18. *Ibid.,* pp. 252–266.

19. *Ibid.,* pp. 227, 264.

20. Torres Lanzas, *Independencia de América,* I, 180. Pérez Sarmiento, *Causas célebres,* I, 164–167.

21. *Ibid.,* I, 265, 272, 274–283, 283–291 297–356, 363–380, 430–465, 487–489.

22. Posada and Ibáñez, *El Precursor,* pp. 269–270.

apparently complete sincerity, but indicated that he thought Nariño had received all that had been promised him by way of amnesty. The viceroy also held out hope to Nariño of more extensive privileges and freedoms if he would, as local authority on the subject, draw up a plan to reform some of the abuses which had put the people of New Granada in a revolutionary frame of mind.[23] As the viceroy put it:

> . . . the exchequer draws very little at present from very rich provinces and yet the people are discontented; if their discontent is unfounded, granting that they do contribute, neither are there forces here sufficient to restrain them and reduce them to just obedience; if their complaints are well founded, it cannot be because of the *amount* of the taxes but rather the method of collection, and in this case a reform of the administration is necessary. . . . It seems that Nariño understands the sickness of the people; he understands that it is very serious and for that reason requires a serious remedy which he indicates should take the form of reform of the administration. It is indispensable that he should explain his concept of this matter with more thoroughness.[24]

Nariño replied that his confession of September 3 had been a mistake since it had not improved his condition as promised. He had helped the government calm the people in time of trouble, and he thought more appreciation should be shown. In fact, he thought the government had showed bad faith. That very day they were taking measures to increase vigilance over his imprisonment for no reason that he could see or understand, nor was explanation made. He desired to cooperate fully in bringing order and public tranquility to the viceroyalty. However, to comply with the viceregal request to write a plan to reform the administration, he needed more data than was available in jail relative to taxes and public opinion on taxes. A worried, sick prisoner, deprived of all sources of information, was in no frame of mind to do justice to the vast, delicate, and dangerous operation contemplated by the viceroy. Nariño regretted, most respectfully, that he was not yet in the condition of freedom necessary for full and intelligent compliance with the viceroy's request.[25]

This not-so-subtle hint for freedom on September 13, 1797, does not appear to have had any immediate effect. Nariño finally wrote the plan for reform of taxation in New Granada which was duly forwarded by Viceroy Mendinueta, along with recommendations for more leniency toward Nariño. This request for leniency, dated December 19, 1797,[26]

23. *Ibid.,* p. 271.
24. *Ibid.*
25. *Ibid.,* p. 273.
26. Torres Lanzas, *Independencia de América,* I, 201.

did not produce any immediate answer or action, and the case dragged on with Nariño still in jail and still complaining.[27] As a matter of fact, the letter sent from the Spanish ambassador in Paris, Nicolás de Azara, to Minister Saavedra in Madrid on July 25, 1798, resulted in a royal order, issued from San Ildefonso on August 21, 1798, to keep a close watch on Nariño, Caro, and Miranda, who were all plotting to destroy the Spanish empire with English help.[28]

Information piling up elsewhere, particularly in Madrid, was not of a kind to encourage viceregal leniency toward Nariño, no matter what his complaints. On August 1, 1798, a confidential royal order went out from the minister of war in San Ildefonso to the viceroy in Santa Fé de Bogotá. It enclosed, from Ambassador Azara in Paris, Nariño and Caro's intrigues with Miranda, and counsel to the viceroy to keep military forces continually alerted against rebellions and invasions, and that only the mutinies of 1797, in the British navy at the Nore and Spithead, had prevented success of the Caro-Nariño-Miranda-Picton joint operation of 1797, against Tierra Firme (Venezuela).[29]

Re-alerted thus, by information which actually antedated Nariño's surrender and confessions, the viceroy became alarmed, either forgetting the time lag or deciding that Nariño was more dangerous than had been realized. Lack of up-to-date information caused him to be both worried and uncertain. He had in his possession two letters, the warning from Spain, possibly outdated, and a November 4, 1798, appeal from Nariño. Nariño was again complaining to the king via *Oidor* Hernández de Alba and the viceroy, about the failure of the government to keep its word and of his "miserable fifteen months of close confinement" in which he "barely existed in submission and silence." He thought sufficient time had elapsed for the court to have acted on the archbishop's and the viceroy's sacred promises of August, 1797, and September 11, 1797. He further reminded the court of the paper he had voluntarily written — an *Essay on a New Plan of Administration for the Kingdom of New Granada.* He reminded the viceroy too of the recent letters of Don José Caro from London and Paris, which had further supported the truth and extensiveness of his confessions of '97. Yet, since the arrival of the Caro letters, his jail treatment had become, if anything, more strict. "Thus after 500 days of jail, here I am still with no more hope than the

---

27. Posada and Ibáñez, *El Precursor,* pp. 274–275. Torres Lanzas, *Independencia de América,* I, 225–266.

28. *Ibid.,* I, 216, 218.

29. Pérez Sarmiento, *Proceso de Nariño,* p. 168. Torres Lanzas, *Independencia de América,* I, 218. Gill, Conrad, *The Naval Mutinies of 1797,* University of Manchester Press, 1913.

day I came . . . it seems as though my sole punishment now is for having told the truth."[30]

The viceroy was in a quandary; everything Nariño claimed appeared to be the truth. It was quite true that the Caro letters proved that the prisoner's confession was accurate down to the minutest details — even to description of conversations, thoughts, and actions. Furthermore, he had done nothing whatever to cause anyone to suspect even his aims for the future; he had, in fact, done all that was humanly possible to cooperate with the government in order to be free once more to join his wife and children, and to live in harmony with his sovereign as a faithful vassal. It was important also, to pay one's debts and to clear one's name of calumny. But how could that be done in jail?

Nariño realized, of course, that the determination of his case was not solely up to the viceroy but hoped that, in so far as it was under the viceroy's jurisdiction, the case would be considered on its merits. It was particularly hard to believe that a man of the viceroy's outstanding character would keep him imprisoned out of caprice or personal distrust. For over a year Nariño had not seen the sun. He hoped that his health would last, but restricted to a cell ten paces long, often without even enough drinking water, and with little or sometimes no food, his strength, his hope, and his courage were rapidly disappearing. Perhaps since this was the "birthday of our most August Sovereign," the viceroy would use the occasion to remember his sacred promise to the archbishop and see that now at last justice would be done without further delay.[31]

Viceregal Alarms

In response to this appeal from Nariño, coming on top of the war department warning from San Ildefonso, the viceroy prepared to send Nariño down the river to Cartagena and secretly prepared another *champan*. If Nariño's friends in Santa Fé, or the daily possibility of attack by European enemies, should force the viceroy to save himself by fleeing down the river to the safety of fortified Cartagena, he could now do so.[32] The viceroy was in a panic, and the fact that the British were reported to have intercepted the September mails did not help matters. Nariño's network of friends, relations, and supporters throughout the first families of Santa Fé were getting more and more restless with the increase of news from Europe and enemy colonies. They might rise, overpower the scant forces and the weak jail, and free Nariño. Hence

---

30. Pérez Sarmiento, *Causas célebres,* I, 180–185.

31. *Ibid.,* I, 185.

32. Pérez Sarmiento, *Proceso de Nariño,* pp. 169, 170.

the viceroy sent secret orders to the port director at Honda on the Magdalena to keep the *champan* loaded and ready to go at a moment's notice.[33]

At that time, November, 1798, the great Spanish empire in America was very thinly garrisoned. Miranda's secret message to the British in September, 1798, reported that the whole standing army in the area of proposed attack — Panama, Cartagena, Chagres, Darien, Santa Fé, Popayán, and Quito — consisted of 3,059 officers and men, two-thirds of whom were centered in Cartagena and Panama. The viceregal guard in Santa Fé consisted of thirty-four cavalry, twenty-four halberdiers, and two lieutenant generals — one of them the viceroy himself![34]

With only fifty soldiers to support him in an atmosphere thick with rumors of revolts and invasions, Viceroy Mendinueta became fearful. He was surrounded by a hostile people and practically unarmed. He held Nariño as a hostage but a word from the hostage might explode the hostile countryside into open rebellion. The nearest reinforcements were six hundred miles to the north, in Cartagena. Under the circumstances, Pedro Mendinueta proved himself worthy of the high trust and ancient traditions of the best of the viceroys. First, he said the king should keep the sacred promise to Nariño given by the archbishop and the viceroy. The king was reminded of the desperate conditions of the kingdom which had necessitated such promises. These promises had been necessary to head off revolts at a time when there was little preventive force available. Moreover, if the king would keep his word to Nariño, other such persons would be urged to confess and reform. What would happen if instead, it became notorious that the word of the viceroy and the bishop, given in the name of the king, could not be trusted?

Public confidence depends directly on impartial, dependable justice of the authorities. . . . The amnesty granted to Nariño could serve as an example to others guilty of similar crimes who would hasten to accept similar amnesty thus lessening the need for forces to resist them. In times like this, amnesty is more useful than force. . . . Up to now Nariño has co-operated fully with us, awaiting long-promised clemency. But how long will this last if we do not keep our word to him? There is, of course, risk involved, but up to now we have been given every reason to believe in the absolute faith and sincerity of Nariño. We have two choices: either we believe him and carry out fully our promise to him, or we don't believe him, in which case he is very dangerous and it is then indispensable that we erase him forever from the pages of history. . . .[35]

---

33. Pérez Sarmiento, *Causas célebres,* I, 176–177.

34. Archivo General de Indias, Seville, Estado, Legajo 61, 125/10 N.1, Memoria y plan de Miranda. Copy in possession of the author.

35. Pérez Sarmiento, *Causas célebres,* I, 178–181.

It would be difficult indeed to have said it any better. Under such circumstances Spain would have had to look far indeed to find a better administrator than Pedro Mendinueta. But the weakness of this colonial system was at the center, in the executive branch in Madrid. The sovereign and his minister, Godoy, continued to delay. They did not send troops. Perhaps they had none to spare. But neither did they approve pardon for Nariño. Worse yet, they did not even disapprove a pardon! They simply did nothing. No answer came to Santa Fé. No answer went to Cádiz either. There in San Sebastian jail on January 15, 1799, Nariño's old friends and jailmates, Mutis, Cifuentes Ayala, Froes, Pradilla, Sandiño, and Cabal, wrote, "please free us for the love of God or bring our case before the Council.[36]

For two months Viceroy Mendinueta sat on his powder keg waiting for an explosion. It did not come. He could stand it no longer. "Please send me some troops now before it is too late," he wrote. "This letter is urgent." Once more he tried patiently to explain the situation in such a way that the king might understand and act. Much had been done through reform and precautions to prevent revolutions since the year when Nariño printed the *Rights of Man* (1794). Many more precautions had been taken since Nariño had surrendered on July 19, 1797. Letters had been sent via the secretary of state. Vargas's plan to invade with British help from Jamaica had been intercepted and mailed to Spain before it could be executed. Don Manuel Vicente Prieto's plan to spread insurrectionary verses and broadsides had been stopped. Dr. Ferreira, the preacher of seditious sermons in Anolayma, had been promptly removed without further incident. Repeated urgent requests had been sent for more military forces. They were needed to uphold respect and authority in Santa Fé. It would be a sad state of affairs if complaints were not to be remedied nor forces sent to suppress the complainers. Still no action or confirmation had come regarding Nariño, except approval of keeping him in jail pending a final decision.

In the meantime, Caro had written Nariño from Paris, and these letters had been intercepted. Since Caro's most recent letter stated that he was en route to Santa Fé because he had received no answers from Nariño, the port officials had all been alerted by some letters arriving August 21, to be on the lookout for Caro, probably disguised as a Negro.[37]

Viceroy Mendinueta obtained further information about the plotters

---

36. Torres Lanzas, *Independencia de América*, I, 228–229.

37. *Ibid.*, I, 229, Pérez Sarmiento, *Causas célebres*, I, 185–187. Also typed copy, in full, in possession of this author.

by opening July and December letters addressed to Barbara Forero from New York by her lover Vargas. According to these letters Vargas was leaving New York for Spain.[38]

On the twenty-fifth of November, at the end of a quiet, empty month, as far as action on his American empire was concerned, King Charles IV dictated a letter to the governor of the Council of the Indies, asking the Council to advise him on the status of Antonio Nariño and his defense attorney, José Antonio Ricaurte.[39] The Council did not comply at once.

Christmas, the new year and the new century of the 1800's found Nariño still in jail and apparently no nearer his promised freedom. Then on February 6, 1800, Nariño opened his "afflicted heart" to "His Grace the viceroy":

Thirty months I have been in jail now and I am still ignorant of my fate, thirty months of expectation and silence, thirty months of indecision, more than enough to crush the strongest heart, the calmest soul. If I don't hear something pretty soon to sustain my hope, time itself will put an end to my work and waiting and end my miserable existence. . . . I have kept my word and I know your Excellency is a man of honor . . . but I am still here in jail. What shall I think? If perhaps my existence threatens that of the state then I am ready to sacrifice my life. I am ready to die. There are only two reasons I still desire to live, one is to pay my debts and clear my name and the other is to help, with the sweat of my brow, my wife and children whose unhappy fate has tied their sufferings to my punishment. . . .[40]

Viceroy Mendinueta was touched by this appeal and forwarded it to the king on February 19, 1800. The judge who had sentenced Nariño apparently approved of this action also, for he added his name, Hernández de Alba.

Review by the Council

A year later, with Nariño still in jail, Spanish justice was grinding slowly but perceptibly toward a decision. By September 8, 1800, the Council had reheard the case and passed it on the king who wrote an *oficio* to the Council asking for a summary of the case from its inception under the *audiencia* of Santa Fé on September 19, 1795, through the viceregal letter of July, 1798. On March 24, 1801, the king issued a "decision of the king in Council."[41]

---

38. Torres Lanzas, *Independencia de América,* I, 239.

39. *Ibid.,* I, 261.

40. Pérez Sarmiento, *Causas célebres,* I, 187–189.

41. *Ibid.,* I, 23, 49, 190.

Between September 8, 1800, and March 24, 1801, the case of Nariño was reviewed in great detail by the highest judicial machinery of Spain. The king and Council reheard it in detail on November 25, 1799.[42] The findings of the *audiencia* in Santa Fé and also in the special session called "plenary session of three chambers," on September 8, 1800, were summarized. In view of the need to send troops to protect the viceroy in Santa Fé, in consideration of Nariño's effort to comply by writing a plan to reform the administration, the Council had been delayed several times during 1797, 1798, and 1799. Three lawsuits had been drawn up: The one against Nariño for printing the *Rights of Man* which eventually was found to have connections with the other two; one for posting of *pasquines* ridiculing the government; and a third for attempted revolt. Nariño, for escaping to Madrid, was found criminal in the highest degree. Because of his repentance, apparently sincere, it was the opinion of the Council that the viceroy's action in giving Nariño amnesty should be ratified and confirmed, and that all past acts of Nariño, Prieto, Espinosa, and other defendants in the suit of the lampoons should have complete amnesty and restitution of each one to the state in which he was before the suit. However, they should be carefully watched in the future. The Council would neither approve nor disapprove the acts of the *audiencia*. Nariño's essay on reform of the administration should be given consideration by the royal treasury. The viceroy was cautioned to gather up and burn seditious French literature, jailing or punishing persons found possessing such works. The government was immediately to issue absolute condemnation of two works mentioned by Nariño: *Espiritú de los mejores diarios* and Capmany's *Filosofía de la elocuencia*.

A more careful censorship of printing was also ordered for New Granada. Ambassadors and consuls in France, Hamburg, and Holland were ordered to assist in capturing Pedro Fermín de Vargas and José Caro, still at large. The king was urged to reconsider commissioning the French Doctor Rieux to go on the royal botanical expedition to Santa Fé since he was a revolutionary subversive implicated in the Nariño plot. They objected also to the large salary of two thousand dollars *(duros)* to be paid to the convicted French doctor.

The five-man Council was split on the vote. The Marquis of Bajamar, governor of the Council, cast a dissenting vote against the opinions of the other four, Jorge Escobedo, Fernando Joseph Mangino, Francisco Rigüero, and Vicente Ibore. Bajamar objected to the trial of Ricaurte which, he said, upon review appeared to have been improperly conducted with no written statement of the charge, had not been confronted with the evidence against him, or been heard in his own defense;

---

42. *Ibid.*, I, 23.

nor had he been told his fate. Yet Ricaurte had been jailed in Cartagena, his property confiscated and his family left homeless by this highly irregular procedure of the *audiencia* of Santa Fé. Nothing, however, had been proved against the unfortunate Ricaurte. For those reasons, Bajamar, governor of the Council, recommended, first, that the lawsuit be ended and permanent silence be imposed upon the case; second, that the innocent wrongly accused be freed and have their property restored; third, that they be restored to their previous positions of honor; fourth, that Nariño, Ricaurte, and others be carefully watched in the future, and, finally, that the viceroy and *audiencia* be commended for having preserved the public peace during a difficult era.

The other four members stressed different aspects of the three suits. Escobedo, Mangino, Rigüero, and Ibore recommended first that laws against foreigners in the Indies be more strictly enforced. They also thought that the Inquisitor General, aided by the proper prelates and curates of both secular and regular clergy, could help to exclude dangerous foreign ideas and prohibited books in any language. Due to the irregularities of the trials and the exemplary conduct of Nariño, it was thought that the viceroy should free the Precursor, Ricaurte, and the ten other Bogotanos. Safe conduct should also be extended to Manuel Vicente Prieto. However, even though some posts might be restored, Nariño and Espinosa were to be forbidden to do any more printing. Furthermore, Pedro J. Caro and Pedro Fermín de Vargas were *not* to be included in the general amnesty. Likewise they urged that Nariño be asked more questions about Caro's interest in Peru, and his relationship with Vargas and Miranda. These four Council members also thought it very unwise to take the ex-convict, Dr. Rieux, and send him right back with the botanical commission to the area in which he had just been spreading French Revolutionary doctrine, namely, New Granada. It did not make sense to hire as a scientist a recently convicted enemy of the state. To avoid embarrassment with France, it was suggested that the botanical expedition be disbanded, thus abolishing Dr. Rieux's position without international repercussions.

Veto by the King

In his final decisions of November 19, 1800, and in the royal decree issued through the Council on November 13, 1800, King Charles IV largely ignored the recommendations of his Council. He would not fire Dr. Rieux nor abolish the botanical commission. He would not free Nariño, Ricaurte, and the others nor relax their incommunicado status in jail. He sent Nariño's plan to be examined by the treasury, but claimed he had already issued orders to take care of Caro and Vargas. He urged the viceroy and *audiencia* in the future to operate within the laws of the realm, and not to compromise or give *salvo conductos,* since such power rested only in the king. Finally, he urged the viceroy of Peru to take special care to prevent the introduction of prohibited books into the viceroyalty.[43]

The case was closed. The king had spoken. Nariño was still in jail. The highest authority had finally and definitively refused to free the repentant ex-revolutionary. Nariño himself was crushed, but not his wife, Magdalena Ortega Mesa. She decided that there *was* a higher authority than the king, namely, the queen. So she proceeded to beseech the queen in most heartrending terms to make one last effort to have the king show a little mercy for the "humble supplications of an innocent woman, victim of the persecutions visited on an unlucky husband. Today Señora I gather together the tears of a lifetime and beseech Your Highness to hear with clemency the simple succinct exposition of my travails. . . ."[44]

She then summarized the trials and tribulations that had followed her family and her husband, causing her to have to beg food to keep alive the five children who were the —

. . . ill-fated fruit of our marriage. And what was the origin of so many calamities and violences? Why, that is public knowledge. . . . My husband translated a scrap of a French book which had been loaned to him by our Viceroy Don Josef Espeleta [*sic*] and had it printed on his own private printing press, on which he printed anything without special license and with the tacit permission of the government, on whose behalf he had purchased and established the printing press. He had not sold more than one copy of this printed work when an official of the viceroy's secretariat who saw it warned my husband not to let it circulate because the circumstances of France could make it appear evil. This single friendly word of warning was sufficient to cause my husband to collect that single copy and another two or three he had loaned and without further ado consign them all to the flames, so that at the time of his arrest not a single copy printed or in manuscript was to be found anywhere to serve as a starting point for the lawsuit in the case.[45]

Doña Magdalena Ortega y Mesa made a very convincing case for her imprisoned husband, Antonio Nariño, appealing to all the finer emotions of mercy, justice, and honor, reminding the queen of the sacred promises given by the archbishop, Compañon, and Viceroy Mendinueta.

Doña Magdalena went on to say that the sacred words of the highest officials in both church and state were —

---

43. *Ibid.,* I, 23–37.
44. *Ibid.,* I, 190–192.
45. *Ibid.*

... above question, not to be doubted, yet three and a half years have passed while my husband remains entombed in jail. In such deplorable circumstances, whom else could I turn to, Your Majesty, with tear-drenched eyes, but you? You, with your great soul, sublime spirit, and what is more important than all else, your sensible and generous heart can render, as fountain of all authority, the justice all others deny me. ... You alone can rescue this afflicted mother, disconsolate wife. You alone can return to me a husband and to my five children a father and to the king a loyal suffering vassal.[46]

If Queen Maria Luisa had possessed any of the qualities so generously, or flatteringly, ascribed to her by Nariño's wife, it is possible that she might have been moved to intercede with her husband. However, this letter of December 29, 1800, remained unanswered. On behalf of the king, some official wrote in the margin just two words: "Está Resuelto" — case closed.[47]

Freedom in Desperation

The story might well have closed here, too, if Nariño had stayed in jail much longer. By June 1, 1802, he was sick and dying. Hoping that the double festivities caused by the peace and the marriage of the Prince of Asturias and the Infanta Doña Isabel, might be a suitable occasion for the king to reconsider their cases, Nariño and Ricaurte had both written from jail that they were sick and dying. On behalf of his clients, their attorney Juan Bosmenial y Fiesco hastened to remind the sovereign that half the generation of 1794, particularly the younger half, had the same ideas for which Nariño had suffered so much.

From the year 1794 to the beginning of 1795, the whole human race was criminal, one half of it fighting against the other half: Nariño and his associates were in that epoch: all Europe has pardoned itself: Your Majesty himself and your wise ministers have given many examples of this ... a father pardons with ease the extravagances of youth and Your Majesty enjoys the reputation of a wise father ... gaining much by conciliation. ... Why then must Nariño be excluded from this reconciliation when he, perhaps, merits it more than many others already pardoned? It seems, sire, also that the same rules which should soften the hard fate of Nariño might equally apply to his lawyer Ricaurte. ... Such royal generosity would secure in dutiful loyalty to Your Majesty many families, many generations of secure good will. ...[48]

By April 26, 1803, the viceroy was alarmed to find his prisoner in the *cuartel de caballería* was sinking fast. Six years of jail had almost

---

46. *Ibid.,* I, 192.
47. *Ibid.,* I, 190.
48. *Ibid.,* I, 193–196.

finished him. Fresh air and exercise were prescribed by Dr. López Ruiz as the only possible means of saving the prisoner's life. *Oidor* Juan Hernández de Alba and Camacho, an official scribe, witnessed the examination of Nariño. The next day, *Oidor* Hernández de Alba re-examined the rapidly failing Nariño with doctors of medicine, Don Sebastián López Ruiz and Don Miguel de Isla. They agreed on the diagnosis of their patient:

> . . . damage to the lung and mediastinum affecting also the external pectoral muscles which may be considered not so much dropsy of the chest as purulent empyema as indicated by fetid sputum mixed with a certain portion of purulent material, glutinous by nature, with predominantly muriatic aklalinity which has to be coughed up late at night or in the early morning, violent coughing of long duration, dry at first followed by copious sweating, palpitations of the heart, fluttering quick spasmodic pulse followed by slowly rising fever and great exhaustion.[49]

The cure recommended for Nariño was "the pure air of the country, freedom from jail, goat's milk, and moderate daily rides on horseback as the patient improves."[50]

Three days later, April 30, 1803, Dr. Miguel de Isla repeated his diagnosis under oath, stating that the patient's case was rapidly becoming more serious with spitting of blood from the mouth, a stage designated as *homotipsis,* difficulty of the patient in resting at all on the left side, difficulty in respiration caused by edemous tumors and casting up of putrid material; all symptoms indicating an advanced state of hidropsy with the increase of abnormal fluids in the chest, and deterioration of lung tissue: in short, a serious, dangerous, deadly malady, very difficult to cure, especially until after extracting the fluid from the lungs. It was again stated that cure would necessitate a strict regimen of life in the country with fresh air and, later, continuous walks and rides on horse-back. The patient's health had been ruined by the sedentary restricted life and bad air of the jail.[51]

The famous Dr. Celestino Mutis, as special consultant, verified both the diagnosis and the remedy urged upon the viceroy by his medical colleagues, adding his own similar diagnostic remarks of even more lengthy and sonorous terminology. Mutis further stated that the malformation of the patient's chest had predisposed him from infancy to lung diseases, adding that it was absolutely necessary to remove the patient

---

49. *Ibid.,* I, 199.
50. *Ibid.*
51. *Ibid.,* I, 200.

from jail to the country if he was to live even a few days longer. Such was the state of his ruined health that the doctors would not care to guarantee recuperation even under the most favorable care.[52]

With this *expediente* of medical advice in hand, Viceroy Mendinueta proceeded to apply the remedy on May 5, 1803. Nariño was freed conditionally under bonds posted by Juan Vergara, Don Andrés Otero, and Doctor Sebastián López Ruiz. Nariño was to be continually watched in the hacienda at Montes by a viceregal guard, and regularly checked by a medical doctor.

The next six years Nariño spent quietly in the country doing everything possible to regain health, wealth, and the confidence of the Spanish monarchy in his absolute loyalty. He achieved partial success in all directions. His health was good enough to see him through twenty more years of strenuous life, a life which was to include not only the ardors of political and military command but also, seven more years in jails.

His wealth was never entirely restored, but after receiving conditional freedom from the king on January 14, 1804, he applied for control of his property and houses in order to pay off his debts, both public and private. The new viceroy, Antonio Amar y Borbón, forwarded this request to the minister of state, Godoy, on November 16, 1807, recommending approval. Amar stated, however, that the senior *oidor* of the *audiencia* of Santa Fé, Juan Hernández de Alba, had advised him to suspend final approval pending royal action. In view of Nariño's repentance of past *culpas* and exemplary loyal conduct, Viceroy Amar wished to advise that in his humble opinion (and in consideration of earlier promises given in the name of the king by the archbishop, the preceding viceroy, and the royal audiencia), he, Hernández de Alba, must feel constrained to comply provisionally with Nariño's request. It was Viceroy Amar's wish that His Majesty would soon approve this action. In order to strengthen the request, Viceroy Amar included the attested copies of debtors requesting that Nariño be granted possession of his property provided only that he be required to give back to each of them proportionately what he owed within the legal limit of ten years, and that at the end of the first four years he would pay back a third, at the end of seven years, two-thirds, and the full amount in ten years. In order to be given more freedom to pay he was not to be required to put up bonds nor pay interest. Twelve creditors signed the original request on August 22, 1805; on July 30, 1806, the viceroy approved the plan. On August 16, 1806, *Oidor* Hernández de

---

52. *Ibid.*

Alba became absolutely opposed to approving Nariño's request because of the reported near success of Miranda's invasion of Caracas. However, a royal *cédula* of March 20, 1806, demanding that Nariño and Ricaurte pay court costs of the case to the Royal and Supreme Court of the Indies, caused Nariño to reappeal for control of his property in order to comply with the royal order. In consideration of the royal *cédula,* and with the further statement that Nariño had made no move to aid Miranda in the excellent opportunity offered by the 1806 invasion, *Oidor* Hernández de Alba consented on November 3, 1807, to Nariño's request, and hastened to add his name and approval to that of Viceroy Amar, in a joint letter to Spain written at Santa Fé, November 16, 1807.[53]

Two years later, Nariño was still trying hard to convince the Spanish government of his loyalty when Viceroy Amar received word on October 15, 1809, that the Precursor *was* involved in a new plot to overthrow the royal government![54]

---

53. *Ibid.,* I, 207–216.
54. Posada and Ibáñez, *El Precursor,* p. 278.

CHAPTER VI

FROM RETIREMENT
TO REVOLUTION

Napoleon, in 1809, was the indirect cause of precipitating Nariño out of retirement and once more into the forefront of revolution. The Napoleonic kidnaping of the Spanish royal family at Bayonne, May, 1808, led to the famous Dos de Mayo revolt in Madrid against the intruding Bonaparte. In Quito, the news of Civil war in Spain brought forth the bloodless rebellion of a creole *junta suprema de gobierno* against the president and *oidores* of the *audiencia*. There, on August 10, 1809, the Quito *junta* invited the *cabildo* of Santa Fé to follow its lead, and on September 6, the viceroy in Santa Fé, Amar y Borbón, found himself reluctant host in his palace to an open *cabildo* which included all prominent citizens, office holders, and priests, both creole and Spanish.

Once adjourned to a second session, on September 11, the two factions, creole and Spanish, found themselves opposed on all basic issues. Only the viceroy's military preparedness prevented an open civil war in Santa Fé.[1]

Troops were called from Cartagena, troops were sent to suppress the Quito rebellion, and troops patrolled the streets of Santa Fé day and night. The *oidores* slept in the viceregal palace. Lampoons appeared on the city walls, and lampooners and suspects went to jail.

Another Arrest

The Inquisition issued an edict excommunicating possessors of lampoons or proclamations from Quito, and the viceroy proclaimed the death penalty for all such activities. Cavalry reinforcements arrived from Riohacha, and on September 23, the viceroy arrested Nariño in his retirement at Fucha, and cast him into a Santa Fé jail with *Oidor* Baltasar Miñano of Quito.[2]

---

1. Henoa and Arrubla, *op. cit.,* p. 193.
2. *Ibid.*

Nariño had not shouted: "Down with the French, we want a *junta!*" or "Open *cabildo* and long live Ferdinand VII!"[3] as everyone else was shouting in the fall of 1809. But Nariño, true to his former principles, wanted more than just Ferdinand and an open *cabildo;* he wanted independence. To get it he was even prepared to share it with his Negro slaves and half-savage Indian neighbors. At least that was the accusation made by Pedro Salgar and others to Viceroy Amar y Borbón.[4]

Surrounded by enemies, actual and potential, the viceroy was inclined to shoot or jail first and ask questions afterward. In answer to his questions, the accusers told the following bloodcurdling story of Nariño's new plan: With the aid of creole leaders, Pedro Groot and Luis Caicedo y Flores, the first attack was to be a night ambush of the viceroy and his bodyguard in the viceregal palace. Incriminating papers had been found in an inner room of the quarters of Dr. Andres Rosillo, prebendary of the cathedral. These papers revealed a plan to bribe the palace guard, capture arms, money, and the viceroy's person, and offer freedom, in return for assistance, to some Negro slaves on the hacienda of Saldaña.

An independent *junta* would then be set up with Groot, Nariño and Caicedo each serving two-year terms as president. In addition to the Negro slaves, six hundred men from Zipaquirá, led by their *corregidor,* and 1,500 from Socorro, led by Dr. Miguel Tadeo Gómez, administrator of the *aguardiente* monopoly, would join forces, at a signal from Santa Fé to be given by José Acevedo, the *regidor* of the city *cabildo.*

Even though the whole plan seemed somewhat complicated, remote, and perhaps improbable, to the viceroy, he was alerting troops. Since his informers indicated that the attack was due in a very few days, timed to begin before Cartagena reinforcements could get to Honda on the way to Santa Fé, all precautions were taken. Socorro was carefully watched, as well as all other critical locations. Dr. Rosillo was observed conferring behind closed doors with other suspects — the lawyer Ignacio Herrera and Dr. José Joaquín Camacho.[5]

On October 16, 1809, the day after the accusations had been made to Viceroy Amar, the royal *audiencia* sent a confidential resolution to the viceroy, urging him to initiate a lawsuit. This body wished to proceed in conformity with the law to press the unnamed informer to repeat his

---

3. Bulnes, *Nacimiento de las repúblicas americanas,* I, 233, 238.

4. Posada and Ibáñez, *El Precursor,* pp. 278, 279, 286.

5. *Ibid.,* pp. 277–278.

charges formally, under oath giving more information, dates, and specific facts, with the understanding, of course, that his name would be kept absolutely hidden from both witnesses and defendants. Carrión and six other members who signed the resolution further approved special watching of the house of the prebend, Dr. Rosillo.[6]

After a four-day delay, the viceroy felt called upon to explain to the king on October 20, 1809, why he had not carried out the resolution of the *audiencia*. It was not desirable to flush his covey of suspects too early. For the king's information, however, the informer was one Pedro Salgar, curate of the city of Girón, momentarily resident in Santa Fé. Salgar had informed Andres Rodríguez, viceregal secretary, who then told the viceroy. The viceroy assured His Majesty that the affair would be handled "in a manner most suited to advance the royal service and the public welfare."[7]

On November 2, 1809, Pedro Salgar gave further testimony to the *audiencia* in Santa Fé. He admitted that he was curate and resident of the city of Girón. At the moment, however, he was also a legal adviser for the royal *audiencia,* in which capacity, on his word as a priest, he wished to swear by all that was holy to the truth of the allegations. Had it not been for the great danger to his person from the plotters he would have testified earlier. Only under promise to keep his evidence hidden in a locked safe with a key placed in a different locked room would he divulge the names and plots mentioned. This accomplished, he began his story about Nariño.

Late one afternoon on or about twenty-three days before October 10, Pedro had been at the house of Prebend Andres Rosillo to see about renting a house. While waiting he chatted with his nephew, Carlos Salgar, and another young fellow named París. They asked for Prebend Rosillo and were told he was inside. Just then someone came in off the street. It was Antonio Nariño. He knocked briefly, waited, then said he would come back at eight. Soon Prebend Rosillo left with Don Sinforoso Mutis and another gentleman named París. Remembering the troubles of Nariño and Mutis in the revolt of '94, Salgar suspected some mischief, and dispatched his nephew to talk to Nariño. Later, the nephew replied that Dr. Rosillo was in a position to find posts in the new revolutionary government for Dr. Salgar. Upon inquiry, Dr. Salgar discovered that some posts were to be filled, but the vicar general and Dr. Andrade were to be excluded. Carlos, a talkative fellow, informed his Uncle Pedro,

6. *Ibid.,* pp. 278–279.

7. *Ibid.,* p. 279.

the curate, that a lieutenancy at least, perhaps a captaincy, had been promised by Nariño to Carlos in the revolutionary government. He further stated that Nariño had set aside a thousand ounces of gold to bribe the troops. Don Antonio Baraya of the palace guards hinted at prison for the viceroy. Plans had been made to get six thousand men from Socorro and fifteen hundred from Zipaquirá. Many slaves from La Mesa would help in return for their liberty. Senor Miñano was to be president of the secret *junta* and he too had promised Carlos Salgar a lieutenancy at the very least.

Two days later nephew and uncle met again at Pedro's house in the afternoon. Plans had been changed. Senor Miñano was not to be president; instead he would proceed to Cartagena to win over the troops in the plaza there. Don Luis Caicedo would be president the first two years, and afterward Don Pedro Groot or Nariño. Groot was due that very day to report on available funds in the strongboxes. About fifty-five thousand pesos were already on hand and there would also be money in the mint. Instead of one hundred thousand as first suggested, the viceroy would get only ten thousand for abdicating. The viceroy's wife would be deprived of eighty thousand pesos of her income in pearls and other jewels, as a penalty for having sold government posts for money and then having gone back on her promises.[8]

Other plans included removal of royal officials from their posts, and beheading of Hernández de Alba and the royal assessor. Carlos likewise told Uncle Pedro that Senor Miñano already had drawn up a summary legally justifying his plans against the royal *audiencia*. In spite of blood-ties with his nephew, and friendship with Dr. Rosillo, Pedro Salgar stated that his conscience as vassal, Christian, and priest compelled him to inform on his nephew and his friends.[9]

A month later, Pedro tightened the noose around the incarcerated leaders, Nariño and Miñano. In previous testimony, he had neglected to mention that Dr. Sinforoso Mutis had promised four hundred dollars *(pesos fuertes)* to anyone who would kill *Oidor* Hernández de Alba. He had neglected to mention in previous testimony that his nephew, Carlos, had informed him that for troops, Nariño also counted on men in Santa Fé to whom he would give one thousand ounces of gold plus a regular allowance extra of an ounce a month; and on Negroes from La Mesa and Villa de Purificación who would be granted their freedom. Don Domingo

---

8. For instance, a certain Canabal from Cartagena had paid 10,000 pesos for a job, but was robbed of the job and the money too.

9. Posada and Ibáñez, *El Precursor,* pp. 279–282.

Caicedo had gone there to make them such an offer while Rosillo's nephew had gone the other way to Charalá with the same object in mind. Salgar's nephew, Carlos, had produced a letter to prove the Charalá offer. When asked by Pedro if there was any written plan, Carlos had replied: "Yes, a very good one, for a new system of government, was in the possession of Don Manuel Pardo." Carlos promised to get a copy for his Uncle Pedro, but did not return.[10]

Extraordinary Session

Threatened with mutiny, murder, and mass rebellion, the *audiencia* met in extraordinary session *(acuerdo extraordinario)* on October 20, 1809. Don Francisco Manuel Herrera presided. Three other *oidores* and two fiscals, one civil and one criminal, were present. Juan Hernández de Alba, Nariño's ancient enemy, was senior member *(decano)*. The additional *oidores* were Don Francisco Cortázar and Don Joaquín Carrión y Moreno. Don Diego de Frías was fiscal of the civil court and Don Manuel Martínez Mancilla fiscal of the criminal chamber of the *audiencia.*[11]

A summary view of the situation indicated a continuing threat from the Quito rebellion. Special sessions of the *audiencia* September 6, and 11, and Ocober 12, revealed an alarming spread of rebellion into the very highest levels of creole society, both secular and religious. Those implicated in an effort to overthrow the Spanish rule and set up an independent Junta Suprema included, besides Nariño, the canon Dr. Andres Rosillo, the *alcalde ordinario,* Don Luis Caicedo, and the royal official, Don Pedro Groot, as well as two lawyers, Don Joaquín Camacho and Don Ignacio Herrera.

Dr. Rosillo was also accused of trying to suborn the viceroy and his wife. He had asked them to join the plotters in a very private conference in the palace, September 25 or 26. He had told the viceregal pair that the real truth about Spain was not reaching Santa Fé. Ferdinand VII was already dead, killed by strangling, dagger or poison, and since the viceroy and his wife were well liked in Santa Fé, they should join the plot to proclaim the viceroy as king. This done, his excellency could count on the support of forty thousand men, already armed and supplied with artillery under the command of a friend of the viceroy. Dr. Rosillo further informed the wife of the viceroy that he had received letters from many who were impatiently awaiting the signal to rise. The signal

---

10. *Ibid.,* p. 283.
11. *Ibid.,* p. 284.

was to be a rather English sounding word: *Charrortón*. The *virreina,* shocked, dismissed Dr. Rosillo with the statement that she wished no more kingdom than the kingdom of heaven.

All this was told by her to the vicar general and governor of the archbishopric, Don Domingo Duquesne. Because of his extreme deafness, the viceroy seems not to have understood about Rosillo's offer. Therefore efforts were made by the fiscals, Frias and Martínez Mancilla, to draw out more information from their friend, Dr. Rosillo. The curate willingly complied. After referring to the success of the Quito revolt, he spoke of the tyranny of the Spaniards in America ever since the Conquest, for which they were now paying. The Spaniards would not give honorable posts in the government to the Americans, but now, out of fear, called them brothers. Dr. Rosillo reported that, a little while before, the Marquis of Selva Alegre, fearing that the Quiteños might win superiority over Santa Fé, had made a plan for the independence of America,[12] and the Marquis spoke critically of the viceroy and his wife for selling government jobs.

When asked to prefer formal charges as basis for court action, the viceroy refused on the grounds that the alleged subversive talk had not been with him but with his wife. Nevertheless, the *oidores* and fiscals continued their case without viceregal specification of charges.[13]

Back in Jail

Exactly one month after the top secret meeting of the *audiencia,* there burst another bombshell which led to the jailing of Nariño. Camilo Torres, speaking for the *cabildo* of Santa Fé, presented his famous *Memorial of Grievances* against the Junta Central in Spain. Spain was given thirty-six representatives in the new Cortes, the vast colonies of America only nine! This was intolerable![14] This memorial of the *cabildo* was generously sprinkled with impassioned demands for equality, sacred equality, and ended with the hope that "Heaven might prevent the wish of the *cabildo* that ideas less liberal should bring about the lamentable result of an eternal separation."[15]

The viceroy, irresolute like his master Charles IV, vacillated between force and compromise. He ordered the eleven signers to be shadowed and their *Memorial of Grievances* suppressed, and he refused

---

12. *Ibid.,* pp. 285–286.

13. *Ibid.,* p. 287.

14. Manuel Antonio Pombo and José Joaquin Guerra, comps., *Constituciones de Colombia* (2nd ed., 2 vols., Bogotá, 1911), I, 27–42.

15. *Ibid.,* p. 42.

to forward a copy to Spain.[16] One of the signatures on the document belonged to an in-law of Nariño, José Ortega. the other ten signers were prominent creoles of the *cabildo,* well known to Nariño and, like Luis Caicedo and José Acevedo y Gómez, persons prominently mentioned in earlier plots against the royal government.[17]

Three days later, on November 23, 1809, Nariño was unceremoniously ordered to accompany the major of the guard, Don Rafael de Córdoba, at 3 p.m., to the viceregal palace. They did not go to the palace, however, but to the barracks jail or *auxiliar,* where Nariño was left without explanation in the custody of the officer of the day, Don José María Bermeco.[18]

Better communications or a more effective executive in Spain, or in Santa Fé, might have prevented an open break at this time. A new and better offer of representation was soon suggested by the *junta* of the Regency, meeting in Cádiz in May, 1810. There twenty-six deputies were allotted to the Americans.[19]

This offer arrived too late to stop the independence trend in Santa Fé and, in the meantime, the viceroy continued his tough policy toward Nariño and *Oidor* Miñano. They had just settled down to sleep in their new quarters in the *auxiliar* barracks when a guard shook them.

"What time is it?"

"Two o'clock in the morning, get up, get dressed, we are going for a ride."[20]

It was still dark when their cavalry escort, without answering any further questions, mounted their horses and led the prisoners out of town. Nariño's mount was a vicious nag provided for the occasion by Don Lorenzo de la Sierra. The brute would scarcely let his rider stay up, even as far as the exit from the city, whence the prisoner had to walk as far as the ridge, at which point one of Nariño's sons overtook the party with a good horse, which, Nariño's jailers fortunately allowed him to use.[21]

On the same day, November 24, 1809, as they rode down to Facatativá, the lieutenant in charge, Angel González, informed his prisoners that he had been given only three hundred pesos for the subsistence of Miñano and not a penny for Nariño. So a peon was

16. *Ibid.,* pp. 27, 42.
17. *Ibid.,* I, 42. Posada and Ibáñez, *El Precursor,* pp. 277, 278, 281, 284.
18. Posada and Ibáñez, *El Precursor,* p. 307.
19. Pombo and Guerra, *Constituciones de Colombia,* I, 42.
20. Posada and Ibáñez, *El Precursor,* p. 307.
21. *Ibid.*

dispatched posthaste to Nariño's wife at home to try to borrow a little money. She had to sell a pair of English boots, just arrived from Cartagena three days before. The ten peso boots brought four pesos. This sum took care of the prisoner's expenses as far as El Banco, whence they proceeded with the aid of another hundred sent through Domingo Nieto at Honda from Pedro Groot, and an additional fifty sent by Ignacio Camacho.[22]

A Brief Respite

Upon leaving Honda, the prisoners were told their destination. One of the viceroy's servants told them they were going to the *castillo* of Cartagena, there to be locked up incommunicado without ink or paper until death. This determined Nariño to attempt flight. A little past Banco, during the dark of a rainy, stormy night, he slipped away, leaving a note for his captor, Ángel González:

> My dear Lieutenant: The imperious law of necessity obliges me to take a step contrary to my sentiments. The company of the *Angels* is fine for a trip to heaven but not for a voyage to a dungeon where I shall be loaded with chains and shackles. For this reason I am impelled to separate myself from your pleasant company.
>
> > Your Obedient Servant,
> > Antonio Nariño.[23]

Accompanied only by his son, he commandeered a two-oared *piragua* and made Santa Marta in three days, and if some "cursed Catalan" had not denounced him to the government, his "ferocious judges and the pious *virreina* would not have had the pleasure of seeing me groaning in jail in Bocachica as they prophesied."[24]

On the afternoon of December 20, 1809, Nariño and his son were found in the house of a curate, the rector of Santa Marta, were loaded with chains and locked up in the windowless jail of the militia barracks. While fastening the chains, the jailer began stripping both father and son of all their possessions. The father flew into a rage at this final insult to his person, but the jailer flung at him a watch, a change purse, and a pocket book before leading him off to prison.[25]

Imprisoned and Chained

Twelve days later, January 2, 1810, he was sent in chains to Cartagena. There he sold his last possessions, some handkerchiefs, to

---

22. *Ibid.,* p. 308.
23. *Ibid.*
24. *Ibid.*
25. *Ibid.*

get a few chickens to eat. In the new jail his light chains were replaced with thirty-six pound chains and he was transferred to the death cell used for convicted highwaymen. It was situated over an open sewer covered only in places by planks and surrounded by sewage filth. There the prisoner stayed until January 5 with almost no air, bread, or water for three days. The chains made sores on his body and the stink was so great the guards would not enter, even with the door open.

On the third day, January 5, when Nariño was no longer able to lift his arms or legs, Governor Montes ordered his chains removed on one leg but increased to a length of seven yards. He was transferred to a new cell on January 20, after the dungeons of Bocachica prison had been remodeled and strengthened. The commandant, the sergeant, and twelve soldiers escorted him to his new jail where he stayed four months until May 21, 1810, sick, loaded with chains, without communication and still with no knowledge of why he had been so treated.[26]

The new administration of Governor Montes was also ignorant of the charges or crimes attributed to the prisoner and asked for some enlightenment in a letter written to the viceroy on May 14, 1810. He also informed his superiors that he had transferred his prisoners to the prison of the Tribunal of the Inquisition in order to keep them from dying. No answer came.[27]

A compassionate citizen named Enrique Samoyar decided to keep Nariño alive and took upon himself the expense of feeding the prisoner in jail. In the latter part of May the new commissioner from Spain, Antonio Villavicencio,[28] took the responsibility of removing Nariño's chains and of countermanding the sentence by which he was to have been sent to Puerto Rico to be executed.[29]

From June 1 to about July 15, Nariño luxuriated in the comfort of the Inquisition jail. He concentrated on regaining his health and strength. No longer obliged to wear irons, he ate well, thanks to his God-sent patron, who spent in all 772 pesos, two-and-a-half *reales*. A friend, Don Juan Vicente Romero Campo, spent on Nariño's food an additional eight hundred pesos.[30]

In the month of July, when Governor Montes finally freed Nariño under bond to cure his illness, open revolt had broken out in Santa Fé,

---

26. *Ibid.*, p. 310.

27. *Ibid.*, p. 288.

28. Antonio Villavicencio was the first victim of Morillo's bloody reconquest of 1816 and is one of the martyrs honored in Bogotá's "Panteon."

29. *Ibid.*, pp. 310–311.

30. *Ibid.*, pp. 301–311.

beginning with the events of July 20, 1810. As Nariño put it, "now begins a new order of things."[31] Nariño expected to be freed in triumph like Dr. Andres Rosillo who had been made a voting member of the Junta, or loaded with honors and income like his erstwhile cell-mate *Oidor* Baltasar Miñano of Quito, or made sergeant major like Joaquín Ricaurte in Maracaibo. At least some slight token seemed reasonable to expect in return for years of suffering for the *patria*. But no reward came.[32]

The Road to Recovery

While other jail-mates passed on to glory, honor, and wealth in the new regime, the Colombian Precursor remained forgotten throughout the summer and fall of 1810 until at last, on October 20, an order came to return Nariño to Santa Fé. *Oidor* Francisco Cortázar authorized Magdalena Ortega to issue bond for a loan of four hundred pesos to pay for the journey homeward from Cartagena. About two months later, around Christmas time, the traveling prisoner was home again in Bogotá; ill, broken, and bankrupt. He now rejoined a sick and dying wife; forgotten by his countrymen, but at last free![33] The greater part of the year that followed — December, 1810, to December, 1811 — was spent in three projects: (1) restoring his health, (2) restoring his wealth at the expense of ex-Viceroy Amar, and (3) entering on his new career which was to lead him to the viceregal palace as president — the career of editor of a newspaper, *La Bagatela*.[34]

---

31. *Ibid.,* p. 311.
32. *Ibid.*
33. *Ibid.,* pp. 312, 314, 320.
34. *Ibid.,* pp. 320–336.

CHAPTER VII

THE PROBLEMS
OF A PRESIDENT

The conflicting aims of royalist versus republican, and federalist versus centralist, which rent Colombia in 1811, guaranteed Nariño a rocky ride to the presidency, many enemies while in office, and the likelihood of a very insecure term. Nariño was outspoken, however, in his views as a republican and a centralist. He refused to compromise. His medium for expressing his views was a new Sunday newspaper, *La Bagatela,* which Nariño wrote and published continuously for thirty-eight weeks,[1] from the first issue on Sunday, July 14, 1811, to the last, on April 12, 1812.[2] The publication was used first as an organ for criticizing such federalists as President Lozano. After Nariño replaced Lozano in September, 1811, it was used primarily to defend Nariño in office.[3]

The growing trend toward independence in Bogotá was accompanied by a mushrooming of newspapers throughout New Granada. The *Diario político,* edited by Francisco José de Caldas and Joaquín Camacho, began to publish resolutions of the Junta Suprema at public expense for presiding officer Miguel Pey. Forty-six numbers were issued beginning with August 27, 1810, and ending with February 10, 1811. It was the bulletin of revolutionary acts of independence and as the supporter of burgeoning centralism in Santa Fé, was opposed, in September, by the rival organ of the Cartagena *junta,* the *Argos,* which soon satirized Cundinamarca President Jorge Tadeo Lonzano as "Jorge I."[4]

---

1. Posada and Ibáñez, *El Precursor,* p. xxi. Otero Muñoz, *Historia del periodismo,* p. 37.

2. See the 1947 reprint of *La Bagatela, passim.*

3. Vergara y Vergara, *Historia de la literatura en Nueva Granada,* I, 82, 97, 247–249. Otero Muñoz, *Historia del periodismo,* pp. 37–38. José M. Vergara y Vergara, *Vida y escritos del General Antonio Nariño* (2nd ed. [facsimile reprint of 1859 ed.], Bogotá, 1946), *passim.*

4. Otero Muñoz, *Historia del periodismo,* p. 36.

A Jubilant Period

On Bastille day, July 14, 1811, Nariño issued a call for total independence with his first issue of *La Bagatela,* thus paving the way for the July, 1813, declaration of total independence.[5]

Why must we live another hundred or two hundred years in slavery to brutalize us still further; they have just tried to persuade us that the American and the African were born to serve a handful of Europeans just because they learned to cheat and to kill before we did; we must agree to stand together; now is the time to free ourselves ... if not, we shall never get free. Our oppression will increase in double proportion to the growth of fear in our oppressors. The events in Quito, La Paz, and the *llanos* were just the prelude of the great tragedy which, for the second time, is being prepared for America. . . .

The talk of liberalism in Spain is a delusion. . . . May heaven preserve us from falling back into the hands of our former masters! The blood which the lash of war has not yet poured forth we will live to see — blood run in rivers turned loose by these cutthroat murderers. Even if this does not happen, what sense does it make for a mere handful of men to rule the whole world from a center two thousand miles away with a vast ocean between them?[6]

Nariño was thus launched for the third time in seventeen years into his never-ending battle for an independent *patria.* Two days later came the death of Nariño's faithful companion of many victories and defeats. José María Caballero entered this notation in his diary for the year 1811: "June 16 — Doña Magdalena Ortega, wife of Don Antonio Nariño died today and was buried in La Candelaria."[7]

President Jorge Tadeo Lozano, in office since May 25, 1811, had not done much to replace the revenue lost by the abolition of royal monopolies but was able to celebrate Bastille day with the happy announcement that July 14 was to be a day of fiesta. After parades, dances of all sorts — Granada, gypsy, wild Indian, cowboy, and ancient Spanish — the program ended appropriately after sundown with a glorious display of fireworks. Six days later the anniversary of Colombia's first real independence day was celebrated in similar fashion, with the addition of illuminated streets at night, a High Mass in the cathedral for the national assembly, firing of salutes by the Provincial Battalion and the Provincial Regiment, and a fine sermon in the cathedral[8] by P. Chavarría, prior of San Agustín.

---

5. *Ibid.,* p. 37. Vergara y Vergara, *Vida y escritos,* pp. 124–130.

6. *Ibid.,* pp. 125–127.

7. Caballero, Diary, p. 138. The Caballero diary ends with the year 1819. It is very detailed from 1784 to 1819.

8. Caballero, Diary, pp. 139–140.

Not much work was likely to get done in this jubilee atmosphere. Perhaps with that in mind, the editor of *La Bagatela* devoted his second issue of the next day, July 21, 1811, to a discussion of pertinent aspects of the constitution of the United States, a long harangue on the need for a more genuine freedom of the press, and an allegorical warning against idle disagreements among the newly liberated citizens.[9] Issue number 3 of *La Bagatela* brought Nariño's opposition to states' rights out in the open:

The Congress of the United States does not have to get the consent of all the respective states . . . except where the articles of the confederation are silent, then only is the unanimity of all the states in Congress required *as well as the approval* of each state separately. . . . It is necessary to distinguish between the object of this so-called assembly, namely a *Convention,* which made that which is called a *Constitution or form of government* and the duties of later assemblies charged with ordinary legislative power, which cannot separate itself from principles established in the constitution. . . . What we need is a *Federative* Congress of independent sovereign states, united, however, for peace and war so as to be recognized as a unit as far away as Europe, China, Tartary. . . .[10]

Meanwhile the new government celebrated by cutting interest rates from fifteen to two per cent, raising a few militiamen, and ringing the bells on August 21 to commemorate the total independence of Caracas. The republican mobs were much inflated by events in Caracas, shouting death to the Regency and death to the Spaniards *(chapetones),* while the Spaniards watched fearfully from behind Bogotá's shuttered windows.[11]

A week later, August 29, 1811, a state reception was held for the "incomparable, unconquerable, immortal hero who today completes seventeen years of prisons and suffering for the *patria,* Antonio Nariño."[12] It was an enormous official celebration. The governor of the state, the *corregidor* of the city, the senior intendant of justice and inspector-judge of the theater were all present to compliment the hero "who has at last seen the liberty of his country in spite of many reverses and whose many sufferings will some day be written down in full."[13]

Meanwhile every Sunday saw another issue of *La Bagatela,* still complaining about a lack of unity in New Granada and lack of force

---

9. Vergara y Vergara, *Vida y escritos,* pp. 131–138.

10. *Ibid.,* pp. 138–143.

11. Caballero, Diary, p. 140.

12. *Ibid.,* p. 141.

13. *Ibid.*

in its chief executive, President Lozano.[14] Today we would find it hard
to conceive of these tiny broadsides as sufficient power to oust a president
and elect the editor as the new chief executive. Nevertheless, this newspaper campaign was the weapon which unseated the first president of
Cundinamarca, and carried Editor Nariño to the viceregal palace as
second president on September 19, 1811.[15]

Events had seemed to augur well for President Lozano. For the
previous two weeks, the cause of independence was seen as winning
everywhere. The counter-revolution in Caracas was reported suppressed
with the imprisonment of fifty-four royalists and the hanging of twelve
others. The new viceroy for Santa Fé, Francisco Javier Venegas, was
falsely reported killed in battle by the Mexicans. Tacón was retreating
in the south from republican Popayán. "More parades, dancing in the
streets and fireworks, shouts everywhere of Hurrah for the valiant
Mexicans! Long live the independence of Caracas and the unconquerable
Baraya!"[16]

A New President

Everybody was happy on September 19, in Bogotá — everybody
except President Lozano for whom the day started badly. Newspapers
said the public was angered with his inactivity. Royalist enemies were
reported still threatening on all sides. Crowds gathered in the streets. The
mob shouted for action as they pushed toward the Palace of Justice:
"Abolish the Company of Challardas! Down with the Spaniards! Long
live the National Guard and the Provincial Regiment!"[17]

At nine o'clock the Junta was called into special session. The
members debated. At four o'clock in the afternoon they came out.
"Lozano has resigned; Nariño has been elected your new president."
The town went wild. At 1 a.m. they were still shouting *vivas*. The new
government finally had to issue a special proclamation to send them
home to bed, as another day was dawning in the east.[18]

Two days later, civil war was brewing in Bogotá. Two hundred
armed men gathered in the barracks of the *Milicias* shouting for Nariño.
The *Nacionales, Patriotas* and *Artillería* companies joined them. Not
far away, the Provincial Regiment gathered, shouting for Lozano. At
four in the afternoon the Junta went into special session. At ten they

---

14. Vergara y Vergara, *Vida y escritos,* pp. 157–209.
15. Caballero, Diary, p. 141.
16. *Ibid.*
17. *Ibid.*
18. *Ibid.*

came out and announced the re-election of Antonio Nariño. This time the chronicler made no mention of cheers, or fireworks, or dancing. The armed rivals remained armed throughout the night.[19]

The Lozano government had lasted a little less than six months. Lozano had initiated the republic of Cundinamarca on March 30, 1811,[20] and had promulgated the new constitution of Cundinamarca on April 4, 1811, closely modelled on that of the United States.[21] Now there was a new president.

What would Nariño do about the old constitution which he had condemned as unsuitable? If he changed it, how would he change it? How long would his ousted rival, Lozano, remain at peace with him? These questions kept the air electrified throughout 1811. They led to trouble and civil war later. In order to maintain support for his new government, the journalist-president created two more publications. In October, 1811, the first issue of the *Gazeta ministerial de Cundinamarca* was created by order of the president. Its directors were Miguel José Montalve and José María Gómez de Salazar. The editor was Manuel de Socorro Rodríguez. In many ways this official journal was the most successful of any created in the new era of journalism. Most important to its influence was its long life. It was issued 210 times up to February 16, 1815, when abolished by the Spanish reconquest. Nariño also ordered published the *Noticias del día* (1812–1815) and *Providencias del gobierno,* consisting primarily of decrees and resolutions of the executive. The Precursor was a great believer in newspapers as political weapons and showed his consistent faith in the power of the pen to the very last year of his life. In his fight with Santander in 1822, Nariño founded *El Insurgente* and a few months later he replied to Santander's *El Patriota* (1823) with the short-lived *Toros de Fucha.* The irony of *El Insurgente* was that it put Nariño in the false position of appearing to defend his old enemies, the federalists, when, in fact, he was merely demanding constitutional reforms.[22]

Struggle for Unity

It was a fact that Nariño had ousted his predecessor Lozano with *La Bagatela.* This becomes crystal-clear from reading the special issue "Noticias muy gordas," which appeared the day of the coup d'état,

---

19. *Ibid.,* p. 142.

20. William M. Gibson, *The Constitutions of Colombia* (Durham, N. C., 1948), p. 8. Pombo and Guerra, *Constituciones de Colombia,* I, 70, 152.

21. *Ibid.,* I, 70.

22. Otero Muñoz, *Historia del periodismo,* pp. 41, 45.

September 19, 1811.[23] That special issue made very clear Nariño's chief problem once in power: how to unite the rival cities and *juntas* in the face of rising royalist sentiments and forces. Soldiers were needed, money was needed, but, most important, the public must learn the dangers of disunity and over-confidence. No final victory was yet in sight. The Cartagena *junta* was jealous of the government in Santa Fé. Santa Marta was full of royalists inclined to accept the new viceroy, Benito Pérez. "While our enemies are sharpening their swords to cut our throats, the deputies of the Congress occupy themselves looking for posts of honor where they can shine, ventilating hair-splitting questions, creating schisms. Will we, in the end, be free?"[24]

The question was rhetorical. The answer was "No," or was apt to be, unless the public could be aroused to its real danger. *La Bagatela* for September 19, 1811 — the same one which had ousted Lozano and raised Nariño to the presidency, outlined the chief dangers. Viceroy Pérez and the old *audiencia* of Santa Fé were in Santa Marta. Talledo had absconded with six thousand pesos entrusted to him by the *junta* of Cartagena for the dike (canal), and was in Santa Marta. Don Domingo Esquiaqui, with troops, was deserting to the royalists. Other citizens of Santa Marta were joining them. In fact, Santa Marta was a very pesthole of royalists. Pamplona and Girón to the north had been captured by the enemy. To the south, Quito's fate was unknown. Reports of Tacón gaining money and men augured ill for Quito. People in Popayán were shifting to his side. And what had Santa Fé accomplished?

We have laid one egg and now we quit to debate! Words will not save us!. . . Bayonets we must oppose to their acts. Let's not deceive ourselves — to them we are rebels, traitors to be treated as such if we lose; lances, not words we will face then. Domínguez Vallejo, Samano, Gutiérrez, Mansilla, Cortázar, and these countless others we let escape with life . . . will give us death. Now all who are not with us are against us. . . . If they do not give us their lives, their treasures, their promised support, they shall be declared enemies and treated as such. If any man prefer slavery to freedom with us, let him get out now! The hour to unite has arrived!. . . No more inaction! Citizens of Cundinamarca, *save your native land or die!*[25]

The Precursor called for action. He got action. Lozano went out; Nariño went in. Two parties were created, the centralists with Nariño, the federalists with Lozano, and from that day to this, two rival parties

---

23. Vergara y Vergara, *Vida y escritos,* pp. 217–220.

24. *Ibid.,* p. 217.

25. *Ibid.,* pp. 217–220.

have with great gusto rushed in to save their native land and die — but usually at the hand of their own fellow-countrymen! This tendency became more apparent when the Lozano group, ignoring Nariño and his government, debated and passed, on November 27, 1811, the Act of Federation of the United Provinces of New Granada, a weak federation in which the provinces "bind themselves by a pact as permanent as the wretched human state permits."[26] To this, *La Bagatela* replied on the next day, November 28, 1811, with withering sarcasm and renewed warning to unite in the face of deadly peril on all sides. Equal sovereign independent states indeed! How long could they hope to remain so if they remained disunited while Spain won everywhere! Santa Marta royalists were advancing on Ocaña; Cartagena remained hostile; Dupar Valley and the Orinoco were open avenues of attack; Quito, Panama, Guayaquil, Cuenca were no longer free. The royalist leaders, Tacón, Nemesio Salcedo, Melchor Aymerich, José Millares, and Joaquín Molina were still alive. Enemies surrounded Santa Fé on all sides, growing in number while the heart of Cundinamarca continued its futile federalist anarchy, arguing about titles, jobs, honors. "Our revolution seems more like a lawsuit over lands than a political transformation to recoup our liberties."[27]

We seem not to see that our liberty rests on our armaments, not our words. . . . Talk! talk! talk! What kind of stupidity is this sort of sickness? What kind of egotism makes us believe we can create an army with a few words and kicks? . . . Do we have some Santiago who will appear in our midst and lead us out of confusion against our enemies? . . . We need troops, not words, arms, money. . . . If we return to slavery we shall have no recourse but tears — that is, if they leave us our eyes!"[28]

Government Begins

Faced with the grim need for united action against the royalists everywhere, the congress of free, sovereign, and independent states that had been envisaged in the constitution of November 27, 1811, was not installed until October 4, 1812, in Leiva. Nariño operated in the meantime as a strong executive with emergency powers. When, later, in October, 1812, the headless congress came into operation at Leiva, its impracticability became so patent that an amendment was finally passed on September 23, 1814, authorizing congress to set up an executive

---

26. Gibson, *Constitutions of Colombia*, pp. 8, 9. Pombo and Guerra, *Constituciones de Colombia*, I, 156.

27. Vergara y Vergara, *Vida y escritos*, p. 282.

28. *Ibid.*, p. 283.

triumvirate elected by congress, the chairmanship of the triumvirate to rotate every four months.[29]

There is no doubt that much of the bloodshed, defeat, and bitter tears of the Spanish reconquest (1811–1816) can be attributed to the incredible anarchy and particularism of those years. But Nariño was fated to be another Cassandra. His warnings fell on deaf ears; his efforts ended in bitter defeat. Enemies dubbed him dictator. Thus he was thanked. For a short time, however, his victory of September 19 was crowned with popularity. The fickle mob rent the air with *vivas* for their new leader. Troops marched off in all directions to promised victories. The senate passed a resolution to hold a *residencia* (investigation) of the outgoing president, Lozano, on November 7. An election was held on November 10 for procurators to the electoral college, everyone voting for a list of eighteen persons. On the twenty-sixth of November came the election of the college, at which time ugly signs appeared on the walls saying: "Death to the President, the commandant, and the Captain of Artillery. Long live the Regency and death to the government . . . bad, all bad."[30]

On December 23, 1811, the electoral college was installed and chose as its president, Don Pedro Groot. Six salvos were fired in his honor in the plaza. The next day, the electoral college chose the interim president, Nariño, as president in his own right. There was general rejoicing and pealing of bells, musical festivals, fireworks, parades, salutes, and speeches, and an illumination of the whole plaza. Dancing and singing in the streets lasted far into the night of this Christmas Eve. Christmas day after the bull fights, the militia barracks were lighted up brilliantly with the following illuminated verses:

> With great tenderness and affection
> Love applauds obediently
> The great patriot Nariño
> Our worthy President[31]

At eight that night, the Provincial Battalion sounded retreat with many flourishes, after passing in review around the plaza. The plaza resounded with the music of several marches and the following day was a repetition for the Provincial Regiment, with more music and cannon

---

29. Gibson, *Constitutions of Colombia,* pp. 11, 12. Pombo and Guerra, *Constituciones de Colombia,* I, 510–519.

30. Caballero, Diary, p. 144.

31. *Ibid.,* p. 145.

salvos. Celebration continued on the twenty-seventh when the government ordered the whole city to be illuminated for three consecutive nights in honor of the installation of the electoral college and election of the president of the state. Bull fights were ordered for the afternoons, parades, candlelight processions, and fireworks for the night celebrations.[32]

A six-months' presidential amnesty beginning on Christmas Eve had already cleared the jails throughout Cundinamarca of all political and of most civil and criminal prisoners. Only those committed for the following crimes remained in jail or were exempt from the six-month amnesty if convicted before the expiration of the amnesty: forgery, sacrilege, sodomy, bestiality, murder, treason, and defalcation of government funds.[33]

The night of the twenty-seventh, the *Milicias* regiment staged a musical pageant under the direction of their sergeants and captains. Over two hundred marched out from barracks bearing giant wax torches, and in the middle, a lighthouse beacon a yard square escorted by armed soldiers who carried a huge *fleur de lis,* standard of the *Milicias,* alongside that, a crown with a palm tree transfixed by a sword preceded by an octave which read:

> La sabia providencia que he nombrado
> I elegido a Nariño Presidente,
> Bienes continuos hanos preparado
> Esperanzas de glorias permanentes
> Riquezas mil y aumentos del Estado
> Todos los pueblos con amor vehemente
> A disfrutar vendrán de su Gobierno
> Digno por cierto, de desearse, eterno.[34]

Arriving in front of the palace, the people raised standards, and troops, filling the streets as far as the eye could see, raised their weapons in unison. Three salvos were fired. Twenty dozen rockets and colored fireworks were set off with two dozen pinwheels. The procession entered the palace, stopped in front of the president's principal living room. The escort of sergeants marched forward to receive the presidential greeting. The president came out to greet his guests and then they all marched in to the candle-lighted rooms to dinner. The chronicler who was there reported:

---

32. *Ibid.*

33. Posada and Ibáñez, *El Precursor,* pp. 338–340.

34. Caballero, Diary, p. 146. "A wise providence which has named and elected Nariño president, has prepared for us continual good fortune; hopes for permanent glories, wealth and increase for the nation, all the peoples enthusiastic with love, eager to enjoy what will come from their government, worthy, for sure, to wish itself eternal."

It was good. After the banquet and dancing in the palace, some señoras danced the *contradanzas* and some the minuet. And the sergeant of volunteers, Nicolás Parada, began a play in praise of the president from the plaza while the music was playing, but because of the music he had to stop.[35]

As the year 1811 came to an end, the problems of a president fell momentarily from view. They appeared to be largely non-existent. Such, however, was not the case.

---

35. Caballero, Diary, p. 146.

CHAPTER VIII

DICTATOR-PRESIDENT
AND CIVIL WAR

Colombia Versus Bogotá

Nariño was probably the most reluctant dictator in Colombian history. He did not want dictatorship. It was thrust upon him by his fellow citizens and by the situation in 1812, which was to be a year of decision. Anarchy and particularism, added to civil wars and wars of conquest, made New Granada a land of chaos. Temporary dictatorship was the only alternative. This became increasing obvious to the centralist-minded editor-president. Rival juntas such as that of Cartagena, rival federalists such as those in the congress at Leiva, personal rivals such as the ousted Lozano, might claim that Nariño was already a dictator long before the official proclamation as such. However, the president put off absolutism as long as possible consistent with the desperate need for unity and order, in the face of enemies, foreign and domestic. Dictatorship, for him, was the last resort.

Liberty, excessive liberty, was the heady wine which made the citizens of New Granada crazy drunk in 1812. Not only were the old sections of the Spanish empire in rebellion against the Peninsular metropolis and in rivalry with each other, but even the cities and towns were in rivalry with each other: Cartagena against Santa Fé, Santa Fé against Tunja, and the federal congress, largely disregarded, against them all. Even worse, sections of cities were against other sections and individuals against individuals, all in the sacred name of liberty.

Liberty, the excessive liberty which leads to license, to anarchy and thence quickly to dictatorship was in the air everywhere. Nariño sensed it, feared it, and tried in vain to warn against this vicious cycle, so typical of all Latin American history since Independence.

We are not able to be simply citizens, free and independent, but we all wish to be sovereign; we prefer this Quixotism of a week, to a permanent liberty. Yet at this very moment, Cartagena is blockaded, a new viceroy, Pérez, is in Santa Marta and it is reported that reinforcements are en route to complete the subjugation of our realm. People of Cundinamarca, your liberty is about to be strangled in its cradle. . . . Away with these foolish rivalries. We must have a single thought, a single voice. Be free or die![1]

Dangers did not dampen New Year revelry in Santa Fé. On the first, there were parades, masked balls, decorated floats, musical plays, victory marches, fireworks, feasting, and dancing. On the fifth of January came more parades with the officials dressed like *oidores* with high Spanish collars, gaily decked horses, and bull fights and masquerades. On January 10, 1812, a regular Roman triumphal entry was arranged for the return of Brigadier Antonio Baraya, with cannon salutes, parades, *vivas,* illuminations, and a magnificent reception in the viceregal palace. More celebrations followed the next day, January 11, with a grand review and firing practice of the *Batalión de Patriotas* and the *Artillería,* and a musicale, fireworks, tableaux, and grand banquet and ball in the palace.

"More bulls, masquerades, and parades,"[2] wrote the commentator for January 12.

A serious note entered the scene when a small expedition went forth to keep San Gil allied to Santa Fé and prevent it from being swallowed up by Socorro. January 12 was also a day of near tragedy for on that date the erstwhile hero, Doctor Rosillo, made an attempt to assassinate President Nariño.[3]

According to Article 34, Title 5 of the constitution, Nariño decreed prison for Doctor Rosillo, but in consideration of the prisoner's clerical background specified the Convent of Candelaria as the place of incarceration. It appears, however, that the officials of the archbishopric refused to confirm the decree of the executive. After a review of Doctor Rosillo's case on January 18, 1812, he was set free without condition on February 7, 1812.[4]

Meanwhile more troops went out from Santa Fé to support San Gil: a second group on January 13, and the greater part of the garrison reserves on January 19, under Don Joaquín Ricaurte. Artillerymen, cannon, ammunition, a band, a chaplain, and a surgeon accompanied this latter group, but little or no news came back.

At least three partisan groups disagreed on the wisdom of the expedition to Vélez and San Gil. Some feared it would alarm other provinces. Some thought the reunification already a year and a half

---

1. Vergara y Vergara, *Vida y escritos,* pp. 290–291.
2. Caballero, Diary, p. 172.
3. Posada and Ibáñez, *El Precursor,* p. 354.
4. *Ibid,* p. 354.

overdue, and many said Bogotá had at last unmasked its own greedy ambition of conquest.[5]

A general amnesty was published on January 21, and a law was passed banning admission of foreigners under penalty of a ten-dollar fine. A pronouncement for "good government" was issued.[6]

Steps Toward Civil War

The steps which soon followed, leading toward civil war, have been outlined in the history of this period by Henao and Arrubla, so will not be repeated here.[7] Suffice it to say that Nariño was twice given dictatorial powers and twice resigned them as soon as the danger had passed.[8]

The Precursor also tasted the bitterness of betrayal by a trusted follower, Antonio Baraya, and discovered plots against his life by Rosillo and Miñano.[9] These and other similar facts illustrate the bitterness, blindness, and stupidity of the revolutionary governments in the face of the enemy — which gave this era the name it so thoroughly deserves, "Patria Boba" [10] — foolish fatherland.

Everywhere foolish Americans still hoped for better government under Ferdinand or the Regency. Everywhere in New Granada there were division, conflict, opposing plans, and material poverty — sovereign states of small size pretending to be rich and powerful. These dreamers could convince themselves they already possessed the qualities of a great state; armies, generals, libraries, cities, industries, universities, printing presses, arms and powder, and factories. Yet to Nariño it seemed "a sad comedy, like Sancho when his master took it into his head to believe, in his madness, that the flocks of sheep were armies." [11] "You can kill yourself trying to tell these truths to these excessive anarchic individualists." [12]

Even independence was not the same to all who desired it. Carácas could declare it on July 5 of 1811, but Santa Fé was still not clearly for it in 1812. Independence, to many, meant the right to be free of Bogotá without first declaring freedom from Spain.[13]

---

5. Nariño, *La Bagatela,* p. 180.
6. Caballero, Diary, pp. 147–148.
7. Henao and Arrubla, *op. cit.,* pp. 220–227.
8. *Ibid.,* pp. 222–225.
9. Posada and Ibáñez, *El Precursor,* p. 354.
10. See vol. I of *Biblioteca de historia nacional* (Bogotá, 1902).
11. *Ibid.,* p. 158.
12. Nariño, *La Bagatela,* p. 158.
13. *Ibid.,* pp. 163–165.

At the beginning of the new year, 1812, Nariño received a copy of the *Argos* of rival Cartagena which called him "an imprudent tyrant who recognizes no other law than his own wishes, whose ambition is so great he no longer tries to disguise it, whose true interest is to subject us to the government in Cádiz. Your president in Cundinamarca is a foolish dolt [*majadero*]."[14]

In the meantime the journalist-president continued the increasingly difficult task of answering his many enemies and critics both foreign and domestic, in the pages of *La Bagatela*. In the most desperate circumstances, Nariño was trying always to provide an example of truth and fair play, even to the extent of printing in his own paper lengthy quotations of other newspapers which attacked him, particularly the *Argos* of Cartagena.

Nariño did not hesitate to print the charges against his operation of the presidency: "Some call me a tyrant without principles or morals."[15] The most subtle and pernicious attacks came from those who pretended to oppose Nariño so that "not a drop of blood nor a penny shall be wasted . . . not even if we shed guilty blood to save the innocent[16] . . . yet no present evil is comparable to the new slavery of the realm."

La Bagatela was also accused by its enemies of being impious, blasphemous, and worthy of being "consigned to flames with its authors, sons and nephews unto the fifth generation."[17] "*La Bagatela* seems to desire monarchy yet on the next line wishes to hand over the kingdom to its enemies. . . . It says America has the same right to claim independence as Gil Blas had to break down the door in the robbers' cave, yet on the other hand states that the electoral college does not have the right to declare for independence."[18]

The electoral college was soundly criticized in this same January 16 issue of *La Bagatela*. As a revisionary body it had been installed on December 23, but after nearly a month of discussion, on January 8, it had accomplished almost nothing specific. It had after much debate desided that "the representative monarchy of Cundinamarca is not the basis of the constitution."[19]

Having destroyed a palace . . . an architect is expected to put some other building in its place. What new constitution has the electoral college put

---

14. *Ibid.,* pp. 168–169.
15. *Ibid.,* p. 180.
16. *Ibid.,* p. 181.
17. *Ibid.,* p. 206.
18. *Ibid.,* p. 207.
19. *Ibid.,* p. 182.

in place of the old? Instead of modifying or replacing the old structure they have merely torn it down. If the public now believes we should be independent and frankly republican, let them consult the wishes of the people and convoke a new constitutional college. Let us have an end of sophistries. If there is to be a new constitution instead of a revision, let it be done now; time is slipping away fast.

The president of Cundinamarca was clearly annoyed at the double-talk of an independent republic, still loyal to Ferdinand VII, and he was not afraid to say so. It was similar to another anomaly which should be stopped, the sending of money in response to the Papal bulls announcing crusades, an anachronistic taxpayer-gouging device, which even the priests admitted "smelled a little," *(olía un poco).*[20]

On January 19, 1812, the *Argos* accused Bogotá of subservience to royalty in that the government could not publish its gazette without previous consent of the king. "Learn from Cartagena which recognizes neither king nor rook."[21] Cartagena boasted that its paper was not like *La Bagatela,* a mouthpiece of the government. "Let the government of Cundinamarca quit publishing ministerial mouthpieces and you quit printing *La Bagatela* so that it will no longer be said, what has been so often repeated, that all Santa Fé thinks about is writing, while Cartagena is busy working."[22] To this Nariño replied in a footnote that everybody knew the commoner usage of *obrando* (easing nature) and it seemed more applicable to Cartagena than "working."[23]

Cartagena admitted being pro-Regency and Francophile under Pombo and Talledo, but boasted that it was better to smell French than to pretend to be American. Meanwhile the *Bagatela* warned of "Those boobs who were crazy enough to believe the Regency would send them a boatload of doubloons and crosses so they could all be rich and noble."[24]

In Cartagena, citizens were plain simple "Citizen" without any such unconstitutional, undemocratic prefixes as "Don" or "Excellency" or "Highness," or such fancy honors of royalty as crosses of Montesa and Charles III — the kind that were given after independence in Bogotá by its president. "In Cartagena there was true republican democracy, like that of North America, an exact copy of the North

---

20. *Ibid.,* p. 183.
21. Caballero, Diary, p. 189.
22. Nariño, *La Bagatela,* p. 200.
23. *Ibid.,* February 23, 1812, pp. 203–205.
24. *Ibid.,* p. 180.

American constitution, a senate. . . . Which makes me proud to be as always a resident of that city where honor is always triumphant . . . Cartagena."[25]

In the February 1 issue, the editor-president bemoaned the reduced state of Cundinamarca, literally and figuratively.

Here we are now the capital of a small and shrinking province with little income and many officials; one part of the populace is discontented with the new form of government. . . . We need troops, money, guns, and printing presses. Yet we are surrounded with incorrigible regentists, an angry rabble, centralists, congress supporters, lukewarm patriots interested primarily in themselves, we seem to be on the eve of our ruination. . . .

Cundinamarca is for the moment the most fortunate portion of our continent, perhaps of the whole world. Cast your eyes for a moment on Mexico, Lima, Buenos Aires, Caracas, Quito; nay even Socorro, without mentioning inflamed Europe, and everywhere you will see the earth stained with blood. Meanwhile here with us, no father weeps for a son destroyed, no wife bemoans her lost husband, no brother laments the loss of a sister; we have not shed a drop of blood, nor a tear. . . . All follow their accustomed manner of life . . . All sleep tranquil in their homes enjoying the fruits of their labor in peace. Everyone speaks and writes with unfettered freedom, without government interference with the development of their ideas.

. . . Although you hear some say religion has suffered, don't believe it! A few practices have altered . . . as always and everywhere a few pessimistic, timid souls go around seeing evil omens in crosses which chance or the wind makes of straws in the alleys, and these folks are always getting alarmed at some minor change of ceremony or worship and predict dire doom. But pay no attention, religion is strong in its purity and there are fewer of these hypocrites than usual around today.[26]

With great sarcasm *La Bagatela* ridiculed the thinking of the weak-kneed, slow-witted patriots who "will embrace their ancient slavery in order to live in peace."[27] To the charge that he was a dim-witted Quixote, the editor-president replied that he seemed to have many followers judging from the "nine thousand copies of *La Bagatela* which have been sold in seven months."

They say the Montalván Junta commands school boys to write replies to the *Bagatela*. . . . It looks like it to judge from their style and lack of logic, their puerilities and filthy sandalmaker language! . . . As final summary, however, let me repeat: the enemies who will reconquer from us our freedom gather increasingly day by day. They hope to gain by our lack of unity. That is what gives them hope. . . . Let us then open our eyes, frustrate the plans

---

25. *Ibid.,* pp. 202–205.
26. *Ibid.,* pp. 185–187.
27. *Ibid.,* p. 209.

of our enemies, internal as well as external. Let us unite the provinces to defend ourselves, without reducing any one to dependency on any other; thus we shall remain invincible and happy.[28]

Ill-Fated Expedition

After two months of preparation, the ill-fated expedition of General Antonio Baraya set out on March 8 to subdue rival Tunja and restore it to the rule of Cundinamarca. Little did the two Antonios, Baraya and Nariño, suspect that their parting as friends was to be followed soon by their meeting as enemies. If President Nariño had suspected that his general and his troops would soon return to attack their native city, it is certain that they would not have been given such a warm send-off and very likely would not have been sent at all. The expedition included fifty men of the *Patriotas* regiment, twenty artillerymen, twenty of the *Milicias,* sixty *Nacionales* and *Provinciales,* and the rest all veteran cavalry. The expedition was well provided with eighty loads of ammunition, two howitzers, and six pieces of light artillery.[29]

In his next to the last *Bagatela,* of March 9, 1812, the author begged the rival cities to give up their costly feud, "for while *Argos* and *Bagatela* argue with each other, the enemy is dividing and conquering our provinces one at a time, just as the Romans used to do."[30]

By March 9, 1812, it was clear to the president that disunity was opening the gates of the republic to all sorts of tragic defeats. France, if she subjugated all of Spain, would proceed to the conquest of America. Whereas if Spain escaped the relentless stranglehold of Napoleon, the colonies would be even less fortunate, since Spain would then be free to fall on America with all her hate and fury. There was, therefore, only one hopeful alternative — unity! Quito, Popayán, Santa Fé, and Cartagena, acting together, could establish a strong confederation. Meanwhile disunity caused a loss of precious time. Once powerful, victorious, and recognized in Europe, the confederation could safely reconsider the relationships of the provinces to the central government, but to attempt decentralization in weakness and face to face with strong enemies could lead only to catastrophe. "Cartagena needs help; what we need in our present hour of crisis is to establish a national militia so that every man becomes a soldier . . . so that America may be and remain free and her independence be recognized by all nations."[31]

---

28. *Ibid.,* p. 224.
29. Caballero, Diary, p. 149.
30. Nariño, *La Bagatela,* p. 218.
31. *Ibid.,* p. 315.

Meanwhile, with Cartagena blockaded by two Santa Marta vessels, cut off from food supplies up the Sinú River, surrounded by the forces of Viceroy Pérez, and with Cundinamarca troops falling back on Mare from Ocaña, Nariño was eager to put aside particularist jealousies, encourage his followers with words of enthusiasm for Colombian liberty, brought by Domingo Caicedo, and repeat once more, "Liberty or death."[32]

On Holy Thursday, March 26, 1812, the earth shook at two-thirty in the afternoon. Rumors of great damage to the patriot cities in Venezuela to the north soon began to cast a shadow across the once hopeful republican cause. By April 16, Santa Fé received notice that most of Mérida had fallen down in the earthquake of Holy Thursday, that eighteen hundred people including the archbishop of Mérida had been buried in the ruins or burned in the resulting fire. Special Masses were said in Bogotá. The chronicler reported, "Our city was overcome with sympathy for all this."[33]

In the last issue of *Bagatela,* April 12, 1812, the editor issued a desperate cry for unity, citing the many dangers on all sides. Montalván proposed to destroy the *Bagatela* and attack its government. Anti-*bagatelistas* accused the president of dictatorial procedure, and of secret greed for a crown. Anarchy was rife in the name of liberty. Cartagena had crushed Mompox, Tunja, Sogamoso, Pamplona, and Girón. Santa Fé was accused of similar greed when it sent troops out to help protect those of its neighbors who desired to be a part of Cundinamarca.

Cundinamarca was everywhere hated and suspected for its wealth and power. Yet Cundinamarca had one of the smallest of districts. Paradoxically, some of the very persons and cities aided by the generosity of Santa Fé abused the freedom of its press to call the president of Cundinamarca immoral, an ingrate, enemy of order and of the just, honorable and wise Montalván. Everywhere the president found himself accused of criminal intention to violate constitutional rights. Even while printing the accusations of his enemies, he found himself accused of suppressing freedom of the press in order to strengthen his tyranny and of planning to convert his title from president to king.[34]

Nariño versus Baraya

On June 23, Nariño himself led forth a large expedition to Tunja to subdue both the federalist congress and his own erstwhile ranking

---

32. *Ibid.,* p. 171.
33. Caballero, Dairy, p. 145.
34. Nariño, *La Bagatela,* pp. 221–222.

general, Antonio Baraya.[35] It was a sad occasion to be marching against one's own countrymen but, as usual, the city turned out with a brave show of gaiety to make a big occasion of the departure. Members of the corporations were there with richly caparisoned horses to escort the departing president-general. Color bearers of the *Auxilar* and the *Milicias* pranced proudly in the van.

Young Lieutenant Caballero had harsh words for Baraya, "that denaturalized, expatriated, disowned ingrate of his country who ... went forth to be bribed, to betray, and plot with those gentleman of congress in Leiva and then aided them to arm this cruel sedition and revolt against his city, Santa Fé de Bogotá, and his own president in this cruel and bloody war."[36]

Don Camilo Torres and Don Fruto Gutiérrez — Torres as president of congress and Gutiérrez as a leading member — were likewise named as principal leaders of the federalist congress and enemies of Nariño. Ambition and jealousy caused them to ignore the royalist threats of reconquest and expose their country to civil war at the risk of both sides losing their *patria* through disloyalty, disunion, and civil war. All this seemed very sad and very selfish to the young chronicler as the expedition moved slowly across mountains and plains toward the offending city of Tunja.[37]

Acting as secretary for the traitorous Baraya on this unhappy day in the movement for independence, young Lieutenant Francisco de Paula Santander explained the mass treason as follows: "The displeasure shown by the towns on account of being deprived of self-government by incorporation with Santa Fé, the protests of Pamplona and Casanare, the opposition of the government of Cartagena and Antioquia against Santa Fé . . . led Baraya to refuse to obey Nariño. . . . It was not an example of military discipline . . ., but I yielded to the voice and order of the chiefs, leaving the responsibility to them."[38]

The expedition proved fruitless. Nariño's forces found Tunja empty, deserted by congress and the joint armies of Baraya, and Tunja's governor, Niño.[39] Negotiations dragged on through the summer in a querulous, inconclusive fashion, satisfactory to neither side. On August 5, 1812, the electoral college, under the leadership of Don Manuel

---

35. *Ibid.*, p. 224.

36. *Ibid.*, p. 149.

37. *Ibid.*, p. 150.

38. F. de P. Santander. *Santander ante la historia* (1869), quoted in Henao and Arrubla, *op. cit.*, p. 222.

39. Caballero, Diary, p. 150.

Alvarez, decided to end their recognition of Ferdinand VII, and, two days later, a frustrated Santa Fé army passing through Leiva, received word their quarry, Baraya, had moved to Santa Rosa. They returned to the capital on August 14, angry, disappointed, and worried.[40]

The suspicions of the Bogotanos that all was not well were justified when the president issued a special edict proclaiming an imminent siege of the city by Baraya. Citizens were warned to prepare to collect their women, children, and old folks when they heard the cannon signal. Inside their houses they were to shut and bar all doors and windows. Meanwhile all male citizens fifteen years old and upward should assemble in the plaza of their parish. All bridges, gates, and entrances to the city should be guarded by cannons. Owners of horses were ordered to saddle up and go to the Huerta de Jaime.[41]

On October 23, 1812, a tremendous mass meeting was held in the wings of the church of San Carlos to consider proposals sent by congress in Leiva. The dean of the ecclesiastical chapter, the heads of all the corporations, the "most serene national representatives," and some three thousand heads of families were crowding into the square by eight in the morning. Prelates of the religious orders, curates, chaplains of the nunneries, syndics, *hacendados,* and merchants were there to listen to the congress proposals which were as follows: That the government of Santa Fé hand over to congress all forces, powder and munitions of war, to be put at the disposal of Baraya, with money.[42]

Various subversive memoranda from congress at Tunja were read. They were full of terms derogatory to Santa Fé and its president. Finally, after debate a motion was made: "Whether the president should leave office for the public good and tranquility."[43] Individual voters wrote their votes on slips of paper, entered through one door, deposited their votes and passed out into the patio beyond to avoid fraud. Guards of halberdiers were posted. When all the votes were counted, it was found that not a single vote was cast for the president to resign. Not satisfied, the president, after this demonstration, invited anyone who had not voted to do so freely, or if they wished they could do so by voice vote, but they all shouted, "Long live our President Nariño."[44]

Only one man, Canon Dr. D. Rafael Lasso, refused to vote at all, even when requested to do so. Since he would not vote yes or no, he

---

40. *Ibid.,* p. 151.
41. *Ibid.,* p. 151.
42. *Ibid.,* p. 152.
43. *Ibid.,* p. 152.
44. *Ibid.,* p. 153.

was asked to leave the province in twenty-four hours. As soon as he heard this he got up from his chair, and he left within the time limit.[45]

Magistrate Rosillo then proposed that there should be decreed a *providencia* (provisional judgment) for the arrival of the archbishop. A motion was proposed, while awaiting the present circumstances of the treaty with congress, that Bogotanos should vote whether to obey or not to obey Tunja congress orders to Santa Fé to join in the federation; two voice votes determined that there was no desire for federation, all of which was to the general satisfaction.[46]

On November 30, 1812, Nariño tried again to arrange peace with Tunja. In this difficult situation, which often required the absence of the president of Cundinamarca as director of campaigns at the front, a *junta* of five men was named November 26, 1812, to assist the president. The secretary of war, Felipe de Vergara, was named to preside. The four other members appointed were Juan Dionisio Gamba, secretary of *hacienda*, José Ignacio San Miguel, secretary of justice, and Manuel Camacho Quesada and José María Arrubla. In case any one of them was incapacitated, the remaining ones would continue to operate as a governing *junta*. They were to have full power to operate internal affairs but must have Nariño's approval for external affairs such as the purchase of arms and supplies from abroad.[47]

Having set up his emergency five-man *junta* to govern in his absence, the next step was to make a proclamation to the people of Tunja regretting the painful necessity which caused him to fight them "in order to extinguish the fire of discord."[48] This proclamation of November 30, 1812, sent from the camp of Ovejeras, did not postpone the conflict, but the president continued his efforts at reconciliation with Baraya and his troops.

Meeting of Antonios

Baraya tried and failed to trap Nariño into parley. Finally, in the convent of San Juan de Dios, December 26, 1812, the two Antonios met. Nariño risked his freedom by riding unescorted into a ring of one hundred men with fixed bayonets backed by two loaded cannon. He jumped from his mount unarmed, walked up to Baraya, embraced him cordially, and without hesitation marched off to the parley tent indicated by the enemy commander.[49]

---

45. *Ibid.*
46. *Ibid.*
47. Posada and Ibáñez, *El Precursor,* p. 356.
48. *Ibid.,* p. 357.
49. Caballero, Diary, p. 378.

Since the parley was secret, both sides could only guess at all of what was said. Undoubtedly, Nariño stressed the tragic shame of Colombians fighting each other when their mutual enemy, Spain, still had troops near by, strong enough to destroy both New Granadan parties and hurl them back to a condition of defeat and slavery.

Baraya, under the influence of Narino's persuasive tongue, seems to have yielded momentarily to the suggestions made for compromise:

1. Santa Fé was to recognize provisionally the power of congress under the pacts of May 18, 1812, and to call a convention.

2. Said convention was to be accredited to the officials of the different branches of government.

3. It was to discuss and pass on revised agreements based on the May 18, 1812, pact and, before disbanding, select a new president.[50]

Unfortunately, Baraya felt this truce agreement could not be binding on him until confirmed by congress in Tunja. All that Baraya would promise was a willingness to parley again if congress proved willing and cooperative. Thus, he felt free to attack later when it suited him, and felt justified in breaking the truce.

An almost immediate renewal of hostilities on December 29 and 30 led the besieged people of Santa Fé to further distrust the sincerity of Baraya. Their dashed hopes led them into an even more united and grim determination to fight to the last house. Baraya's ultimatum to surrender the city to him at Usaquén, not later than 10 a.m. on December 30 or be treated as rebels and traitors against the armies of the Union of New Granada, contained appeals for unity which were but thinly disguised threats of dire punishment in case they chose to fight on. An assembly of men, women, and children, including Doña Manuela Barona, wife of Don Francisco José de Caldas, ally of Baraya, issued one more urgent appeal to the besiegers to stop the fratricidal bloodshed in a note dated December 31, 1812.[51] Caldas and Baraya chose to believe the appealing letter was either a fraud and a trick of Nariño's or extorted from Manuela Borona under threat of torture. They became more determined to punish the stubborn city of Santa Fé:

You may torture, threaten and decapitate this innocent, virtuous woman and do the same with my little son and other relations of mine whom you hold there in this unfortunate city. But that does not intimidate me at all. If they die at the hands of your faction, they will die with honor and virtue and they will not stain my reputation by weakness. This innocent blood you are about to shed will call down the awful vengeance of Heaven upon you and close

---

50. *Ibid.*, p. 379.

51. *Ibid.*, pp. 382–383.

our hearts to forgiveness. We will pardon nobody. The life of one of our women will cost you a thousand dead. Do not think this is a vain threat. . . .[52]

So wrote Caldas on the last day of December, 1812. Nariño, in Santa Fé, tried to reply in the same calm manner he had used in replying to the heated tones of Baraya.

He reminded Caldas that they were old friends, well known to each other, and that all wild talk about decapitating Caldas' wife and son was utterly silly.

I am always the same Nariño you knew at Fucha. . . . If C. had not acted in bad faith, he would have told you how your wife came to my house along with the other ladies. They deplored the misfortunes about to be visited upon us and how they were the first victims whom inhuman husbands, fathers, and sons were about to immolate. Tell me now honestly . . . if my innocent tender daughters, whom I have with me here on this battlefield, should die under the fury of your troops, would it not be just for those related to these killers to die first? . . . But we still speak the language of reason here. I have no such idea . . . nor do I intend to save myself and slip away . . . there is my honor at stake . . . and so here we are about to die in a war which will also kill our chances to be free because even though Nariño yields all, we demand, we yield him nothing, isn't that what you must admit to yourselves? You are now avenging yourselves for hurts which exist solely in your imaginations. More than the state will perish therewith. Liberty will perish! To what end? To get a fine name for ourselves as great heroes of the universe? Will the name American acquire a new lustre in this battle of passions? I swear to you in the bosom of friendship that if I outlive this action, you can kill me in cold blood before I will take part in any government founded on such principles. So then, buried in some corner, far from this climate you may write your history of my tyrannies and I will justify them. But now I do not have the time. If you, my friends, wish to contribute to peace, the serenity and calm of Cundinamarca and New Granada, if you wish to end this civil war in a fashion most praiseworthy of the name American, you can do so by adding your influence to the calming of base passions; to looking at matters in the large; and if without this minor preparation, you agree to my proposals and that we should embrace again as brothers, spouses, fathers, sons making known completely the naturalness and pleasure of having terminated with the stroke of a pen, how much better to end thus, what so unjustly was about to end in blood and fire.

May you recognize the greatest sincerity and good faith of your most affectionate,

Antonio Nariño[53]

---

52. *Ibid.,* p. 383.
53. *Ibid.,* p. 385.

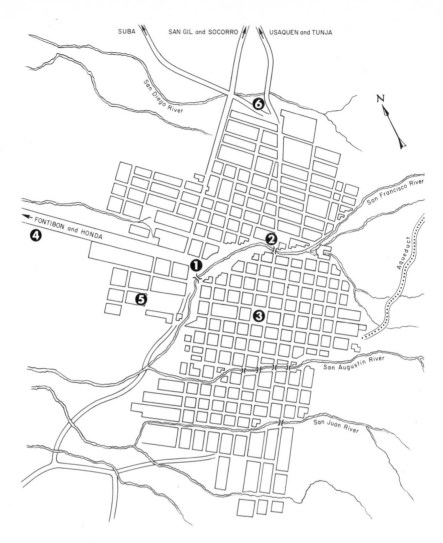

SUBA   SAN GIL and SOCORRO   USAQUEN and TUNJA

San Diego River

N

San Francisco River

Aqueduct

FONTIBON and HONDA

San Augustin River

San Juan River

STRATEGIC LOCATIONS IN BOGOTA

BOGOTA WAS FOUNDED IN 1538 on the site of an earlier Indian city, located far inland on a high plateau, surrounded by mountains. It is about six hundred miles inland from the Caribbean coast and about half as far in from the Pacific coast of Colombia. Only four degrees and a half north of the equator, Bogotá is nonetheless at a chilling altitude of nearly nine thousand feet above sea level. It lies in a fertile valley sixty miles long and twenty broad, with the heights of Monserrate and Guadalupe standing like sentinels between the city and the rising sun.

The rains, coming almost every afternoon from February to June, pour torrents of water down the steep flanks of the mountains into the city via the San Francisco and San Augustín rivers, between which lies the triangle containing the heart of the ancient city, centered on the plaza.

The city plan (in 1823)* was a regular grid, composed of 25-foot wide streets, crossing each other at right angles, paved, and provided with running water from an aqueduct. Seven stone bridges spanned the three main streams, the chief bridge being San Victorino (1), defended by Nariño against Baraya. The loss of that bridge and San Francisco (2) and two heights in the east forced Nariño's troops to stand and fight at the heart of the city on the Great Square (3).

It was important for Baraya to capture the city in January for two reasons: first, the beginning of the rains in February would delay or stop battle preparations; second, the heights would be enshrouded in mist and rain, and be of little use for observation and artillery fire, once the rains began.

Consideration of the nature of Bogotá streets and houses indicates why Baraya's defeat became an utter route. His men approached from the west, up the straight boulevard leading in from Fontibón and Honda, past the cemetery (4) and through the garden of Saint James (5) to converge on the square and bridge of San Victorino (1). His other force, coming in from the north — from Suba, Socorro, and San Gil, converged there in part. Crossing the Fields of San Diego (6) and two bridges, the north flank joined forces from the north — from Usaquen and Tunja, and took the left fork of the road after crossing the San Diego, in order to strike upstream at San Francisco bridge (2). They, however, lacked the extra striking force of Girardot and his men, stranded by Nariño's forged order, on the heights to the east.

In the heart of the city, the narrow side streets and barricaded doors afforded no escape, and the balconies were vantage points for the defenders to attack from above. Bache and others mention that the plaza was sometimes thus barricaded for a bull ring. In January, 1813, Baraya was the bull, and it was Nariño who skillfully led him, by an apparent retreat, to the center of the ring where (Baraya) received the neat final thrust, in which Nariño's artillery played an important part.

---

*Material describing Bogotá and its environs in 1822 can be found in Captain Richard Bache, *Notes on Colombia Taken in the Years 1822–23* (Philadelphia, 1827), pp. 222–232, and in Charles Stuart Cochrane, *Journals of a Residence and Travels in Colombia During the Years 1823 and 1824* (London, 1825), vol. II, pp. 1–150.

Nariño's statue facing the observatory in Bogotá shows him braving the Royalists at Pasto who demanded his head when he surrendered in May, 1814, rather than hide in the mountains to escape death.

CHAPTER IX

BOGOTA VICTORIOUS

From Dictator-President To

President-General

The new year January 1, 1813, found the two armies entrenched in the suburbs of Santa Fé waiting for the end. The chronicler wrote that it was a good hot day, but the population was beginning to suffer from scarcity of food. "Baraya hopes to conquer us by starving us out."[1] Usaquén, Puentegrande, Bosa, Fontibón, Santa Catalina, Las Lanches, and Cabanuela were held by the attackers. Report had it that Congress had moved to Zipaquirá. On Monday, the fourth of January, came a general call to arms. The inhabitants took their battle stations and attached sheepskin devices to their hats as a distinguishing mark. One lone cannon ball swished through the streets. No one was hurt. Finally, on Tuesday, January 5, the battle began in earnest. It was a clear day. At two-thirty, Colonel Anastasio Girardot, a congress commander, was seen attacking the heights of Monserrate. Musket and cannon fire was heavy from all directions until 2:45.[2] Shortly after, Monserrate Heights fell.

The loss of this position to Lieutenant-Colonel Girardot caused a general panic inside the city. From the bridge and heights of Monserrate the enemy could now rake the besieged city with artillery and destroy it. Weeping, consternation, and panic swept over the city. The people were certain their fate was in enemy hands. Apathy, fear, and defeatism reigned, even among experienced troops. Soldier and farmer alike abandoned their posts. Disregarding commands and pleas of their officers, they fled from their camps to their houses whence they burrowed down as if hoping to hide in the very bowels of the earth. Silence was so great it seemed as though the citizens feared to breathe. Such was the state of affairs when Nariño again attempted to negotiate.

From Santa Fé on January 6, 1813, he made further proposals of compromise:

---

1. Caballero, Diary, p. 155.
2. Posada and Ibáñez, El Precursor, p. 387.

1. He would give up the presidency and return the government to its constitutional form as of September 10, 1812.

2. Congress should be recognized, but Cundinamarca should be left its right to object in a called convention to those portions of the act of federation which were prejudicial to it, or did not give it a fair share in relation to the other federated provinces.

3. All arms would be left to the disposition of the Supreme Congress.

4. On the moment of surrender of his government, he would be given passports and assurances for transporting himself and his family outside the state of Cundinamarca.

5. The same guarantees would be granted to all other persons requesting them.

6. The past was to be completely forgotten by both sides and, conse-questly, the deputies of Cundinamarca held prisoners in Tunja and all others in Tunja similarly jailed because of their political beliefs, should be set free.

7. Baraya and deputies with him will guarantee the individual security and properties of all inhabitants of this city and the whole province of Cundinamarca.

8. To avoid disorders, Baraya and his troops will not enter this city in greater numbers than absolutely necessary for security and for taking charge of the orderly transfer of command here.

Neither now, nor later, shall the Supreme Congress prefer charges against Nariño for anything in the past, and he shall be free to live wherever suits him best, in, or outside of New Granada.

10. The proposals to be ratified by both sides as treaties to be executed within five days from date, suspending all hostilities as soon as both parties agree and entering then into a conference to settle all doubts, if any still remain.[3]

Baraya refused to accept Nariño's terms of conditional surrender. In arrogant and bloodthirsty language based on assurance of a near victory, he demanded unconditional surrender of Bogotá to the union troops.

During the next three days, January 6–9, 1813, Baraya's confident troops moved closer to the heart of the beleaguered city, threatening to bring dire ruin upon the inhabitants if they refused to surrender:

Your usurper . . . who has invaded Tunja . . . wishes to erect his throne on the ruins of your rights and the religion of our ancestors . . . He is a *parricide* who abandons you to foreign enemies, puts insuperable obstacles in the way of forming congress, and then tries to destroy congress with a hostile army . . .

You may be sure that as soon as I win this victory, I will pardon *nobody*. I will not leave a stone unturned to punish all rebels with death. I will omit no act to punish the many who persecuted those who attempted escape from you. Rest assured that I have closed my heart to any impulse of compassion and

3. *Ibid.*, pp. 357–358.

pity. Your blood will flow in torrents in the streets of your city. The soldiers and troops of the union are resolved to slaughter everyone who hinders their purposes of punishing all our enemies.[4]

Further exchanges of letters between the two Antonios proved equally fruitless, until, finally, the last note was struck with this one:

Antonio: I have just received your letter replying to mine and I see it is no use now; that all parley with you is fruitless. Let us now involve our fatherland in bloody mourning, since that's how you must have it! Perhaps then you will disillusion yourself of the certainty of expected triumphs. As far as I am concerned, I shall never close my ears to reason — whenever you may happen to propose it to me . . . Good-by, perhaps forever, Antonio Nariño.[5]

Baraya's demand for unconditional surrender had exactly the opposite effect from what he intended. The people and the troops became furious at this madman's determination to destroy his native city. Now at last it was clear to all how a bloody, inhuman, and barbarous fate had been reserved for them by this ambitious general and former neighbor.

A Daring Attack

The president, having tried in vain all efforts at reconciliation, now resolved to shift from a dogged defensive strategy to a daring and risky attack in hopes of rebuilding the courage and spirit of the city. At ten o'clock on the night of January 6, 1813, several officers and two hundred volunteers under the command of Antonio Baylli moved out to attack the enemy division at Cabo de Suba. However, since the bridges there were broken they had to move first against a large detachment under Antonio Morales at Usaquén. The first attack was a complete success. Morales was utterly routed, leaving fourteen dead and thirty prisoners behind, along with guns and supplies. By 7 a.m., January 7, Baylli was seen advancing toward San Diego and the field of San Victorino.

This sudden shift electrified the besieged city. Where all had been gloom and fear, now valor, hope, and joy burst forth. With energy and enthusiasm, groups of citizens rushed forward. Even women, children, and the beggars of the city rushed in groups toward San Victorino to attack. As the adversary retreated, the mob pushed on to the enemy quarters in Fontibón, and wishing each other luck, they rushed to the attack, secure in the belief God was with them, and greatly relieved to have shed their intolerable burden of fear.

---

4. *Ibid.,* pp. 367–373.
5. *Ibid.,* pp. 374–375.

At this psychological turning point, General José de Leiva agreed to allow Nariño to release four hundred reserves under Baylli for an attack on Fontibón bridge. Even the sight of two thousand under Baraya, grouping for a counter attack, did not terrify the little army. When the advance guard of Baraya fired and failed to budge Baylli, the enemy turned and retreated. Supper time brought Nariño one more "final" ultimatum to surrender to Baraya in four hours or be destroyed. To this the council replied:

"General . . . the residents of Santa Fé are resolved to fight to the last drop of blood."[6]

Nariño's final victory resulted from a shrewd combination of daring, bluff, and stratagem. On the seventh he had dared and attacked with success against greatly superior odds. The following day he trapped Baraya into attacking by letting a pretended spy inform Baraya at night that the city army was divided into three columns for an attack on Fontibón bridge and Monserrate Heights, and that the trenches were thus deserted.

Baraya apparently decided his hour of decision had at least arrived. At 4:30 a.m., January 9, he launched his full-scale attack under the cover of darkness. Some shots near Estanzuela gave the first warning that he was massing all his four thousand men on the plains for attack.

With only fifteen hundred men, the defenders of independence formed their units in good order and waited. Soon a torrent of attackers moved in through Estanzuela gate, overwhelmed the Juerta de Jaime, took possession of the bridge and square of San Victorino and of all the alleys leading out of the Prado, and left the defenders penned up in an area of four-hundred square rods, literally with their backs to the walls.

It was 5:30, the break of day, and raining, when the city defenders, three hundred strong, opened fire. Twice the attackers moved forward into the square, and twice they were thrown back up the streets by the trapped defenders. Neither side could escape by side streets since these were blocked by Nariño's artillery. The president and his daughters, along with the city officials, stood firm in the block of defenders, many of whom fell wounded.

Suddenly a piercing bugle sounded the attack. Baraya's forces panicked in their haste to escape. With the narrow streets blocked, the walls of houses and masses of their own men behind them made escape impossible. There was no alternative to death but surrender. Baraya's forces had been neatly trapped. They surrendered. So fearful were they

---

6. *Ibid.,* p. 390.

that one group of four hundred men surrendered to a cavalry detachment of fifty before realizing how few their captors were. Even the women joined the fray, capturing supplies of slings and knives near the militia barracks. They rushed forward and disarmed startled soldiers by holding knives against their chests.

A forged order from Nariño kept the Monserrate and Fontibón forces idle until the town battle was over. Then they, too, had no recourse but surrender.

Nariño the Victor

Within a few hours, Narino had converted imminent defeat into a smashing victory. At the moment of supreme triumph,[7] he again demonstrated the magnanimity and moderation which made him the admiration and despair of his enemies. Bandages, medicine, food, and tender care were rushed to the enemy wounded. All fighting stopped immediately following surrender. Baraya, Niño, the governor of Tunja, and all other captured officials and prisoners in the mass of one thousand or more were treated, not like enemies but like prodigal sons, which, in many cases, they were. Early plans to jail the leaders were soon put aside, and all were pardoned, invited to go home to their families and aided with food and transportation for the return journey. A big celebration was now in order, and official cedulas of honor for the "Conquerors of the Month of January" were printed on the government press and distributed to all residents of the brave city.[8]

Technically, Nariño was still dictator when he issued an invitation to his defeated rivals to help him form a new government on February 6, 1813.[9] However, a combination of internal chaos and external danger from Spanish royalists seemed to require a strong executive if Santa Fé de Bogotá was to weather the storms brewing in all directions. In the south, royalists under Toribio Montes controlled the Pasto and Patía area; in nearby Tunja, the pardoned troops of Baraya remained a potential danger; in the north, royalists were still strong around Santa Marta, and continued to be a threat to rival Cartagena. In the central Magdalena Valley area, Bolívar, by defying the orders of his superior, Labatut, was beginning his reputation as a conqueror with whirlwind campaigns against Tenerife, Banco, Chiriguaná, Tamalemeque, and Puerto Real. In spite of his resounding victory at San José de Cúcuta,

---

7. *Ibid.,* pp. 390–393.

8. *Ibid.,* pp. 393–396. Caballero, Diary, pp. 160–163.

9. Posada and Ibáñez, *El Precursor,* p. 396.

February 28, which netted a rich booty of a million pesos, Bolívar felt the need to request help from Tunja and Bogotá before pushing his attack over into Venezuela in May.[10]

It was this precarious situation which caused Nariño to attempt to strengthen and centralize a congressional government in Santa Fé. As he had pointed out in the invitation of February 6, he found the names *tyrant* and *dictator* equally distasteful, but necessary, until such time as the chaos and threat of invasion ended, or congress demonstrated ability to govern effectively.[11]

The new plan of centralization proposed to congress allowed one deputy for each fifty thousand population for the central *junta* of the government of the republic, on sole condition that the deputy be over age twenty-five, natives of their province, and not involved in lawsuit. Under this plan several deputies soon left for the provinces: Pedro Groot and Manuel Pardo for Antioquia, Pío Dominguez and José María Castillo for Cartagena, José de Jaén for the Llanos, Joaquín Bonilla for Popayán.

During the next month, a round of fiestas, bullfights, night dancing in the coliseum, and a fair at Candelaria failed to hide the disunion and chaos threatening on all sides. There were rumors of an attack by an army of four hundred from Socorro,[12] still unwilling to be a part of a Santa Fé-dominated state. The same day an edict went out ordering all pigs off the street under penalty of confiscation. Shortly after, on the eleventh and twelfth of March, came word of Bolívar's great victory over Correa in Cúcuta. This was an occasion for the usual celebration, fireworks, dances, and parades led by the president and an Englishman named Perry, carrying the banner of liberty and wearing the liberty nightcaps, shouting *vivas* to liberty everywhere. "Only the *chapetones* stayed inside sulking."[13]

About the time the congress envoy, José Félix Ribas, arrived to negotiate with the president, Nariño became very ill. Negotiations were broken off and special Masses said for his health until far into the night. Good news arrived from the delegates to Cartagena, and a compromise was finally made with Colonel Ribas on March 30. The next day *pasquines* against the government appeared on the city walls, a bad sign as always. Nevertheless, plans went forward to send out posters

---

10. Henao and Arrubla, *op. cit.,* pp. 235–238.

11. Posada and Ibáñez, *El Precursor,* pp. 396–399. Caballero, Diary, p. 169.

12. *Ibid.,* pp. 169, 173.

13. *Ibid.,* p. 174.

announcing an election of delegates to choose a president and deputies for the great convention, while troops were dispatched to Carácas and Papayán.

Sunday, April 4, was election day. Nariño's family and the París family made peace publicly in a friendly banquet which included the president, José Maria Cabal of Popayán, Dr. Ignacio Vargas, the cripple, and José París with his sons and daughters, all declared enemies of Santa Fé and Nariño. Tuesday, April 6, more troops marched off toward Cúcuta and Bolívar. On Holy Thursday there was a special Mass and state banquet attended by the president and all the officials of the government as well as halberdiers, grenadiers, and cavalry. Easter Sunday was saddened by another evil omen. Señor Miñano, *oidor* of Quito and former friend of the president, went crazy. He walked up and down the streets yelling that there was no government, then took out a pistol and pulled the trigger. Luckily it misfired. He was soon captured and taken to the hospital.

Wednesday, April 28, was another ominous day. Antonio Baylli, the hero, was mortally knifed in a scuffle with one of his young mulatto slaves. After stabbing Baylli in the stomach, the thirteen-year-old slave ran to the palace and surrendered to Nariño. This incident postponed until April 29 the planting of the Liberty Tree — a very grand and solemn affair — preceded by the usual parade on horseback. The myrtle was finally planted in the Masonic triangle, decorated with four circular laurel wreathes, poems to liberty, and crystal lamps for illumination. At the top of the tree there were painted symbols of Jesus, Mary, a tree, and the sword of Justice. Four cannon salutes and a parade ended the celebration, but not until the young mulatto who had killed Colonel Baylli was publicly shot in front of the jail. Father Ley and Canon Dr. Rosillo preached a brief sermon on the theme that liberty could not tolerate anarchy, as had just been proven.[15]

After the French colonel, hero, patriot, and martyr of liberty had been duly interred in Veracruz with all pomp, and following requiem Mass in the cathedral, the crowd retired to the coliseum where a great ball was in full swing.

Meanwhile, Miñano had been sent as a prisoner from the hospital to Cartagena. A special edict went out ordering the wearing of the symbol of Jesus of Cundinamarca and not the symbol of the Union. Rumors of a new alliance of Tunja and Socorro against Santa Fé were

---

14. *Ibid.,* p. 175.
15. *Ibid.*

heard on the streets. Three stray Frenchmen wandered into town with little or no explanation of their presence. Tobacco monopolies were restored, whereupon a tobacco huckster had a fit of epilepsy, and drowned himself in the waters of the pontoon bridge near Carmen. The mother of the traitor, Anastasio Girardot, made no secret of the bidding in of her son's property in a sale of belongings of the self-exiled enemies of the city. Such was the troubled state of the city of Santa Fé de Bogotá on June 13, Nariño's saint's day and the day set to install the new electoral college.[16]

On June 13, 1813, Nariño resigned his dictatorship, but the electoral college would not accept his resignation. Royalist and regency supporters were, however, noticeably few in the new electoral college. Having taken the usual oath, the president gave a "long and learned" discourse after which he was elected dictator for life.[17]

To a certain extent, this occasion was the dividing line between the dictator-president and the president-general, for not long after, on June 28, the electoral college voted their dictator-president the rank of lieutenant-general in preparation for the expedition against General Sámano and the royalists.[18]

Farewell to Dictatorship

The speech of June 13, 1813, represented Nariño's last act as civilian executive of Cundinamarca, and, as such, measured up creditably to the solemnity and seriousness of the occasion. Many external and internal dangers threatened all liberty-loving Colombians. In fact, the fate of all South America seemed hanging in the balance, and Nariño did not hesitate to say so.

Today I have the pleasure of ending voluntarily my so-called tyranny . . . But I would be failing in my duty to the post I still occupy, if before proceeding to the installation of the electoral college, I neglected to outline to you the work ahead . . .

It seems to me, gentlemen, this way: You are acquainted with the system Spain has followed in America from the discovery right up to our times. Content to take out all the riches of our soil, she never thought of enriching it. As for us, we were kept in complete ignorance in matters of government, and not only did Spain prohibit us from any part in it, but even forbade here the study of international law whence we might have obtained education in matters of government. The House of Bourbon died at Bayonne. Suddenly we were masters of our house, filled with holiest and most praiseworthy desire to

---

16. *Ibid.,* p. 178.
17. *Ibid.*
18. *Ibid.*

improve our fertile lands. Instead of beginning a well-planned gradual reform, we embraced the reckless plan of desiring to destroy and rebuild everything in one day. The universal shout went up to copy the system in North America!

So what did we do? We chopped up our country into as many states as there had been provinces and townships before! Each state was to have all the powers of self-government attributed to the central government of New Granada, collection of all taxes, a sovereign legislature for every thousand people, whether any of them knew law or not, a separate executive, separate courts, separate senates, constitutions, treasuries, arms, roals, buildings and so forth . . . even separate church units for each tiny state! Here were the grandest principles ever based on the idea of perfect stability of governments.

Nevertheless, three years have gone by and no province has any treasury, money, army, cannons, powder, schools, roads, banks. All they have is an endless number of functionaries eating up what little tax money exists, and defending this new system with all their strength. They claim that liberty would perform all miracles were it not for this intruder president of Cundinamarca; the state would be well organized were it not for him. But this unnatural son, because of blind ambition wants to run everything and reduce us all to slavery under his corrupt capital.

And so we have had to send out expeditions against this intruder president and his corrupt capital — six in all — in a year and a half. But since Cundinamarca is the cow we all milk and gives us sticks instead of food, the cow must die and the provinces so soon will have nothing. Do I have to be any great prophet to prophecy for you the fate that will soon await us? Is it necessary to seek mysterious causes of our ruin? Is it not obvious we have caused it ourselves? . . .

. . . To the proposals of congress I reply: to establish a strong state out of weak pieces is a contradiction, an absurdity, the craziest insanity of a lack of ability to understand humanity. . . . You may reply with the example of North America, but I will answer a hundred times, if necessary, we cannot be compared to peoples who were always free, and who also had the aid of France and Spain to defend themselves. These fine unworkable constitutions will ruin us if we do not pretty soon open our eyes to reality and learn from experience . . .

As the famous Smith has pointed out in his *Wealth of Nations . . .,* what works perfectly for one economy, will not necessarily work in a very different one. Plants which flourish in the north die here, and vice versa. There is no government equally suitable to all climates and parts of the world. No man should expect a universal system equally suitable all over the world.

I tell you, sirs, if we don't soon change our ways, we'll go to our execution and ruin, buried under these fine unworkable constitutions, cursing the cruelty of our political-theorist bureaucrats who failed to give us three more years to work on our favorite system. I hope to God my prophecies prove unfounded and that instead you will put your fate in skillful hands, such as those of that last illustrious convention . . . However, it is better to be aware of the sickness and prevent it than hope for a cure . . . Our greatest present evil is partisanship and division.

It is perfectly clear that congress cannot exist without Cundinamarca. It is equally clear that Cundinamarca cannot last without congress and the help of the other provinces. We cannot go on divided as we are now.

If congress is stubborn and will not compromise, if Cundinamarca will not yield either, another civil war is inevitable, because then only force of arms can decide the question.

Then, if we wish to continue our existence, it will be necessary either to change the general system or join Cundinamarca in federation with other provinces. There is no way to avoid it, gentlemen. We are forced to these alternatives: a new civil war, change the general sytem, or join the confederation. The first is a barbarous alternative leading to almost surely mortal blows at our liberty.

The second I have proposed to all the provinces, writing them to call together the great convention as the sole body which can legally determine a strong and uniform system which would embrace all of New Granda in order to save its existence. But, unfortunately, this proposal has been unconditionally rejected by some, dallied with by others, and all have looked upon it as my idea and Cundinamarca's, that is to say, that even though it is as clear as day, and the most useful possible, it should never be adopted because it comes under the guidance of Nariño.

And should we follow his example? No, never! . . . and so the sick provinces must die and we die too . . .

My opinion then, is that we should join a federation, not because it is the system for us but because in the present circumstances it is the only road remaining to us by which we can avoid the immediate end of our liberty, of our very existence. Nay, I say more, that when we decide to embrace this plan, it should be without reservation, placing our fate entirely in the hands of the national body.

Then may we not hope that the rest of the provinces will follow our example and join up in peace, as friends? . . . Thus unity will replace division.

Congress can accelerate the reuniting of Great Colombia and gradually invite the provinces to simplify their governments, reducing them to an executive power, a judiciary of first and second instance, and a senate composed of three bodies forming a general legislature composed of the most learned men of all provinces, prorated in proportion to the general intelligence and to the importance of the matter in hand. There could be a supreme court of three or four highest tribunals of last resort. The saving resulting from the reform should be put in a common fund to maintain veteran troops. Let's not delude ourselves with impossible visions of perfectibility: without money, no troops; without troops, no force, and without force there is no liberty. . . . Let us pass on to our constitution.

Revision of the constitution is, in my opinion, an absolute necessity. It will be perhaps more convenient and simpler to revise the first one because the latter is so defective that it would take much more work and time to revise it than to make it new from beginning to end . . .

It is a misfortune with us that our list of officers lengthens as our list of competent officeholders shrinks. Until now we have been buried under a profusion of legislators. The executive and judicial power should be primarily instruments to carry out the resolutions of the legislative body. All of human wisdom is needed to make a law but honor and common sense are sufficient to execute it. What then can we say of our present ratio of one legislator for every thousand souls? Only that the laws will not be made by the most intelligent, only by the most populous. When it is a matter of raising armies, opening canals, cultivating the ground, people are what we need; but when it is a question of making laws, then we need intelligence, because it is no longer mobs of men that are needed if they do not have the intelligence required.

Perfection in government is born from good legislation, yet "we must begin where we must begin," as Abbé Raynal said. The general mass of a nation feeds not on sublime ideas but on sensations. Let us then make them sense the advantages of liberty and they will desire it. The people reduce the circle of their ideas to these simple two points and to these only: administration of justice and means of subsistence. The general security is a good negative unknown, until about to be lost and it belongs solely to those who do the governing . . .

. . . It is difficult to erase what is written on us, the creases that are in us, the habits of our machine. Use your left hand and you are soon persuaded by your reason how advantageous would be the use of both. Just try though, to put this idea across and you will be warned against any easy victories. France with its guillotine and torrents of blood was unable to make this lightning-like metamorphosis. And that was the primary cause of the ruin of our system. Gradually we must pass from the known to the unknown, that is what logic should teach us. All that love of liberty can do is to accelerate these steps, but never turn everything upside down without the danger of making all changes utterly fruitless.

Three examples and no more I will give you to demonstrate weaknesses of our overheated democrats: they are infatuated with jobs, distinctions, and idleness. Anything worth while requires long and patient work. But just offer them a long arduous task and watch their patriotism evaporate! . . .

The constitution should be reduced to simple general terms not changed every year for each minor detail. I would like to consider many other points but time does not permit. One of our troubles arises from indeterminate boundaries and the disorganized system which we adopted three years ago in the beginning. Today what is Cundinamarca is tomorrow another province, and this confusion is a true cause of our weakness since the transit of peoples from one province to another and of goods dissipates their value and taxable income, resulting in nothing but discord and poverty.

You have already seen, gentlemen, that the federal system is the most perfect yet discovered by man for people to govern themselves after they have reached adolescence in intelligence, income, and the force to defend themselves. Yet this is the weakest possible and last appropriate to a people just being born and still threatened, like ourselves, with being invaded from Europe. Yet you have seen how we have made of federation an epidemic sickness all over Spanish America, because of contagion from English America.

. . . Fix the bases of a righteous and intelligent administration of justice in which man can live secure and calmly in the shelter of his innocence; give the initial impulse to the encouragement of agriculture and commerce, not only for the support of public taxes but also as a sure means of increasing the population. Establish a system of economy in the government, seeking new sources for the exchequer for the raising of troops and the buying of arms, and leave the rest to time.

You must penetrate, gentlemen, the inner truths of the importance of the posts you now come to occupy today. Cast your eyes upon your fellow men whose fate depends perhaps, on one single word you let fall from your lips.

When once our fate used to depend on a few high proud souls, all we needed to know was how to obey. Now that it depends on ourselves, we must know how to think, how to suppress our passions, our resentments, our vices; we must learn how to sacrifice unstintingly our personal interests, our very lives. Be warned that you are already embarked on the open ocean, it will no longer suffice to be sorry you embarked until you arrive again in port. You must not turn loose the oars if you wish to escape the storm. May the sacred fire of liberty pierce your hearts, inflame your souls, illumine your intelligence! Aye! may this pure fire, this holy fire, which is more than just kindness and love of fellow-beings, make you worthy of the high rank to which today the destiny of the New World calls you! Nothing so draws a man close to Divinity as the action of improving the lot of his fellow man, of breaking his chains, of drying his tears and of bringing him happiness. Virtue is the base, the foundation of all liberty. Without virtue all is confusion, disorder. May assiduous work, mature, deliberate reflection, and integrity, in the face of all tests of intrigue, seduction, and bribery, be the distinctive marks of your character. May Heaven bless the work of your hands, and we and all our posterity will sing hymns of joy and thanks to the restorers of peace, to the liberators of the fatherland. [19]

19. Posada and Ibáñez, *El Precursor,* pp. 399–412.

CHAPTER X

CAMPAIGN IN THE SOUTH
From Victory To Defeat

On June 28, the dictator-president was elected lieutenant-general, with additional powers granted to carry out the new campaign in Popayán and Pasto against the royalists, under Sámano. Several months of preparation elapsed, however, before Nariño was ready to move south against Sámano. In the meantime, the electoral college met and on July 4, 1813, elected Nariño's uncle, Manuel Álvarez Casal, as governor of an emergency council, and Ignacio Herrera as councilor. On the seventh of July, congress voted a levy of three hundred thousand pesos to the president-general to be raised from taxes on businesses, on the *hacendados,* and upon the clergy, both secular and regular, with the salt works, the sales tax, and the mint as collateral.[1]

News both hopeful and ominous filtered into the city from far-away campaigns. On July 11, the Cartagena mail arrived with news that two mails had been detained, and that *piringas* (river pirates) had set fire to the town of El Banco, and had captured munitions, supplies, and prisoners from the Samarians, including Menéndez and Moreno, the cripple, while the Samarians had invaded Tenerife and other places. Everybody was very excited and confused, happy and fearful. A new draft was levied for the expedition against Popayán, but disturbing reports from stragglers of Sámano's cruelty in the south caused great uneasiness. Sámano was reported headed for Santa Fé, determined to enter and recognize the Regency. Meanwhile, the treasury was empty. Congress, paralyzed with fear, refused to act. There were rumors that church ornaments would be melted down for money. The diarist, J. M. Caballero, felt that such a move would be the end of everything.[2] The dispatch of cavalry and artillery units increased the tension within the city.

---

1. Caballero, Diary, p. 179. Posada and Ibáñez, *El Precursor,* p. 413.
2. Caballero, Diary, p. 180.

On July 15, 1813, the college met in the presence of President-General Nariño to discuss voting on the disavowal of Ferdinand VII. Of the fifty electors, only two stubborn royalists, José Antonio Torres y Peña and Archdeacon Juan Bautista Pey, refused to make the vote unanimous for liberty and independence. In the hope that these men would change their minds, final vote was postponed to July 16. The following day, more discussion went on until noon. By that time all were so exhausted with debate that it was at last agreed to vote on the motion. Dr. Torres and a *chapetón* (Spaniard) named Fernando Rodríguez voted adamantly for Ferdinand VII, while the majority now rushed out shouting for their declaration of independence. More handclapping, more *vivas* for Independence and Liberty filled the air with noise. Finally, it was unanimously decided to elect as patroness of the state, Holiest Mary of Concepción.

Independence Proclaimed

Two days later, the mayor of the city, Azuola, issued a proclamation of independence.[3] Patriots now went up and down the street shouting *vivas,* setting off cannon and fireworks as they passed. That night, a portrait of Liberty was paraded in the streets with more shouting, cheers, music, and illuminations. Only the royalists hid themselves in fear and disgust. It was Sunday, and what a Sunday! Streets were lighted all night. A Tree of Liberty was propelled into and out of the chapel. Only one event marred the joyous mood. On Santa Inés street, posters against Nariño appeared.[4]

Preparations for departure continued apace, punctuated, as always, with a mixture of the sad and the gay, of deaths and dances, of bullfights and fiestas. The padres of Santo Domingo decorated the *colegio's* windows and balconies. Band concerts were mixed with parades and cannonades. Beautiful ladies in their silks, and gentlemen mounted on expensive saddles paraded to the accompaniment of artillery fire and roman candles. Ceremonies were concluded by planting the olive tree of Liberty in a triangle. The president and the national representatives then went to the church of San Juan de Dios to carry the statue of the patron to Santa Librada en route to the cathedral in preparation for the fiesta of Santa Librada.

---

3. The full text of this proclamation was still readable in 1962 on the outside front wall of Bogotá's city hall. Parts of it are translated verbatim from the words of Jefferson and Franklin in the Declaration of Independence.

4. Caballero, Diary, pp. 179–181.

During the fiesta of Santa Librada, July 20, 1813, all troops were gathered along with the national representatives in the cathedral to hear a sermon by Father P. Florido[5] on "Independence." Mass ended in a Te Deum. Returning to the electoral college, the president spoke about enforcing the oath of allegiance; then followed a ceremony in which the president put his hands in those of the secretary and took the oath of allegiance. All corporations, prelates, ecclesiastics, collegians, syndics, and eccleciastical and secular *cabildos* followed suit.

After Mass and the oath of allegiance came a ceremony at the presidential palace in which the president ordered the royal arms cut out of the flag of the Battalion of the Patriots. All troops took the oaths of allegiance to independence, cannon were fired, people shouted, streets were lighted, and in the evening there were bullffights, a play, and the election of Camilo Manrique and Don Manuel Álvarez as *alcaldes*.

On Wednesday, July 21, one hundred and fifty men left for Popayán to join artillery, militia, and patriot units. The number was swelled by jailbirds whom the president freed to fight.

The next day an edict was issued ordering all who had not yet taken the oath of allegiance to do so immediately. A motley crew of two hundred nobles and jailbirds under Don José María Cabal set out for the south. Five days later the arms of the king were chiseled off the gateway to San Bartolomé by the rector and his collegians, replaced by a gilded Jesus. Some bystanders were reminded of the year 1767, time of the expulsion of the Jesuits, when Spain ordered Jesus chiseled off the portal. One Sr. Cobo had prophesied, "You may chip off Jesus today but we shall live to see it replaced some day."[6]

August 6, Friday, marked another fiesta of Santa Barbara in San Francisco. The following Sunday a badly organized gang of boys from Tunja came straggling in, half-armed, en route to fight Sámano. Jokes and taunts were hurled at the miserable material provided by congress, a group which until six months earlier had tried to force the city of Bogotá into their congress-led, Tunja union. The diarist feared for the future of the president if he were left to count on such worthless, troublesome fellows. Added to their disorder, disloyalty, and extreme youth was their lack of rosaries, and their frank avowals of freemasonry.

Another union troop of one hundred and fifty unarmed federation men came straggling in, trailing five lances, their total equipment for battle. Angry onlookers became caustic and frightened when rumors

---

5. Father Florido was chaplain to Nariño's army, see Espinosa Diary, p. 23.
6. Caballero, Diary, pp. 181–182.

passed that Sámano had just captured Popayán, taking (and killing) many prisoners and much ammunition and artillery. On August 14, the president had to suppress a riot led by a Caraqueño named Mojica who had to be jailed as a revolutionary in order to suppress the riot.

By Monday, August 16, some order was procured among the Socorro troops as they left for Popayán and the enemy. Promise of an ounce of gold helped some, combined with an order condemning Regency supporters.[7]

Such sunshine patriots augured ill for their leader, the president-general, "just like the people of Tunja, famous for throwing a rock, then hiding their hand."[8]

Tuesday, August 17, was a happier day. An Indian *cacique* from near Popayán came to ally with the president and offer a force of five thousand armed lancers, blowgunners, and archers. This *cacique* from the Andaquíes was met with all due ceremony, was decorated, uniformed, and given gifts and the rank of captain, complete with gilded epaulets. Three days later, more preparations included the publication of general amnesty, testing of the range of cannon from the precipice of La Peña, and a drill in carrying heavy artillery toward Popayán in which some men, staggering under the weight of the load, were crippled as they fell, while others vomited blood. Three days later an emissary arrived from Sámano, demanding the surrender of the city.

Notice was published swearing in a triumvirate of interim governors during the absence of Nariño. Bernardo Alvarez was to be assisted by councilors Diego and Herrera. On Friday August 31, the new flag of the *Auxiliar* was blessed with all pomp and ceremony in the cathedral.

From the north came good news of Bolívar's reconquest of Caracas. From the south, September days brought only silence and doubt. It was toward Popayán, to the south, that two hundred more men went forth on September 7, 1813, carrying the new flag. On the eleventh, two hundred more departed, waving the banner of Jesus and the motto "First Battalion, die or conquer — Cundinamarca," and another banner with an eagle carrying a sword and a pomegranate wearing the liberty cap. On September 16, the royal arms were chipped off of the palace gate and replaced with a liberty cap while troops, moving out, cheered.

On Saturday, September 18, 1813, special supplicatory Masses were held for the president. Prayers to Our Lady of Topó and the Virgin Mary were recited to avert the dangers threatening the president and the

---

7. *Ibid.,* p. 184.
8. *Ibid.*

future of liberty. Sunday all the highest functionaries attended special services in the cathedral. Following Mass, a holiday was decreed. A great banquet was finally rained out, about five in the afternoon.

Expedition South

On Monday, September 20, all preparations for departure were complete. The president met the national representatives and delivered his final exhortation. While his coach and escort waited, he debated with the representatives, from eight in the morning until twelve thirty. Finally, at two o'clock, congress reluctantly agreed to the departure. At night the *Milicias* marched out of their barracks preceded by a portable chapel for novenas. Special Masses were said in the barracks square.

By 10 o'clock the next morning, September 21, 1813, the expedition for the south was on the move, headed by the president-general of Cundinamarca. Scorning the coach provided for his comfort, he cantered forth confidently, the feathers of his three-cornered cap floating in the breeze, each feather colored to match one of the tricolors of Independence. Next came the cavalry company, armed with broadswords, pistols, and guns. Then came the empty coach. A crowd gathered on all sides as the little "army of the South" passed out through the gates and disappeared, at last, in the direction of Popayán.[9]

Days and weeks passed with no news from the south. Little events affecting the new government augured ill. It was reported by mail that Caracas had been reconquered. The same mail brought ugly threats from Sámano and the royalists near Popayán. On October 1, 1813, the Tribunal of Vigilance supported an emergency decree demanding that all arms drawn from the state should be returned under pain of death. Meanwhile the royal arms were chipped off once again, this time from the door of the mint, and replaced with those of Cundinamarca. On October 23, two hundred unarmed troops, led by an English brigadier, arrived from Socorro. The stripped city still distrusted them on account of the previous year's civil war and refused them arms until they had marched out to Neiva and Villa de Purificación. On November 3, the government issued an edict against rioting and meeting of men in the streets. The same order made it illegal to joke or talk critically about the government. Anyone with objections should present them to the justices. Billiard players and gamblers meeting in the evening were warned not to criticize the government. The diarist wrote: "The government is trembling with fear. And well they may, for the party of counter

---

9. *Ibid.,* pp. 186–188.

revolution is great, full of proud royalists and regentists who grow bolder . . . unless we soon have a victory."[10]

The royal arms over the customhouse, San Carlos gate, and the cathedral were replaced with the Republican Jesus symbol during the week of December 16. Prayers to Saint Joseph were revised to remove all reference to Spain and the king. Otherwise pre-Christmas festivities proceeded with the usual Masses, processions, and purchase of holiday needs.

December 19, however, was an ill-omened day. The first word from the south told of the near death of the president-general. Jealousy and rancor left over from the civil war with Baraya caused smoldering ashes of the recent civil war to burst into flame. A desperate attempt had been made to assassinate Nariño, along with Colonel Campomanes, an English leader, and several Socorro leaders. A resentful congress, still smarting from Baraya's defeat, was said to be responsible for the plot. "Great men never lack enemies; if this is the evil influence of Congress, we shall soon fall to the common enemy, God help us then. If we fall in their hands, there won't be so much as a cold earthworm left!"[11]

The year ended on a note of Spartan austerity. By special edict, the government on December 30 banned the customary "fiestas of Egypt" and all other celebrations until such time as word came of victory in the south. Instead, patriots were exhorted to kneel to their altars and pray for victory in 1814.[12]

Leaving his elected triumvirate in the hands of his uncle, Manuel Bernardo Alvarez, and an appointed Tribunal of Vigilance and Security (seven men), Nariño with his little army of twelve hundred infantry and two hundred cavalry was pushing south over the frozen *páramo* of Guanacas. Colonel Antonio Nariño, his son, was in command of the cavalry. Brigadier José Ramón de Leiva, a Spaniard, but an enthusiastic patriot, was second in command. A large train of supplies followed and proved cumbersome, especially when crossing the icy *páramo* of Guanacas.[13]

As usual, Nariño was quite willing to prevent bloodshed and avoid war, if Sámano were willing to negotiate. In a November 17 letter from near the Mesa of Juan Díaz, received by Sámano on December 2, the president-general tried out his most persuasive line of reasoning, though remaining firm and clear throughout as to his stand on independence.

10. *Ibid.,* p. 189.
11. *Ibid.,* p. 191.
12. *Ibid.*
13. Henao and Arrubla, *op. cit.,* pp. 247–249.

Nariño noted that General Sámano was in agreement with his superior, the captain general of Quito, that a conference should be held. He reminded Sámano of the many friends he had once made on a long stay in Santa Fé even during the recent troubled years. He observed that one demand included the return of Colombia to rule by the government of Spain, and reminded Sámano that this government of Spain "no longer exists,"[14] since one part of Spain was loosely ruled by an ephemeral government similar to the many *juntas* in America. "I would be thought crazy to desire reunion with such a ramshackle chaotic government."[15] Winning freedom from such chaos in order to surrender to Bonaparte was even more unthinkable. Not only did Americans remember clearly Spanish barbarity, but they also could see that the dawning era required a new type of government for America. To reunite a healthy limb, Colombia, to the sickly, moribund, gangrenous body of Spain would constitute utter stupidity. No American of honor and sense would accept being considered insurgent by the insurgents of Spain. What could America gain by giving up freedom and her new constitution to return to royal subjection? Not security obviously; Spain could not even defend itself, much less America, from Bonaparte. The only reason Bonaparte delayed extinguishing the small part of free Spain was to wait until it had reconquered its lost empire in America. Sámano was thus just a blind tool of Napoleon's despotism. "Give up this stupid error and join the more just, human, and holy cause of humanity, for a just, moderately democratic republic which hopes to wipe out the tears of three centuries of slavery — join us. . . ." General Sámano's reply from Popayán was curt and to the point: "I proposed to you peace or war. You gave me the same reply under opposite terms from my conditions. Very well then, I choose war! May God keep you many years."[16]

More Efforts for Peace

By December 18, the president-general was in Plata camped for the night. It was from there, surrounded with the thousand and one tasks of operating an army in enemy territory, that he wrote what he may have thought would be his last letter home. It was addressed to Uncle Manuel Alvarez. He spoke of the many details filling his life — Congress, cannons, mules, spies, counterspies, etc. — enough to make a man almost prefer battle to the million details of paper work.

14. Posada and Ibáñez, *El Precursor,* p. 418.
15. *Ibid.*
16. *Ibid.,* p. 420. See *Joaquín Camacho* by Luis Martínez Delgado, pp. 133–168: Diary of expenses of Nariño in South.

Campomanes, Serviez, and Scharburg were reputed doing well near Cartagena, so now it was up to Nariño to do as well, against Sámano at Popayán. Letters for congress and the executive branch were enclosed with this letter. "On to Popayán, which, if God wills, will soon be captured by your Antonio."[17]

Alto Palacé fell to the advance guard of Major General Cabal on December 30, and the new year, 1814, found Nariño in possession of his primary objective, Popayán. Pushing south after the retreating royalists, Nariño gained a third victory over Sámano and Asín at Calibío on January 15. In this battle some two thousand royalists were killed, captured, or routed by the enthusiastic charge of an inferior number of republican troops. Nariño then decided to give his men a much-needed rest in Popayán before advancing on his final objective,[18] Pasto.[19]

While resting in Popayán, the president again shifted to diplomacy in an effort to obtain further victory without bloodshed. In a letter to Señora Ana María Polonia García, wife of the royalist leader Tacón, he reminded her of her generous conduct toward prisoners who had earlier fallen into her hands during battle in Popayán, and stated that he would be failing in his principles to the lovable and compassionate sex if he neglected to offer her and her husband safety and honorable asylum in the event that they became his prisoners in Pasto. "Cundinamarca would be pleased to count you among the virtuous ladies who adorn it."[20] Señora Tacón politely but firmly refused the offer in a reply sent from Quito on February 15, 1814. She thanked him for his kind thoughts but assured him that she never confused duty and generosity. "I am easily moved to pity . . . but this does not cause me to forget the debts I owe the nation which gave me birth. I have a husband, whom you will see by the enclosed newspaper is considered brave. He will render me, as I desire, the help which you offer me, and to which in any case I would always prefer death. . ."[21]

Not daunted by one rejection, Nariño continued his efforts to win over the enemy in Pasto with his persuasive pen. His appeal was directed first to the creole *cabildo* of Pasto (March 4, 1814). He informed them

---

17. *Ibid.,* p. 421.

18. Don Carlos Simmonds present owner of the great fortress-like house at Calibío took this author over the battlefield and into the house. In one room Col. José I. Rodríguez cut off the head of Asín, for which Nariño reprimanded him. He later deserted Nariño in the fateful battle of Pasto.

19. Posada and Ibáñez, *El Precursor,* p. 422.

20. *Ibid.*

21. *Ibid.*

that they deceived themselves about their common enemy, Spain, and its representative in Quito, Don Toribío Montes.

If we fall into their hands, they will chop off our heads; if they fall into our hands, we treat them with kindness. Obviously to be *royalist* is the only safe recourse . . . Obviously, fine principles for perpetuating discord, destroying clemency among Americans, which is one of our finest qualities.

When will the day come when all Americans will open their eyes and see that the present plan of Europe is to keep us divided in order to dominate us? Just cast your eyes over America and see this principle in action. From Buenos Aires to Mexico, from Lima to Caracas, they make bloody war and if we go to examine it what do we find? How many Spaniards are killed in this bloody civil war? Not one in a hundred! But each one is a fiery torch setting fire to all others, a fury arming Americans against Americans. How would Spain make war were it not for Americans taking her part? What did Montes lose in the battles of Palacé and Calibío? Just one man, Asín! And how many Americans died? More than four hundred. So you see, win or lose, they always gain — *that many fewer Americans!* That's how it is all over America . . . You want us to do the same? So tomorrow Montes in Quito like Monteverde in Caracas can go away laughing at us while we Americans kill each other.

I propose peace and conciliation instead . . . .[22]

Montes replied on March 27 and the *cabildo* replied on April 1, both rejecting Nariño's appeal, but the psychological warfare continued on both sides, with a barrage of offers and counter offers until April 8, just four days before the great battle at Juanambú. Nariño's attempt to split American royalists or weaken their Spanish commander was thus a failure, yet not a total failure, since they deigned to write him answers to his arguments. In fact, Montes hastened to warn the *cabildo* that "this seductive fellow hopes to win more by the persuasiveness of words than he can get by the force of his soldiers."[23]

Montes flattered Pasto for loyalty and unwillingness to be led by the siren call of Independence. He played on the feeling of superiority to nearby Popayán, which had fallen into the independence trap and was now paying for it in lost trade and higher taxes, confusion, and disorder, "which new systems always inspire."[24]

To Nariño, Montes replied with some exasperation, "since you know my heart is *always* Spanish," that if he continued toward Pasto he could expect finally "the same fate as Caicedo and Macaulay — defeat and death by execution . . . and your printed propaganda of blown-up

---

22. *Documentos históricos de los hechos ocurridos en Pasto en la guerra de la independencia,* Edición oficial (Pasto, Colombia, 1912), pp. 109–110. (Hereinafter *Hechos ocurridos en Pasto.*)

23. *Ibid.*

24. *Ibid.,* pp. 110–111.

lies is useless here, too, since this area has remained calm and voted me five hundred horses and much money."[25] Then followed a resumé of Spanish victories everywhere: in France, in Austria, in Ayahuma, Peru, in Buenos Aires, in Chile, about to surrender, in Mexico, even in the nearer Caracas, and the Cartagena area. Even North America, faced with the burning of Havre de Grace, was reputed to be treating for peace through Russian intervention. Furthermore, Spanish troops were even then pouring into Guayaquil as reinforcements for royalist Pasto. As for Brigadier Sámano and his executive Asín, if they appeared unduly harsh and cruel, Nariño need only appeal over their heads directly to Montes for a reasonable truce.[26]

Still trying to split the creole *cabildo* from the Spanish commander, Nariño claimed that their separate replies seemed confused and contradictory; that he for one was not fighting for opinion, but for existence; that it was a case of conquer or die. No alternate course remained open. Spaniards, of course, would not admit it, but in fact they were being punished for the crimes of the Conquest by the loss of America.

By the bowels of Jesus Christ, do not *force* me to proceed against my principles. I do not come to destroy, nor for personal revenge, nor even victories because they come easily — only peace, harmony, and a justice of rational intelligence which our ancient innocent customs and the purity of our Holy Religion supports are my desires.

With this in mind I await your reply before attacking Juanambu . . .[27]

On April 4, the *cabildo* of Pasto replied sharply, rapping the president-general's knuckles for profaning "the bowels of our Redeemer Jesus Christ" and assuring him the royalists loved peace, and had no desire to force him to go against his principles. But *"it is you who come here to make most unjust aggression against us. . . ,* you talk of freeing us, giving us liberty in the same moment you advance to destroy us and our European brothers to whom we are tied by many bonds."[28]

By April 6, Nariño's patience was wearing thin, his tones becoming more threatening to the citizens of Pasto.

I see it is useless to use papers or reasons with you. I did not rush together my Santa Fe troops until Don Toribío Montes, in the name of a king whom we still recognize here, declared war on us with what legal support, I know not . . . Recent news indicates success against the perfidious French who wished to

---

25. *Ibid.*

26. *Ibid.,* p. 113.

27. *Ibid.,* p. 114. Signed at Caldera, April 3, 1814.

28. *Ibid.,* p. 115.

enslave not only Spain but us. But the corrupted Spaniards do not realize that we fight for the same principles of freedom there which we desire here ...

You must know I didn't gather all these forces, go to such great effort and expense, win two victories in order now to reverse my march.

So I say to you for the *last time* if you fire as much as one shot at me, trusting in my indulgence, which I used in all the other cities along my line of march, Pasto will be destroyed to its foundations ... You must decide, before firing starts, to join us in our common cause or be destroyed and destroyed so thoroughly that Pasto can never again be inhabited. [29]

Fight or Surrender

The Pasto *cabildo's* reply of April 8, 1814, left it finally up to Nariño to fight or surrender. They called him an aggressor, an invading tyrant, a disloyal subject, and an ambitious barbarian misusing the holiest name of Jesus to cover unjust bloodshed: "In short, we place our fate in the hands of the Lord who knows how to knock down into the mud with the tiniest stone even the most colossal self-inflated big-heads like you." [30]

The gage had been thrown down to Nariño to fight at Juanambú,[31] and it was there between April 12 and 29, that Nariño gained his third great battle of the south.[32]

Juanambú was more like a series of engagements than a single battle. One hundred men and two officers were lost, capturing the heights of Boquerón and Buesaco. On April 19, Pedro Monsalve and one hundred troops from Socorro defeated a royalist flanking attempt of eight hundred against Juanambú. A rising river prevented swimming horses in the river from reinforcing Monsalve.

Enrique Virgo, with six hundred troops, on April 26 tried a counter-flank to catch the royalist enemy between two fires. With the river still rising, it was a very risky operation. At the Tablón de los Gómez, efforts were made to penetrate enemy lines strongly entrenched throughout the previous three months by the Indians of Pasto. On April 28, Virgo detached four hundred men under Cabal to attempt to swim the river since the bridges had been destroyed. Tied together with ropes, holding their rifles over their heads. Nariño's army forded the stream, climbed the banks, and captured the outer trenches. Then the corpses began to pile up in the rocky headquarters of the royalist army. It was a slaughter for Captain Calvo, Lieutenant Pedro Girardot, and others of Nariño's

---

29. *Ibid.*, p. 116.

30. *Ibid.*, p. 117.

31. *Ibid.*

32. Posada and Ibáñez, *El Precursor*, p. 422.

forces as well as of his enemy. Nariño's troops finally withdrew again across the river, covered by their own artillery. During the dark and rainy night and the early dawn of April 29, the two forces drew near to each other across Gómez Tablón. Again Virgo's division occupied the heights in the murky dawn. By two o'clock, royalist General Aymerich was in full flight toward Pasto again, leaving three bridges and a wreck of a camp behind him.

At this point, April 29, Nariño wrote his *oficio* of the battle to the governor and councilors of Cundinamarca, begging for more men and mules to gain the final victory:

For here we are marching always in the enemy country, crossing frozen páramos, jagged and pear-shaped, dying of a pestiferous climate, reduced to cooking with tallow, and without a scrap of smoking tobacco . . . but today we are erecting rope bridges to continue on to Pasto where I think we shall be by May 2 . . . so far not a single deserter.[33]

News like the above was well received in Bogotá and Caracas. From Caracas, Bolívar himself addressed a congratulatory letter on May 4. The Liberator of Venezuela conveyed his grateful appreciation for Cundinamarca's help in freeing America from Spanish power and hastened to confer on Nariño membership in the newly instituted Order of Liberators.[34]

Defeat and Capture

In Bogotá, the city prepared to celebrate, as they had for the earlier victories of Calibío and Palacé.[35] But the good news was so slow in arriving (on June 3, 1814), that the terrible shock of Nariño's defeat and capture arrived almost simultaneously, and the diarist, Lieutenant J. M. Caballero, noted no dances, illuminations, musicals, bullfights nor fireworks for June![36] What had happened?

The stubborn people of Pasto had refused to admit defeat. Nariño's threats at total destruction apparently hardened their loyalty to Spain and their determination to fight to the end. Only in Pasto did the royalists refuse to admit Nariño's victory and their defeat at Juanambú.[37]

We won two glorious victories at the battlefields of Boquerón and Matabajoy . . . When Nariño approached in March and April we marched out to oppose

---

33. *Ibid.,* pp. 424–426.
34. *Ibid.,* p. 427.
35. Caballero, Diary, pp. 193–196.
36. *Ibid.,* pp. 196–199.
37. *Hechos ocurridos en Pasto,* p .139. Dept. de Pasto, Pasto, 1912.

him to a man without *any exceptions.* Our new General Aymerich decided to fall back on this city for reasons we do not understand, moving the cannon out as far as the provincial borders of Pasto. Nariño drew closer, but sallying forth from here we won a new victory at Cebollas. We withdrew again to return to the attack on May 9 and it was an unfortunate affair. On this occasion our General withdrew five leagues. Our troops and arms were left without cover but reanimated by faith and trust in heaven, we invoked the aid of Holiest Mother Mary whose image was carried on the feeble shoulders of women and we sallied forth, not over two hundred strong, to destroy the forces of Nariño — eight hundred, a thousand and more — later capturing Nariño who had hidden himself.[38]

Apologists for Nariño tell the story of his defeat and capture a little differently. Henao and Arrubla's official history claims that Nariño won at Palacé, Calibío, Juanambú and even at Tacines on May 9. On May 10 a sally of three columns from the city met the usual stiff resistance from the president-general in the center, but his flank commanders panicked and fled to Tacines. At Tacines, the panic spread to Colonel José Ignacio Rodríguez who decided to destroy his artillery and retreat. By the time Nariño and Cabal reached Tacines, their army was reduced to wounded stragglers. Cabal and Nariño's son pushed on to stop the rout and Nariño was attacked, May 11, by Pastusos. Nariño's routed forces did not reorganize until they reached Popayán. In the meantime, after hiding in the mountains for three days, Nariño surrendered to an Indian and a soldier. This is the story Henao and Arrubla tell of the tragic defeat at Pasto.[39]

This summary is largely based on the documents of the Spanish commander, Field Marshal Melchor Aymerich, as well as the words of the president himself, who was called on in 1823 to defend his actions in the Colombian senate. He remembered with vivid clarity what happened next. The people of Pasto demanded his head.[40]

After three days of waiting I saw there were only two exits — to Pasto or to eternity — so I tried to treat for armistice with the president of Quito . . . I knew I would die in Pasto but I would die serving my country and this was the consideration which caused me to expose myself to die usefully on the gallows, rather than futilely in the shade of some trees . . . When I arrived in Pasto I had had nothing to eat or drink for a week, and I remained until May 14, under some briar bushes, awaiting the return of the troops, not over fifty paces from the spot where the artillery remained. Then when the people of Pasto heard of my arrival, they shouted in unison for my head. Immediately I was imprisoned, a set of heavy chains was placed upon me, twice the president of

---

38. *Ibid.*

39. Henao and Arrubla, *op. cit.,* p. 252.

40. Posada and Ibáñez, *El Precursor,* p. 578.

Quito ordered me shot. He did not say, nor could he say, that I owed my having escaped the furor of the partisans and the orders of Montes to my firmness and serenity.[41]

Nariño could guess, but could not know, what documents found after his death reveal, about this close escape from the Pasto mob. Aymerich had a certain grudging admiration for his official enemy, Nariño. He spoke of Nariño's admirable control of his troops in Popayán and of the fact that not a single person was molested by his troops there. No religious temples were profaned, even the poorest huts were untouched, and the great turbulence created earlier by Sámano had been quelled. Robbing and sacking was abruptly halted upon Nariño's arrival in Popayán. Field Marshal Aymerich with his "accustomed generosity and magnanimity of soul"[42] had therefore placed Nariño, after his capture at Lagartijas on May 14, 1814, in a prison "until a brief could be filed for final decision of his fate."[43]

While Aymerich proceeded formally to draw up suit against Nariño through a lawyer, the people of Pasto kept shouting for Nariño's head. Meanwhile, Captain General Toribío Montes of Quito urged Aymerich to obtain from Nariño, before decapitation, all possible information relative to the location, strength, etc., of Cabal's fleeing republican forces. Another factor which may have delayed Aymerich's execution or decapitation of his important prisoner was the alternate threat of reprisals and offers of as much as seventy prisoners suggested for exchange by Andres Ordóñez y Cifuentes, president of the Constitutional College of Popayán and José de Leiva, Nariño's third-in-command. Among the seventy offered by José de Leiva were two captured Spanish colonels. These combined offers and threats did stay the executioner's hand as Aymerich readily admitted in his letter to Montes of June 4, 1814.[44]

Thus Nariño remained in chains, and in prison, but to the disgust of the Pastusos still alive. Discipline and moderation in victory had again been justified as the wheel of fate quickly turned Nariño from victorious general into defeated prisoner. When his Uncle Manuel Bernardo Alvarez wrote to Aymerich of Nariño's natural moderation and scrupulous observance of the law of nations, he spoke a truth which Aymerich quickly admitted.[45]

---

41. *Ibid.*
42. *Ibid.*, p. 435.
43. *Ibid.*
44. *Ibid.*, pp. 437, 438, 439.
45. *Ibid.*, p. 440.

Pleas for Freedom

By June 28, 1814, Nariño was up to his old tricks of charming his captors. And had it not been for an express order from Montes in Quito to keep the smooth-talking prisoner incommunicado, and without ink or paper, Aymerich might soon have been considering another of Nariño's now famous plan-projects — "for reforming the Spanish government of America." Even under strict orders for imprisonment and isolation, Nariño was finally able to penetrate the barrier of silence on July 4, 1814. On that day from his jail in Pasto he wrote two letters which reached Bogotá.

In the first letter, he urged the president and councilors of the executive power of Cundinamarca to learn from the tragic lesson of his defeat the price of disunity, to forget the past and to heal the breaches which led to his defeat. "Then you must make it known to the world that this great struggle is not a frenzy, is not a madness and that when they open reasonable roads to conciliation and peace, we will adopt them."[46]

To the presiding officer of the Supreme Congress, in a second letter of July 4, he wrote of his earlier efforts at truce and a demarcation line based on the *status quo*, "until all could see how things stood in Europe without further useless shedding of blood. . . ."

However, the fate of this kingdom "does not depend on present forces wherever they may be."

As I see it, . . . America is today a theater of desolation and blood and even though this vista is a little far off, we must know that its fate does not depend on the forces now in the fight. To what purpose then are we slashing each other to bits if the final result will yield neither victory nor defeat of either army? Today one side triumphs in this area, tomorrow the other side wins in another area, and all we get, both sides, is tears. Nothing is decided. We must have truce, however short, an end to these miseries; remaining, if necessary, in the state in which we now find ourselves. While the horizon of Europe clears, let us, both sides, see what best suits us, since it is quite obvious that one more rifle shot will not bring co-ordination of opinions at this point in this case.[47]

With these parting words of a wisdom gained through both victory and defeat, the president-general now entered a new and yet familiar phase of his career. Once again he was transferred from prison to prison, shut off from the outside world, and seldom heard from, except through the Spanish authorities who made the usual methodical copies and records of complaints of their long-suffering prisoner.

---

46. *Ibid.,* p. 446.
47. *Ibid.,* p. 447.

Argos, a newspaper in Cartagena, reported the departure of the prisoner, their former president, to Lima and Spain.[48]

Restrepo in his *Historia de la revolución de Colombia* says Nariño stayed prisoner in Pasto three months, whence he was carried to Quito. In Quito some daring friends tried, in vain, to free him from his escort by attack. Montes blocked this plan and sent him to Lima whence he was sent to a Cádiz jail by way of Cape Horn.[49]

By his own admission, Nariño listed no less than ten prisons where Spain had jailed him, which included in this third and longest imprisonment, Pasto, Callao, Lima, and the royal jail of Cádiz.[50]

For his last incarceration, the sea voyage around Cape Horn was a long one. It was not until two years after his defeat at Pasto in May, 1814, that he was at last placed in the Cádiz jail on March 16, 1816, and there he remained until March 23, 1820. Such a fate might have killed less determined souls, as indeed it did kill Miranda. But the Precursor of Colombian independence had not finished his life work. Somehow, fate had spared him from the mobs, from shooting, from hanging, from death in battle, or in earlier jails. Perhaps Nariño was destined for further life and further work. In any case, he survived this last ordeal and was still alive and complaining, as always, about his jail and jailers, when the Riego revolt freed him suddenly for a third life.[51]

---

48. *Ibid.,* p. 449.

49. Restrepo, I, 263, quoted in Posada and Ibáñez, *El Precursor,* p. 449.

50. Posada and Ibáñez, *El Precursor,* p. 573.

51. Torres Lanzas, *Independencia de América,* IV, 455, 473. Posada and Ibáñez, *El Precursor,* p. 474.

CHAPTER XI

HERO'S RETURN

A Third Life

Were it not for the Spanish proclivity to establish and preserve archives, including prison records, very little would be known of Nariño's four years in the Cádiz jail. However, the Spanish authorities saved no less than thirteen letters either about Nariño, or written by Nariño to his jailers at regular intervals throughout his unwilling visit of four years as "guest" of the Spanish government which he had tried so hard to destroy in Colombia.

The first of these letters was written on March 25, 1814, by Don Blas Lamota in Cádiz to the Secretary of State (Universal Dispatch, Grace and Justice), relative to biographical sketches on Dr. Rosillo, Antonio Nariño, Geronimo Fernández, Pedro Groot, and Gregorio Nariño — all persons referred to by the archbishop of Bogotá, Juan Bautista Sacristán. Sacristán told how Nariño had urged him to leave Bogotá in 1811 and 1812 and had later deceived the government of Spain with flattery while simultaneously urging independence. Dr. Rosillo had relayed this information about Nariño to Spain via the archbishop.[1]

It seems that Nariño had first, in October, 1811, tried to discourage the archbishop from settling in Bogotá by presenting him with a copy of the oath which all prelates were required to take in support of the new Republic of Cundinamarca. When persuasion failed, Nariño had decreed the expulsion of the archbishop on December 30, 1813. At that point, his friend, Francisco Gerónimo Fernández, had urged Sacristán to seek refuge with him in Kingston, Jamaica.[2] Such information against the ex-president of Cundinamarca tended to keep his jailers from giving him special or lenient treatment in the *calabozo* of Cuatro Torres in Cádiz. In fact, Nariño later stated, in 1823, that he was left "naked and starving in these jails for many long endless years."[3]

---

1. Torres Lanzas, *Independencia de América,* III, 98, 99, 249, 441, 473.
2. *Ibid.,* III, 441.
3. Posada and Ibáñez, *El Precursor,* p. 573.

Some, like *Oidor* Jurado, who pitied the lot of Nariño and his family, paid for their kindness with the loss of their jobs.[4] The only safe way to handle Nariño seemed to be with the official precision and impartiality of the viceroy of Peru, who wrote the "Universal Secretary of State for the Indies" from Lima on November 4, 1815, that he was sending to Cádiz, aboard the frigate *Preciosa* under registered departure "the traitor Antonio Nariño, ex-President and General of the revolutionaries of Bogotá or Cundinamarca."[5]

By 1816, Bogotá had suffered in quick succession no less than three destructive attacks and sieges; first, Baraya's January, 1813, attack and defeat; then the successful attack of Baraya, Bolívar, and the Tunja congress in November, 1814, and, finally, the bloodier attack and siege by the Spanish generals Morillo and Sámano in May of 1816.[6] In a way, Nariño was lucky to be in jail in 1815 and 1816, for he was still alive while many of his compatriots like Caldas, Lozano, Valenzuela, Gutiérrez, Pombo, García Rovira, José Ayala, Ignacio Camacho, Bernardo Alvarez, and even his old enemy, Antonio Baraya, had been executed by Morillo and his Spaniards, who used a variety of means including hanging, decapitating, and shooting with the arquebus.[7] Spanish strategy seemed to involve the mass killing of all the rich and intelligent of Bogotá so that "she shall live forever in ignorance and darkness."[8]

Lenience at Cádiz

Meantime, Spanish justice in Cádiz was milder toward Nariño.

By March 15, 1816, another *expediente,* summarizing all of the captive's activities and his connections with troubles and revolts in Santa Fé from 1794 to 1814, was collected in one document. To this mass of information was added a summary from the files of the Supreme Council of the Indies, and public papers dealing with the insurgents of New Granada.[9]

On September 16, 1816, Councilor Juan Lozano de Torres drew up an official report analyzing the *expediente* of March 15, 1816, and urging that Nariño be kept incommunicado in the Cádiz jail, at least until all papers about him could be collected.[10]

---

4. Torres Lanzas, *Independencia de América,* IV, 141.
5. *Ibid.,* IV, 142.
6. Caballero, Diary, pp. 204–253.
7. *Ibid.,* pp. 253–257.
8. *Ibid.,* p. 255.
9. Torres Lanzas, *Independencia de América,* IV, 166.
10. *Ibid,* IV, 217.

Four days later, on September 20, 1816, at the royal palace in Madrid, the president of the Council of the Indies accepted a copy of a royal order demanding the council's opinion on the case of Nariño to be presented to His Majesty one week from date.[11] By September 24, the governor of the Cádiz jail, Alonso Rodríguez Valdés, was in great haste to inform His Majesty that recent orders to keep Nariño incommunicado had been promptly and strictly executed.[12] For two years Nariño stood this solitary confinement without complaint. But on October 9, 1817, he could stand it no longer. Through some friend named Ignacio Marcos Arroyo, he memorialized the king. He reminded the king that he had been on short rations and totally incommunicado for over two years, and requested, as a small favor, that ten *reales* a day be spent for his food as was normally done for other prisoners convicted of the same crime.[13]

The same Ignacio Marcos Arroyo forwarded Nariño's second appeal for mercy (January 26, 1818). In this plea, Nariño complained that the general amnesty of the previous year which had freed other leaders of insurrection in America had apparently forgotten or neglected to add his name.[14]

A year later, on February 20, 1818, in his third memorial, forwarded from the royal prison of Cádiz by Policarpo Herrero, the imprisoned leader reminded His Majesty of the great leniency that he, Nariño, had shown captured Spaniards who had fallen into his hands in the Pasto campaign, and begged the king, in consideration of these many kindnesses and services to captive Spanish troops to set him free.[15]

By November 1, 1819, the king was again ordering the president of the Council of the Indies to speed up justice and put an end to Nariño's undecided case. The previous pleas for liberty were denied but the jailers were ordered to spend ten *reales* daily for his sustenance as was done for other political criminals from America.[16]

The last royal order from Madrid was an urgent message to reimprison Nariño. On May 5, 1820, the king ordered the captain general of Andalusia to find and jail the prisoner immediately. "This President of Cundinamarca, as he styles himself, has by some inexplicable blunder been freed by the interim governor of Cádiz." [17]

---

11. *Ibid.,* IV, 218.
12. *Ibid.,* IV, 219.
13. *Ibid.,* IV, 305.
14. *Ibid.,* IV, 342–343.
15. *Ibid,* IV, 354.
16. *Ibid.,* IV, 455.
17. *Ibid.,* IV, 473.

His Majesty was mistaken. The freeing of Nariño was no blunder! It was the careful work of the friends of liberty, democracy, and Nariño who led the Riego revolt of 1820.

A Liberating Angel

Something like a secret lodge of Friends of America stepped in to free Nariño, "Jaureguí, my liberating angel, appeared suddenly in front of my prison door."[18] General Manuel Francisco Jaureguí had, like Nariño, been in jail until a few days earlier. But on March 23, 1820, the wheel of fate turned. The prisoner, Jauregií, was made jailer, and quickly released Nariño. Short though his authority was, it lasted long enough to free leaders of the movement for freedom of both America and Spain. For two months, Nariño was an associate of Quiroga, Riego, López Baños, Arco Agüero, O'Dali, Infante, Ballesa, and Alcalá Galiano — all working for Spanish liberty and American liberty simultaneously on the island of León. At the first session of the Patriotic Society of San Fernando, Nariño was elected president, and "the majority of them contributed actively to save me from the clutches of the constitutional government of Spain."[19]

Even previous to being freed, Nariño must have experienced increasing liberty, for he was able to smuggle out three essays under the pseudonym "Enrique Samoyar" on March 2 and March 12, 1820.[20] The gist of these essays was that there was much contradiction in calling the insurrection in America "criminal" and the insurrection in Spain "holy"; that many leaders desiring representative government for Spain desired little or none for the Spanish colonies and, finally, that the bloodthirsty generals, Morillo and Sámano, suppressors of American Spaniards, were mistakenly and hypocritically described as heroes in Spain. Nariño and others found themselves in the paradoxical situation of being alternately and simultaneously courted and hunted by different factions of the new Cortes of Cádiz. One faction wanted to raise new armies to reconquer America and throw Nariño in jail. Another faction, also fighting Ferdinand, wanted to grant representation to Spanish America and even elected Nariño as deputy from New Granada![21]

Yet some second sense caused Nariño in May to flee Cádiz for Gibraltar.[22] Direct warning from Quiroga that some Spaniards "would

18. Posada and Ibáñez, *El Precursor,* p. 479.

19. *Ibid.*

20. *Ibid.,* pp. 452–466, 474.

21. *Ibid.,* p. 481.

22. *Ibid.,* pp. 474–475.

like nothing better than to return you to a cell in the Carraca"[23] strengthened Nariño's decision to flee the new Spanish government.

It was with considerable reluctance and sadness that Nariño fled "liberal" Spain for Gibraltar. When first freed from jail by General Jaureguí, the flowering Spanish countryside had looked too beautiful to leave, even if one were threatened by imminent capture and death.

You know it was nine at night when I left the jail. My fate seemed to depend on the caprices of four anti-American governors. My first stop was in the tavern near Chichana, where I took my first drink of freedom, with bread and cheese, drinking to the health of those who directly or indirectly had aided in setting me free. I set forth with an easy gait under a night sky clear enough to distinguish objects. What a multitude of pleasant thoughts and observations! After twenty-six years of suffering, nevertheless here I was a fugitive, fleeing from a free Spain, yet, at the same time, I was being saved and protected by these very same Spaniards! From these thoughts I turned to enjoy objects surrounding me, comparing them with those of home. There, one one side, I made out the shape of a tree, which seemed to grow about like our silk cotton ceiba or our alders. I was transported in my imagination to Chocontá or Guaduas. Now a flock of sheep, then the mooing of cows by the roadside in the moonlight made me believe I was walking along near Sesquilé or Tunja; a little further and I came upon a level prairie of brambles and dwarf trees which made me think I was going hunting at Tibabuyes. Thus I continued my way until three in the morning (pay close attention to these details of terrain and distances, I said to myself; it may save you some day). And so I arrived at the country inn of Verjel or Verger, after an unbroken journey of six hours. Giving thought to the horses which might show up in an hour or so I continued my way in the growing light of day. The first objects which then met my eyes were some straw thatched huts on a terrain very like that of Bogotá, which, if Father Padilla had been journeying with me, would have soon resulted in Indians rushing out in their *jichones* to ask his benediction. What a beautiful countryside! A great country house, all of tiles, with a great drove of Saldaño bullocks nearby, made me think I was in Tilatá, and I had a sudden urge to go in and ask if any of the LaTorre family were at home. Thus, musing, charmed by a day that was serene and cool, I arrived at another country tavern, whose name I have forgotten because there was nothing special about it except that it was three mortal hours distant from the other. "Might you have a couple of eggs?" I asked the tavern keeper. No, he had none, for the good and convincing reason that someone else had already eaten them. After this tavern, the road was level and grassy until I came at last into the beautiful *campiñas* of Tarifa. What comparisons! What agreeable sensations of memory were awakened in me! The landscape was broken and craggy and though I was not able, fixing it in my mind's eye, to convince myself that it was the beautiful rolling plains of Bogotá, nevertheless, in spite of that, its vast green sweep transported me into ecstasy. For the moment I forgot that here I was, a fugitive, in a free Spain, yet without in the very least having killed, or robbed, or even

---

23. *Ibid.*, p. 485.

disturbed the quiet of any citizen. The rest of the trip took four hours more until its end — I moved along without stopping at faster than normal step.

From here on, the scene changed rapidly. Before me rose the ridges of Ojel. And would you believe it? The steepness of the road, its ancient gnarled and twisted trees, and the whole appearance of the mountain which to others was merely a discomfort, was for me a new source of novel sensations! Now the road climbed to Mave, now it dropped down into Tena. A moment later, I was in Sargento. But among all the things which caused me agreeable sensations, the most pleasing were the ripplying wheat fields of Verger and the deep arroyos of crystal pure water cutting deep down into the ravines; the first I had seen for so many, many years. Thus it was that I, almost always on foot, prostrated myself before the Nymph who ruled these streams, kissing her as I drank in large draughts of water and pleasure. Up to here the good part. Its crossing takes more than six hours to Algeciras. The descent, intolerable, and even more so since both man and horses, soaked with sweat, are tired to the very marrow. Down below, the asylum of the persecuted shows itself from the first shoulder of the ridge, this table to which both the man of good and the man of evil turn for asylum and refuge. And yet four more hours remain to the end of the journey. The most frustrating part of it is the discovery of Algeciras, so close you can reach out and touch it with your hand, but after you have gone a league, there it is further off than before.

But at last I arrived at three-thirty in the afternoon, at this place which seemed so very far from America yet appertains to and touches America in many ways, for through it Americans can depart for America with much ease.

And so today I find myself free, saved from the clutches of Sr. Porul or Queipo or the devil whoever he may be! Amen.[24]

Nariño at Gibraltar

Safe under the British flag at Gibraltar, Nariño waited watchfully the outcome of events in Spain and America before deciding to give up permanently his precarious seat in the new Cortes and return to America by way of London. Chaos and confusion reigned in the revolutionary constitutional monarchy of Spain in 1820. And the life of a freed American republican, caught in its contradictory cross currents, was precarious in the extreme. As a result of his "Enrique Samoyar" letters of March, 1820, Nariño had apparently incurred the undying hatred of the wife and friends of General Morillo, who were determined to recapture and jail or execute the outspoken American leader.[25] As Nariño himself said, these American Spaniards in Cádiz who had been elected to the new Cortes were in an ambiguous position. On the one hand, requisitions went out to return him to his former domicile in jail, and yet another faction considered him a duly elected portion of Spanish sovereignty. Quite rightly Nariño judged that the real revolution in

---

24. *Ibid.,* pp. 474–476.
25. *Ibid.,* p. 486.

Spain "had not yet begun; it was only in the fourteenth day of fever."[26]

Even the liberal merchants of revolutionary Cádiz were not to be trusted. Most of them wanted the war of reconquest to continue, since it meant more ships, supplies, and profits. There were a few noteworthy exceptions, some of whom were apparently Jews or may have been freemasons, but, in any case, they honestly desired freedom for Spanish America. Judah Benolid, millionaire merchant, with the help of Andrés Argüibel, Buenos Aires American in Cádiz and governor's secretary, O'Dali in Algeciras, with this Venezuelan associate, Carabaño, and Santiago Cuervo, supervisor of mails on the island of León — these men were a source of help to Americans from both Americas, these men gave refuge, money, protection, and passage to England or America to the hunted, friendless exiles.[27]

Observing the Europe of 1820, Nariño found few governments worth imitating. Most were corrupt and decrepit. They should be studied primarily to avoid their errors. England, to be sure, was rich and powerful, but "more rich and powerful than they [the citizens] are happy."[28]

By June 2, 1820, liberal Americans in Madrid, such as Antonio Arboleda, were hearing rumors that Nariño had at last fallen victim to the *serviles* and friends of Morillo. But, a month later, Francisco Zea wrote from London to Bolívar, that Nariño, though elected deputy from Colombia with Sandiño, had escaped the trap, thanks to the warning of Quiroga. By September 6, Francisco Zea in London was writing Bolívar in Angostura of Nariño's imminent departure.[29]

Briefly, Nariño had been considered for a permanent post as agent for American independence in Gibraltar, where it was thought that nearness to Cádiz and some liberal spending for printing, mail, and spies, would accomplish much. Instead, he acted as a courier from Zea in London to Bolívar in Angostura, carrying word and explanation of the failure of Méndez's mission to London — "largely his own fault."[30]

From London, Nariño proceeded on October 19 to France, where he embarked on a French vessel for Martinique.

Meeting with Bolívar

By the fifteenth of March, he was in Angostura traveling toward Achaguas to meet Bolívar. Never too busy or too tired to write, the

---

26. *Ibid.*, p. 479.
27. *Ibid.*, p. 480.
28. *Ibid.*, p. 481.
29. *Ibid.*, p. 485.
30. *Ibid.*, pp. 485–486.

Precursor made brief entries in his diary as he moved up stream to his historic meeting with the Liberator.[31]

Bolívar's victory in Boyacá in 1819 had led to the Riego revolt in Spain, and now the Riego revolt in Spain, in turn, led to truce negotiations in America.[32] Into this new and happier state of affairs stepped the Precursor, to lead once more, for the third time, the struggle for Colombian independence. His welcome may be judged by the letters he received from Bolívar.

Writing from Achaguas, on March 24, 1821, Bolívar spoke of the "transports of satisfaction which I underwent upon receiving notice of the Precursor's February 25 arrival. It was one of the many favors which fortune had at last conferred on Colombia to have restored the talents and virtues of one of its famous, illustrious sons. . . ."[33] Bolívar urged the Precursor to hasten his march so that he could soon anticipate "embracing you in my arms for the first time."[34] The Precursor was urged to press on to Achaguas or San Fernando de Apure in order to assist in two historic events: the installation of the first general congress of Colombia, and the negotiation of peace with the Spanish commissioners in which "your knowledge and luminous information will greatly facilitate success."[35]

Nariño had already been informed by José M. Vergara in Paris of the many changes — faces, government, place names. Santa Fé was now Bogotá; Nariño was elected to its *cabildo, in absentia;* Bolívar, elected president of Colombia for four years, Zea, vice-president, and Santander, vice-president for Cundinamarca, as Roscio was vice-president for Venezuela, the two chief provinces of "New Granada." Quito also had a vice-president. This same newsy letter informed the Precursor that Bolívar commanded the main army of Ocaña which had Santa Marta as its immediate objective. Admiral Brion commanded a small fleet based on Río Hacha. Other leaders were scattered around the Americas and Europe in various military and diplomatic posts. Vergara expected the Precursor to begin his new duties as a freed patriot as deputy to the congress of Colombia.[36]

Another letter from Bolívar indicated that Nariño was destined for

31. *Ibid,* pp. 487–490.
32. Henao and Arrubla, *op. cit.,* pp. 341, 342.
33. Posada and Ibáñez, *El Precursor,* p. 493.
34. *Ibid.*
35. *Ibid.*
36. *Ibid.,* pp. 491–492.

a much bigger post in the new government. The sudden sickness and death of several of the older leaders caused Bolívar to carry out a suggestion he had been considering since March 9, 1821.[37]

On April 21, 1821, he wrote F. Peñalver that he was "tired of being dubbed usurper, tyrant, and despot," and therefore tendered his resignation to congress urging them to accept General Nariño or Santander as president. He felt that Colombia required a military president and that "the only way to preserve the unity of Colombia is to elect a general of Cundinamarca as president."[38] A letter to Nariño on the same date included the offer of the presidency to the Precursor and explained Bolívar's reasons for the offer. He felt the Precursor to be better fitted than anyone else to overcome the difficulties likely to hamper the inauguration of the congress. Until congress met, the twenty-two cleared provinces would find the constitution "a book which is meaningless to everyone."[39] All else was transitional. Two vice-presidents had died. Ministers were absent abroad. A central treasury was lacking. Other executive branches were missing. Bolívar himself had to be absent to conduct the war, leaving the republic in a state of orphanage. It was all too much for one man to do. "One man cannot, in a very limited time and with scant knowledge do it all, either badly or well . . . amidst this amazing chaos of patriots, *godos,* self-seekers, whites, mulattoes, Venezuelans, Cundinamarca federalists, centralists, republicans, aristocrats, and the *good* and the bad. . . ."[40]

Chaos was indeed the word for it! Yet the Precursor was willing to embark on this sea of trouble and undertake to do all requested of him by the Liberator *except* be president. To be presiding vice-president was quite enough honor and work. Thus his interim appointment by the Liberator on April 4, 1821,[41] as vice-president remained in effect, and the returning hero proceeded with all possible speed to assemble congress.

Congress Assembled

It was at this point that chaos became organized opposition. Due partly to bad and dangerous roads, and partly to disunity of purpose,

37. Simón Bolívar, *Selected Writings of Bolívar,* compiled by Vincente Lecuña, edited by Harold A. Bierck, Jr., translated by Lewis Bertrand (2 vols., New York, 1951), I, 260, 264, 265.

38. *Ibid.,* I, 263.

39. *Ibid.,* I, 264.

40. *Ibid.*

41. Posada and Ibáñez, *El Precursor,* p. 495.

only fifty-seven of the ninety-five deputies arrived. Nariño became impatient and decided to open the sessions without the required quorum on May 6. The deputies met in the vestry of the church at Rosario de Cúcuta.[42] After his installation speech, Nariño asked the assembly if they approved having congress installed under such unorthodox conditions and received a unanimous vote of approval. Congress was then declared in session and the oaths were taken.[43]

Congress ratified Nariño's appointment as interim vice-president of Colombia. Since he was also to be vice-president of Cundinamarca, one office had been abolished and the republic was thereby saved a salary, a worthy purpose, but one which added jealousy to the stormy sessions and quarrels which began immediately between Nariño and congress.[44]

Thoughts of a Patriot

What thoughts occurred to the recently liberated patriot as he stood before congress at Rosario de Cúcuta on May 6, 1821 — the historic day of his installation as vice-president. Some of his thoughts, at least, we can divine from his speech. This was, perhaps, the proudest occasion of a long, arduous life of continual service to the cause of Colombian independence. Understandably, the Precursor felt that this was the time, if ever, to make an accounting of the services he had rendered; of the historical events which had led him to this, the summit of his career, and of his hopes for the future.

Nariño began his discourse in a modest apologetic tone. It was not necessary to tell them of the progress of the liberating armies since the installation of the Congress of Angostura. This great story was common knowledge. Taxation and commerce were important subjects, but he chose to pass over them momentarily. Mention should be made of the November armistice concluded with Spain "which does much honor to American philanthropy, but which we have been forced to break."[45] Special attention was reserved by the president for what he considered the two most important topics: external independence and internal liberty. To Bolívar and his heroes, Colombia owed much of its external

42. One half of this church is now in ruins (July 18, 1962 visit). The rest is badly kept, as is Santander's home, a mile north of the church on the road to Cúcuta.

43. Rodolfo Osvaldo Rivera, "Francisco de Paula Santander: His Role in the Making of Colombia," Unpublished Ph.D. thesis, Duke University, 1932, pp. 130–133.

44. Ibid.

45. Posada and Ibáñez, El Precursor, p. 497.

liberty. At that very moment, Bolívar and his troops were in the process of expelling the remaining armies of oppressors. However, merely to be independent would not be enough for Colombia. Spain was independent under Ferdinand's arbitrary government; Turkey under its despotic sultan was independent. Institutions were needed to assure all men the peaceful enjoyment of their rights. A non-arbitrary system for administering the republic well must be set up. A well-organized physical force to guarantee freedom from new invasions was yet to be established.

I see with pleasure mixed with some bitterness the few stalks of corn that the destructive reaper has left standing here. You are the fecund grain which must now propagate throughout the republic the intelligence which a ferocious system of pacification tried to blot out entirely here. You are the plank which, having escaped from the shipwreck, must save those of us who are yet alive.[46]

In destroying the chains of bronze which united Colombia to Spain, government had also been destroyed. A new one would have to be created. Breaking the bonds had required the creation, on short notice, of soldiers, politicians, and lawmakers, from men who had been scarcely more than slaves. Greatest of all weaknesses was the lack of allies. Weak and new, unlike the new United States, the new republic could not turn to strong France or Spain for help. Spain, Portugal, and Naples changed governments in a day, but they were in possession of their independence and resources. Not so with Colombia — a mere handful of men scattered over a hundred thousand square leagues of earth, fighting in all directions against the forces of Europe, the ignorance of their own peoples, scarcity of supplies, were now asked in such a crisis to make laws for themselves which might some day even serve as a model for their oppressors!

But, if their problems were immense, their situation perilous, yet they could console themselves with the knowledge that what freedom they had won, they had won on their own. They owed no nation anything for help.

We are today the sole nation on earth able to promise ourselves with assurance the most perfection possible, if only we conduct ourselves with maturity . . . The main thing we must watch is not to expect perfection in a day. The first stones must be wisely and securely set together. Then the majestic building of the future can come later, gradually. The three chief tasks now are to plan our form of government, our methods of electing, and our ways and means of financing it.[47]

---

46. *Ibid.*
47. Ibid., p. 499.

The dissolution of the chains of the old government left not only whole peoples and cities in isolation but even individuals. Thus individual wishes constituted supreme sovereign law. Unable to exercise sovereignty in isolation, individuals chose a national representation or congress to represent them. But the faculties of the representative sovereignty were not without limits — they must operate within the circle of their political attributes *to form a constitution, name their agents, and that is all.*

All forms of government had their abuses. In democracies there was the furor of mobs, in monarchies, the abuse of despots; but representative governments held a potential for progress which might be likened to the dynamics of lightning, for if it did not destroy it would illumine, and the light that was cast would be the clear light of principles founded upon reason.

The three elements of government — the executive, the legislative, and the judicial — should be separated to preserve liberty. The constitution should clearly set the limits of each, making them interdependent. Some officials of government must be able to count on a certain durability in their posts, for the sake of efficiency; yet perpetual or hereditary positions were to be avoided, for fear they would nullify the will of the people as expressed in elections.

The unique feature recommended by Nariño was the single-house legislature, which he admitted was contrary to prevailing republican trends. The constitution should not establish "discordant wishes, for that would mean . . . a system of civil war established by the constitution."[48]

Indirect Elections

Rome, Athens, and England pointed the way to governments in which elections prevented despotism, yet were subject to abuses. Many of the abuses resulted from the people's direct election of the highest officials! The rich, the powerful, and the intriguing orator were all capable of seducing the voting mob. If elections were to become indirect, many such abuses might be avoided. Each little town could then elect an individual judged to be superior, someone the citizenry knew to be better. The chosen electors would gather in each province to pick out the second group of electors, and these, in turn, would gather in the capital to select a third group, which would finally choose the officials from the best leaders of their acquaintances. Specifically,

---

48. *Ibid.,* p. 501.

there would be states divided into provinces, provinces into departments, departments into municipalities, and municipalities into judicatures.[49]

With indirect elections as protection from mob influence, qualification on the basis of money or property would become unnecessary. All men of virtue would have equal rights to vote and hold office, and the poor man of virtue and ability would not be eliminated.

Since in national emergencies all citizens would be required to defend their country, the skeletal organization of a militia should be held in reserve at all times. Nevertheless, a garrison state must firmly be avoided. Neither Rome nor Sparta was an ideal model. If all were soldiers, none would be left to feed them, and, as in Sparta, the army would require a permanent group of slaves to support it, and probably neither the arts nor trade would flourish. A small permanent professional force or regular army of trained soldiers would constitute the cadre of training for the militia when emergencies arose.

Since men in general tend to get as many advantages for as little sacrifice as possible, monopolies, privileges, and low taxes for special groups would have to be carefully avoided. Governing officials should not be merchants, traders, or monopolists. The national income should be made public at all times. Taxes should always be raised and lowered relative to income rather than to capital investment. Also they should be levied in proportion to ability to pay, and should not exceed actual needs of the government. Levies excessively vexatious or excessively expensive to collect, should be discarded. With regard to indirect taxes, great care should be exercised not to stultify in particular agriculture, mining and commerce, while taxes on the transfer of property, though easy to collect, tend to destroy capital. Finally, government-acquired lands should be used, not primarily to pay government expenses, but rather to aid the peoples of the nation in proportion as the productivity of the lands would permit.

Even though taxes represent sacrifice and appear to diminish national capital, they actually help to preserve the rest of the taxpayer's property, and to aid him by providing for coined money, postal services, and roads. If kept within bounds, such expenditures add to the national income by lowering the cost of transportation, easing communications, and bringing markets and people closer together.

The income of the republic can be produced only from the total national wealth; and, if commerce, agriculture, and nascent factories do not prosper, but continue deteriorating, then the wisest of laws and the

---

49. *Ibid.,* p. 502.

most detailed of regulations become quite meaningless. The national income grows only with progressive increase of the wellsprings of national wealth.

Once the nation has been regenerated with new institutions, the convention representatives cease to function. Then the newly elected officials take charge under the new constitution. Far from being sovereign, on the contrary, the government is the servant of the people.

I cannot, sirs, speak any more of these matters because the time does not permit and I have been with you this time only nine days and am therefore ignorant of some matters. Nevertheless, I thank you for your attention to my passing remarks and rapid observations which I assure you come only from my ardent desire to aid my country. Europe, gentlemen, the whole world contemplates you at this moment and expects from you a great document . . .[50]

Immediate reactions to Nariño's speech were favorable. Article VIII of the new constitution was a direct application of Nariño's suggestions regarding subdivisions of the republic.[51] Other aspects such as separation and balance of legislative, executive, and judicial powers, indirect elections and general lack of property qualifications, also were a consequence of Nariño's ideas of government.[52] Safeguards were provided excluding and limiting the voting privileges of insane, illiterate, and criminal citizens.[53] However, the property requirements of electoral voters were not in line with Nariño's recommendations and the two-house Colombian congress ran directly counter to his recommendations.[54]

The recommendation of a unitary republic was quite consistent with all previous actions of Nariño, the ex-president of Cundinamarca, but represented a reversal of Bolívar's thinking in 1815. The Liberator, who had once aided the Tunja congress to defeat centralist Bogotá in 1815, had now been persuaded (by the logic of the bloody Spanish reconquest), of the inefficacy of federalism in the face of domestic and foreign wars.[55] By 1821, Bolívar was like Nariño, strongly opposed to federalism.

The constitution of Cúcuta of 1821 thus represented a vindication of the political wisdom of Nariño. Much of his wisdom was written into the document. To be sure, the Liberator also put his stamp of approval

---

50. *Ibid.,* pp. 502–508.
51. Gibson, *Constitutions of Colombia,* p. 42.
52. *Ibid.,* pp. 40–44.
53. *Ibid.,* pp. 43–45.
54. *Ibid.,* pp. 44, 46.
55. *Ibid.,* p. 37.

on it, particularly on its centralizing tendency; but the similarity between Nariño's speech, Bolívar's desires, and the convention's final constitution certainly owes much of its cement to the man who represented all three founts of wisdom and tried to force congress to merge all of them into a completed document stressing centralism and unity.

Mounting Opposition

In trying to push the convention faster, Nariño at first won praise, but this soon turned to jealousy and opposition. Bolívar sent his congratulations on May 7. The *cabildo* and postal department of Bogotá on May 17 and 24,[56] and President Santander of Colombia on May 14, 1821.[57]

But the praise did not last long. Opposition mounted. The work of constitution-making led to heated debates. The honeymoon of welcome to the hero-exile changed immediately to the rancor of disagreements, and Nariño's downfall was rapid. In less than two months he was out of the presidency. In less than two years, he was sick and dying. The underlying causes of his rapid downfall were many: jealousy, rivalry, ambition of younger men, a bitter feud with Santander, the abortive effort to unify Colombia and Venezuela, the eternal arguments over constitutions and principles of government — all these were important causes. The immediate cause of Nariño's downfall, however, was a woman, the widow of Colonel English, whom the Irishman, Colonel D'evereux, claimed Nariño had insulted.[58]

---

56. Posada and Ibáñez, *El Precursor,* p. 510.

57. Francisco de Paula Santander, *Cartas y mensajes de Santander,* compiled by Roberto Cortázar (7 vols., Bogotá, 1953–54), III, 144.

58. Posada and Ibáñez, *El Precursor,* pp. 535–38.

CHAPTER XII

TO THE BITTER END

The last three years of the Precursor's life were busy ones, and included three major events involving his political career: the Congress of Cúcuta, the D'evereux-English affair, and the fight to disqualify him as senator, a conflict which led to his defense speech and death. The D'evereux-English affair developed suddenly after Nariño had readied the Congress of Cúcuta for consideration of his constitution.

The Congress gave him a chance to present his political views to the world. Actually it was a constitutional convention, whose main purpose was to create and put into operation an instrument of government for Colombia. For the first task, the writing of a constitution, the Precursor felt himself particularly well qualified. He had written projects of government before. Within a month from the opening of congress, he was ready with his constitution, which was presented to that body on May 29, 1821.[1]

Congress was in no mood to accept anybody's constitution ready-made, not even one constructed by Nariño. Azuero soon found sufficient support for a motion to defer discussion of this proffered document until it had been discussed by the legislative and constitutional committee. After much debate and efforts to alter, amend, or reject, the motion passed.[2] Santander openly ridiculed the constitution.[3] He also informed the Precursor that he was too busy to read it.[4] It is perfectly obvious, of course, these two statements could not both be true. He had, obviously, read the constitution, and found that it did not suit his federalist ideas. But he could not openly oppose centralism when both Bolívar and Nariño favored it, as did many senators. By choosing to call the plan "federalist," he thus hoped to defeat it. He stated scornfully that it was

---

1. Roberto Cortázar and Luis Augusto Cuervo, comps., *Congreso de Cúcuta, libro de actas* (Biblioteca de Historia Nacional, vol. XXXV [Bogotá, 1923]), pp. 2, 114.

2. *Ibid.,* pp. 114–15.

3. Posada and Ibáñez, *El Precursor,* p. 546.

4. Santander, *Cartas y mensajes,* III, 209, 210.

"a constitution of eight or ten so-called 'equinoctials,' not much in conformity with a central system . . . a patchwork quilt of pieces of a federal system."[5]

Santander was not really concerned about the federalist or centralist nature of Nariño's constitution. He was disturbed about something much more vital to his own political career. He was afraid that its adoption would put him out and Nariño in. "It provides, in urgent cases, for a dictator, probably Nariño himself."[6]

Nariño's own interpretation was very different. He described his proposed constitution as providing "union, division of territory, centralization for the present, federalism for the future, and nothing provisional."[7] In order to assure independence, the immediate need of the republic was massive unity, sufficient to meet all forces of external or internal disruption. Everyone agreed that unity of action toward a common goal was absolutely necessary. "To unite us now, the government which is most suitable for the present is the *central* form of government."[8] Santander had been a federalist in 1813, and might be again, but Nariño had never been a federalist and never intended to be one in the future. As a matter of fact, the unique innovation in his project, the one-house constitution, was described by its author as a change made "primarily to promote *centralist* unity."[9]

Bolívar handpicked Nariño in order to assure a centralist victory at Cúcuta. In his choice, the Liberator pointedly ignored Santander "in spite of my apprehensions."[10] If Santander actually had any genuine apprehensions about the sincerity of Nariño's centralist view, he could easily have dispelled them by reading his projected constitution and its prologue which began as follows: "Because of the present state of war, because of our lack of money, supplies, and experience, we must not multiply our expenses and governments; we must not, we cannot for the present establish a federation."[11] But Santander was "too busy to read it,"[12] so it was very easy for him to misrepresent its contents to himself and to the world.

---

5. Posada and Ibáñez, *El Precursor,* p. 546.
6. *Ibid.*
7. *Ibid.,* p. 513.
8. *Ibid.,* p. 514.
9. *Ibid,* p. 515.
10. Santander, *Cartas y mensajes,* III, 158.
11. Posada and Ibáñez, *El Precursor,* p. 518.
12. Santander, *Cartas y mensajes,* III, 210.

Projected Constitution

This constitution, presented to congress in May of 1821, may actually have been the joint work of the Liberator and the Precursor. By this time, Bolívar was just as adamantly opposed to federalism as Nariño. He called it a "delirium" which is "the road to anarchy."[13]

The projected constitution began by invoking the aid of "our single and Supreme Sovereign, Father of all Intelligence . . . to assist the duly elected Representatives of the people of the Equinoctial States of the Republic of Colombia, gathered together in general congress to decree the following Constitution or Fundamental Code of the Republic. . . ."[14]

Appropriate to the ideas of Nariño, the first part of the constitution was concerned with the rights of individuals. Part Two dealt with public rights, or the rights of nations. Part Three concerned territorial boundaries and divisions, national sovereignty, and divisions of government. Part Four listed the powers of the legislature, restrictions on these powers, immunities and privileges and functions of legislators.

Nariño feared a constitution too specific in nature, which would foolishly attempt to lay the dead hand of the present on the needs of the future. A comparison of his constitution with the one which the convention finally evolved in opposition, clearly demonstrates the flexibility and general breadth of the Precursor's concept. He was interested in the whole world, in international justice and government, in the future as well as the present, in justice and morality in general, and for all times and places.[15]

The convention was more interested in the flesh than the skeleton, more interested in the present than the future, more interested in Colombia than in the world. They tried to be very specific about everything; who could vote; who could not vote; who could qualify for office and who could not qualify for office; what were the duties of officials and what were the powers of officials. All of this they tried to specify and limit in advance and for all times. As a result, they produced a constitution twice as long as Nariño's and much more rigid which was to last less than ten years, as Nariño had predicted.[16]

Many of the statements of principle made by Nariño were completely omitted in the constitution of Cúcuta. This lack of a general statement of purpose suggests excessive attention to minutiae and a

13. Bolívar, *Selected Writings*, I, 266–67.

14. Posada and Ibáñez, *El Precursor*, p. 518.

15. *Ibid.*, pp. 522–24, outlines a League of Nations to be started in the New World.

16. Gibson, *Constitutions of Colombia*, pp. 40–66, 67–80.

general lack of understanding and sympathy for the Precursor's broad principles.

Basic Precepts

"Fundamental Principals" was the title of the first part of Nariño's projected constitution. These principles included: security of property, liberty of the individual, equal protection under laws, and equal responsibility in duties. Rights ended where duties began. Duties were the rights claimed by others. Duties and rights both were born in the necessities of man, and in the means of satisfying these necessities. Therefore, since these needs and means were unequal among men, rights and duties were also unequal. The poor man had more right to increase his wealth. The rich man had more duty to use his superior means to aid the poor man. The line between rights and duties is established by laws, not by individuals. The laws constitute a *Civil Code*. Those laws pertaining to the infringement of the rights of others constitute *Criminal Laws*. Laws must follow the rights of humanity and the political laws, or the *Constitution* which obtains its legitimate force from the general will. The general will of all individuals is infallible, since it is an expression of the public welfare. Elected officers execute the general will and these national representatives are elected by *all* the citizens, thus constituting an expression of the general will. The national representatives make laws which bind the whole nation and defend and conserve the rights of the people. Duly elected officials are not recalled. They may not impair the right of the individual freely to dispose of his property.[17]

In the division of powers, Nariño closely followed both the ideas of Montesquieu and the Constitution of the United States. The government he outlined consisted of three parts. The general will is made into laws. Justice imposes penalties for infractions of the laws. Tyranny results if these three powers are ever merged into one body or are held by one person. The jailing of Milciades by the people of Athens, and the exile of Cicero by the Roman senate are examples of such tyranny, resulting from similar merging of separate functions. Non-separation results in the substitution of the right of the strongest; loss of individual security soon follows; anarchy then replaces sovereignty. Judges must be permanent, but they must not be hereditary. Other officials are neither permanent nor hereditary. Their term is limited to prevent ambition from resulting in tyranny.

Nariño's views on international law were far ahead of his times. His ideas closely resembled those of Woodrow Wilson in regard to the

---

17. Posada and Ibáñez, *El Precursor*, pp. 519–21.

need for a league of nations, except that he was not fooled by the term "international law." The principal purposes of laws of nations were the same as those for the rights of individuals: to dispose of property as one wished, in security. The major difference between laws of men and laws of nations (international) was that the former had acquired some *moral* force, whereas laws of nations depended still on national force. As Nariño saw it, international law was still in its infancy, in fact, in a savage state of barbarism. States still claimed the right of vengeance and reprisal. He believed, however, that reprisals do not right wrongs; the only just war is a war of defense. Moral force among nations can result only from a federation of all nations with the power to judge wrongs and put an end to or reduce the sad *right of war,* and punish infractors of the *Universal Pact.* Such a federation would never have any effect among governments with unlimited authority or not truly in accord with the wishes of their peoples.

A true federation, Nariño believed, must begin in the New World, (where governments are founded on reason, justice, and common interest), and can be extended outward. Colonies which have sufficient extent, population, and intelligence should govern themselves. But the rights of all nations will only be secure under a true international code stating that no nation has the right to alienate by treaty the rights of its citizens, nor can any nation dispose of its territory without the consent of its people by means of plebiscite. National agreements to nullify the rights of other nations are, *per se,* null and void. This does not free nations from sacrificing their goods, their repose, and their lives for the common good of their nation. But no sacrifices shall be demanded except as the result of laws duly passed. Nations have no right to increase by war. They may, however, increase by legitimate commerce, agriculture, improved laws, religion, intelligence, and virtue. In the words of the Greeks, in answer to the proposal of Themistocles, through the intervention of Aristides, "nothing is useful if it is not just." [18]

Needs of a New Nation

In the second part of his projected constitution, Nariño turned from international law and basic principles to the more specific needs of the new Colombia. The republic would own all towns and *baldíos* (unoccupied and unassigned public lands) within an area bounded by the southern bank of the Orinoco River, the Peruvian boundary, the boundary of the province of Quito, the Pacific, the province of Panama, the

---

18. *Ibid.,* p. 525.

sea of the Antilles, and as far as the mouth of the Orinoco, including the island of Margarita.

Within the national territory of about one hundred and five thousand square leagues, the estimated four million people were favored by great national wealth which needed ports for its development. Therefore, each of the seven states of the republic — Quito, Popayán, the Isthmus, Cundinamarca, Mérida, Caracas, and Orinoco — should be guaranteed some seacoast and at least one suitable port.

The subdivisions of Nariño's constitutional republic have already been described and were the foundation stone of Nariño's centralist system. Further strength along centralist lines would evolve from the *National Congress*, elected by all citizens. The congress not only would make and enforce the constitution of the republic but also "name the officials who shall, under the constitution, govern it [the republic]."

As in the United States, the national representatives would have the inviolable, sacred right and duty of free speech, and could not be sued or held liable for opinions given in the exercise of their function as national representatives. However, they should have no troops at their disposal. Their special rights and duties would be limited to a span of four months, considered long enough for each session of congress.[19]

In the legislative arm of the three-branched government previously described, the senators were to be few in number, half as many as the judges in the High Court of Justice whose functions were limited to judging civil and criminal cases. The high court, in turn, was two-thirds as large as the legislative body, and that body was to be two-thirds of the national representation, which was flexible in number but proportionately fixed so each man would represent the same number of citizens.[20] Thus an increase or decrease in any one body would result in a proportional change in all other political bodies of the nation. Totals were to be flexible but ratios to remain fixed for all time.

Ministers of the executive power were to be named by the executive but subject to approval of the legislature (simple majority?). The legislative power could dictate partial and temporary *acts* and *decrees* as well as regulate permanently the administrative, civil, criminal, military, and ecclesiastical laws of the republic. The legislature could set up inferior courts and set their pay, could decree war and ratify peace, and could ratify, correct, or cast aside treaties, both in peace and in war. It could also set taxes, contract debts, assign public lands *(baldíos)* to individuals, fix weights and measures, and indicate salaries to be paid

19. *Ibid.,* pp. 526–27.
20. *Ibid.*

in sufficient amounts to take care of the president's estimated annual budget. Once a year the legislature would determine for the coming year the size of all land and sea forces, it could also permit or refuse the passage of foreign troops, and pension or reward national heroes. In addition, the legislature could choose the capital, and in emergencies name a temporary dictator from among the citizens of the republic.[21]

A special body called the Grand National Council would also be created by the executive from the legislative power when called together as such in emergencies. Thus the machinery for a stronger, more centralized government was provided for during such chaotic times as those through which Colombia was passing at that moment.[22]

Portal-to-portal pay for legislators, equal to that of the salaries of justices of the high court, was to be provided for by the treasury, along with a tricolor sash, and a medallion of office to be worn during all sessions of the legislature. As in the United States, the legislature would adopt its own rules of procedure, name its own police, and appoint its own secretaries and recorders. Certain laws were prohibited in advance, however. No guilds could be legalized and no *permanent* patents granted by the legislature. Congress could not make laws approving primogeniture, entailed estates, taxes on foundations, or monopolies, and should carefully prevent accumulation of great fortunes by such devices as endowing by will and adopting to endow by will (a custom until recently practiced by the Japanese business monopolies, Mitsui and Mitsubishi). Congress should do everything possible to prevent the increase of inequalities of wealth. Likewise the legislative power was forbidden to create special jails, tribunals, and "imaginary values for the currency."[23]

Bill of Rights

The third section of the constitution, on guarantees of members of the legislative body, included a partial bill of rights, not unlike portions of the American Bill of Rights. While they were guaranteed complete freedom of speech in an official capacity, the legislators could be tried at the expiration of their terms for civil offenses committed during the term ("residencia" idea). However, they could be arrested and tried and jailed for criminal offenses only if caught in the act. Trial for criminal offenses could be initiated if two-thirds of the legislature approved. The accused must be heard in person, and the high court of

21. *Ibid.,* p. 529.
22. *Ibid.,* p. 530.
23. Ibid., p. 531.

justice must prosecute. However, twenty-one members of the legislative body would constitute a jury. The accused could challenge not more than seven of the jury, and the high court an equal number. In case of conviction, the accused legislator would end his term immediately and be removed from office. However, capital punishment, if imposed by the tribunal, could not be executed until the new one-third of the legislature had been elected.[24]

The fourth section, on making and passing bills, is extremely specific. Nariño provided very little variation here. Apparently the rather unique veto system was one of his favorite projects.

He planned that a bill would have to pass through many stages, so many as to eliminate the likelihood that bills would be declared unconstitutional, and so lengthy in duration that the public could often, indirectly, influence a bill or express its opinion for or against it. Nariño desired solid public support for bills.

In the first stage, a new bill would be read and considered for discussion, and rejected if two-thirds of the house voted not to consider it. If the house agreed to consider, the bill was printed and a date set for the hearing after three readings and the passage of four days or more. During the next five months, the public could comment on the proposed law, and send in written proposals. These read, the legislature would discuss the bill three more times, then set a date to vote. Voting was to be by name and limited to two words: "admitted" or "rejected."[25]

In the second stage the bill would go for approval to the executive power. Ten days were granted to the president for decision. During that period, the president must consult his ministry in private session. If as a consequence, the president approved the bill, he and all his ministers, including the opposition, must sign it. If passed at this point, the bill would immediately have the force of law. If the bill were rejected, the president would cite his reasons, and the senators would check the proposed bill stating whether or not they considered it constitutional. At the end of five days, if the senators found it contrary to the constitution, they must say so and cite cases, adding "the passage of this law is not permitted."[26]

An unconstitutional law had alternative futures after senate action: amendment or nullity. If declared null, the bill returned to the president via the legislative power, delaying not more than five days at each stage. It was then up to the legislature or the president to decree the law, or for

---

24. *Ibid.,* pp. 531, 532.
25. "Admitida o desechada." *Ibid.,* pp. 532–33.
26. *Ibid.,* p. 533.

one or the other to declare it null and void. If unsatisfied with passage over its veto, the senate could initiate a case of infringement of the constitution. Should the legislature insist on passage over an executive veto, it could insist just once more that the president reconsider the law as necessary and just. The executive, after private conference with the sponsors of the bill, could now veto a second time, in which case the final decision would rest with the senate. At this point, should a law be declared by the senate null and void because unconstitutional, no one could propose the same law again until the next meeting of national legislature.

On the other hand, if approved by the senate, the bill was to be published by the president with the following wording:

The Executive Power ordains that the present law, approved in all its parts by the Senate, shall be published, authorized by the great seal and the signatures of the five Minister-Councilors; it shall be complied with carefully and executed throughout the Republic.[27]

What did Bolívar, the fighter in the field, think of the Precursor, his appointed legislator at Cúcuta, and of the problem of centralism versus anarchy? He felt very strongly against a loose federation and trusted Nariño completely. In no uncertain terms he let Santander in Bogotá know how he felt. Writing from San Carlos on June 13, 1821, he said:

Many in Cundinamarca are said to favor federation. But I console myself with the fact that neither you nor Nariño, nor Zea, nor Páez, nor I, nor many another venerable authority in the army of the free has any taste for such delirium . . .

Some gentlemen . . . have not troubled to notice the Caribs of the Orinoco, the herdsmen of the Apure, the seamen of Maracaibo, the bandits of Patía, the indomitable citizens of Pasto, the Guajibos of Casanare, and all the savage hordes from Africa and America who, like deer, run untamed in the solitudes of Colombia.

Do you not suspect, my dear Santander, that those lawmakers, more ignorant than ill-intentioned, more presumptuous than ambitious, are leading us on the road to anarchy, then to tyranny, and, in any case, to ruin? I believe this; in fact I am sure of it. So if the *Llaneros* do not complete our destruction, it will be accomplished by the tranquil philosophers of a legalistic Colombia . . . The victory of Carabobo we are going to win . . .

Your friend,

Bolívar.[28]

---

27. *Ibid.,* p. 534.
28. Bolívar, *Selected Writings,* I, 267–68.

Victory and Centralism

Bolívar awaited victory at Carabobo and centralism at Cúcuta with equal confidence. He was not disappointed in either. Independence for Venezuela was assured by the great victory of Carabobo of June 24, 1821,[29] and a strongly centralist union of Venezuela and Colombia was secured, though for a few years only, at Cúcuta by July 12.[30] Nevertheless, the great year of victory for Bolívar was a bitter year of defeat for Nariño. To defeat Spaniards and win independence proved far easier than to defeat federalists and win unity. Some echoes of the struggle emerge even in the rather dry official daily records of the Congress of Cúcuta.[31] Reverberations finally were heard everywhere, thanks to the "crazy action of D'evereux,"[32] who threatened Nariño with a duel.

In 1821 the price of a workable centralist government for Colombia was high. Immediate reaction at Cúcuta against centralism destroyed Nariño. Later reaction destroyed Bolívar. Not all Bolívar's trouble with the English and Irish was accidental. One troublemaker, Colonel Henry Wilson, later proved to be a hired Spanish spy. His near success in separating Páez from Bolívar was part of his job. Spain had planted him in the British Legion to destroy both it and Bolívar, and he very nearly succeeded.[33] Natural jealousies of the patriot leaders greatly aided provocative agents such as Colonel Henry Wilson. However, the long arguments between Nariño and Santander in 1821–23 probably dated back to the civil war of 1812, when Lieutenant Santander had been captured, pardoned, and freed by General Nariño in the abortive siege of Bogotá carried on by Baraya and his congress forces from Tunja. Humiliating defeat and the debt of life, pardon, and freedom which the younger owed to the older Precursor must have rankled with Santander,[34] and increased his bitter rivalry with Nariño. Santander was able, briefly, to congratulate Nariño upon his appointment by Bolívar in a letter of May 14.[35] But from that day forward, the official friendship of the two vice-presidents showed increasing signs of slipping. Bolívar's relationship to the two leaders was not unlike that of President Washington to

---

29. *Ibid.,* I, 269.

30. Rivera, "Francisco de Paula Santander," p. 133.

31. Cortázar and Cuervo, *Congreso de Cúcuta.*

32. Bolívar, *Selected Writings,* I, 272.

33. Alfred Hasbrouck, *Foreign Legionaries in the Liberation of South America,* (New York, 1928), p. 78.

34. See Santander, *Cartas y mensajes,* I, February letters, *passim.*

35. *Ibid.,* III, 144.

Hamilton and Jefferson. Bolívar needed both men but Santander, at least, found it difficult to accept, or even to feign friendship. A week after congratulating Nariño, Santander wrote sarcastically about him in a letter to Osorio: "I continue now by talking about myself, though not 'forced to,' as Nariño once said on another such occasion."[36] On June 11, 1821, he wrote Osorio that he had received Nariño's letter asking for comment on his projected constitution, but that he did not have the time to answer.[37] Bolívar condemned the "crazy action of General D'evereux" as soon as he heard about it, on July 10, 1821, and deplored its effect on Nariño as a "real misfortune because it compromises the government and its officers.... I have felt this misfortune keenly... all is chaos...."[38]

Destruction of a Hero

General D'evereux, "professional grafter, liar, braggart, coward, and prince of malingerers," who never fought a battle, but made huge profits by recruiting the Irish legion, used Mrs. English's need for money as a pretext to destroy Nariño.[39] There is absolutely nothing in Nariño's earlier career to indicate any reason for Nariño having been offensive to Mrs. English. Fifty-six years old, just returned from six years in Spanish jails, loaded down with honors and heavy responsibilities, at the peak of a career he had dreamed of through twenty years in ten different incarcerations, D'evereux's charges of Nariño having made improper proposals to Mrs. English could scarcely have any foundation in fact. But the mud splattered, some of it stuck, and in short order destroyed one of Bolívar's trusted assistants. If that was the plan of Nariño's enemies it was eminently successful, and as revenge against Bolívar for appointing Nariño, it was quick and effective. Santander, meanwhile, said little about the matter until it looked as though Nariño's resignation at Cúcuta would bring the Precursor to Bogotá where he might be more dangerous to Santander than before, because "Nariño has an irrevocable ambition for the presidency and knows how to make his revolutions in this town of Bogotá."[40] In the same letter to Bolívar, Santander also claimed that Bogotá was still full of *godos* whom he

---

36. Santander, *Cartas y mensajes,* III, 156.

37. *Ibid.,* III, 210.

38. Bolívar, *Selected Writings,* I, 272. Manuel Villaveces, "El proceso D'evereux," *Boletín de historia y antigüedades* (Bogotá, March, 1932), No. 218, pp. 119–43.

39. Hasbrouck, *op. cit.,* pp. 165–170, 186–188, 357, 384, 400. Thomas Rourke, *Man of Glory, Simón Bolívar* (New York, 1937), pp. 188, 193, 196, 197, 207.

40. *Ibid.,* p. 347.

feared more than another Morillo. Without actually accusing Nariño of plotting with liberal monarchists, Santander juxtaposed his two chief fears in such a way as to suggest to the Liberator that a union of Nariño with revolting Bogotá liberal monarchists was a distinct possibility.[41]

Nothing could have been further from the truth, and Santander, later, at Nariño's death, freely contradicted his own unjust accusation.[42]

Unjust accusations by D'evereux and Santander were only a part of the bitter dregs Nariño was forced to drink at this time. Coupled with his resignation from the vice-presidency at Cúcuta, came a return of ill health. The old hidropsy of the lungs which had nearly killed him in jail now returned. Without sidestepping in any way the D'evereux accusations. Nariño prepared to leave Cúcuta and return home to Bogotá in search of better health.[43]

Thus came to an end the affairs of D'evereux and Mrs. English which had nearly broken up sessions of congress from May 25[44] to July 5, 1821. With them ended the vice-presidency of Nariño at Cúcuta. And thus were delayed or postponed many important issues such as manumission of slaves, centralism or federalism, union of Cundinamarca and Venezuela, taxation and the national debt, location of the capital, the name of the country, and even the very paramount and necessary question of adopting a constitution, while the Osorio-Santander faction ballooned Mrs. English's need for money into a scandal involving threatened duels, the jailing of General D'evereux, the splitting of congress into two factions, and finally the resignation of a sickened vice-president, in utter disgust and frustration, on July 5, 1821.[45]

Congress lost no time in electing a vice-president to succeed Nariño. A special session was held the very same night. José María Castillo showed a distinct lead of twenty-seven out of forty-eight votes on the first ballot and a clear and sufficient majority of thirty-five on the second. Castillo made an appropriate show of refusing, which congress quickly overruled. With no further extraneous maneuvering, Nariño's successor was immediately sworn in.[46]

The federalists, the friends of Santander and General D'evereux, and those who opposed Nariño merely from jealousy, had won a swift

41. *Ibid.,* p. 348.

42. Posada and Ibáñez, *El Precursor,* p. 546.

43. *Ibid.,* p. 538. Sick by July 5, 1821.

44. Cortázar and Cuervo, *Congreso de Cúcuta,* p. 81.

45. *Ibid.,* pp. 81, 83, 84, 92, 124, 130, 133, 134, 138–43, 144–47, 157, 182–85, 204, 212, 221, 231. Posada and Ibáñez, *El Precursor,* pp. 535–40.

46. Cortázar and Cuervo, *Congreso de Cúcuta,* pp. 235, 236.

victory over the sick and dying Precursor. His one consolation at this point lay in a warm sentiment of approval and offers of hospitality made to him on his way home. At Chiquinquirá, the *alcaldes* and *vecinos* of the town signed a joint note of sympathy for his sufferings on behalf of his country. They begged him to come through their town en route to Bogotá and enjoy the free use of any house he might choose.[47] Four months later, the Precursor thanked them "with grief in my heart, that my sickness caused me to delay so long in answering your kind and generous offer."[48] The Precursor's misfortunes caused no grief in Santander's heart, however; only a gnawing fear that Nariño's popularity might make more trouble, once the Precursor was resettled right under his (Santander's) nose in Bogotá rather than far away in Rosario de Cúcuta. Santander's position was a precarious one in 1822 and 1823, for he faced attacks from at least three directions: Caracas separatists, extremists of both federalist and centralist persuasions, and now the personal followers of his deposed rival, Nariño.[49] Faced by this much opposition, Santander did not try very hard to disguise either his fear of his rival[50] or his own joy at reelection as vice-president of Colombia in September.[51] The fact that he began three letters on September 15 using the identical word "surprised" seems clear indication, if any were needed, that Santander was certainly "relieved" at his election to the vice-presidency of Colombia but definitely *not* "suprised" at the honor which now came to him as a result of Nariño's downfall.[52]

Fight to the Death

How could Santander, Nariño, or anyone else, knowing the facts of the bitter rivalry, be surprised, then, at the growing political feud which now enveloped these two Colombian leaders? Sick as he was, and admittedly dying, Nariño plunged into politics in Bogotá and managed to get himself elected as senator of the republic for the department of Cundinamarca.[53] With congress moving from far away Cúcuta[54] to

---

47. Posada and Ibáñez, *El Precursor,* p. 541.

48. *Ibid.,* p. 542.

49. Rivera, "Francisco de Paula Santander," p. 157.

50. Santander, *Cartas y mensajes,* III, 347.

51. *Ibid.,* III, 359. Letter of September 15, 1821, to Bolívar.

52. *Ibid.,* III, 358–62.

53. Posada and Ibáñez, *El Precursor,* p. 545.

54. On July 12, the Cúcuta congress adopted a new constitution and chose Bogotá as provisional capital. Cortázar and Cuervo, *Congreso de Cúcuta,* p. 235. Henao and Arrubla, *op. cit.,* p. 352.

Bogotá, the Precursor would be increasingly more dangerous to Santander. Drastic action seemed called for, and Santander marshalled his forces for a double assault. The open, frontal attack consisted of a barrage of newspaper attacks in *El Patriota* to which the dying Precursor responded in the short-lived *Los Toros de Fucha*.[55]

The second and flanking attack, less obvious, more insidious, and more successful, consisted in a plan to disqualify Nariño for his post as senator and blacken his name so as to preclude forever his having any future in politics. The same Diego Gómez who had structured the troublesome D'evereux-English frame-up at Cúcuta now leveled three charges at the Precursor, all ridiculous, but all destructive.

This final attack on Nariño by Santander was withheld until October 9, 1821,[56] a month and two days after the bitter contest of strength in which Santander defeated Nariño for vice-president only after eight successive ballotings. This bitter election of September 7, held at Rosario de Cúcuta, at first showed Nariño second only to Bolívar in popularity. The final vote was thirty-eight to nineteen in favor of Santander. We may judge the heat of the contest by the fact that two members retired sick, that it took so many ballotings to elect Santander, and that his final victory was by the small margin of exactly two-thirds, no more![57] Two days later, without mentioning any names, Santander forwarded to J. M. Castillo in Cúcuta an anonymous letter which he claimed threatened him with assassination. Castillo was urged to show the letter to all the deputies.[58] A week later, September 15, Santander was dutifully proclaiming his own unworthiness and surprise at the election results.[59] A week later he left Bogotá for Cúcuta by way of Tunja, Soatá, Cerrito, and Pamplona, arriving in Cúcuta after a journey of ten days on October 1.[60] The inauguration of Santander and Bolívar as vice-president and president respectively of Colombia began at eleven o'clock on the morning of October 3.[61] Diego Gómez and the Santander faction began their attempt to remove Nariño as senator and destroy him forever in the eyes of the voters six days later, on October 9.[62]

---

55. Posada and Ibáñez, *El Precursor,* p. 545.

56. *Ibid.,* p. 549.

57. Cortázar and Cuervo, *Congreso de Cúcuta,* p. 558–59.

58. Santander, *Cartas y mensajes,* III, 349.

59. *Ibid.,* III, 359–61.

60. *Ibid.,* III, 372–80. In summer, 1962, the author took two days by truck for this trip via the same towns.

61. Cortázar and Cuervo, *Congreso de Cúcuta,* pp. 718–21.

62. Posada and Ibáñez, *El Precursor,* p. 549.

Attack by Gómez

Diego Gómez' attack consisted of three charges:

1. That Nariño was an absconding bankrupt (*deudor fallido*), never having paid back money which he had lost when, as treasurer of tithes in 1794, his arrest prevented him from paying his official debts as treasurer.
2. That Nariño was a traitor to his country for having surrendered "voluntarily" at Pasto in 1814.
3. That he was constitutionally and legally unqualified to be senator because he did not meet the residence requirements, having "voluntarily absented himself from his country and not in behalf of the republic."[63]

Of twenty-six candidates for senator from Cundinamarca, Nariño was clearly the winner, with twenty-nine votes as against twenty-five for his nearest competitor, Colonel Rieux. It was at this point, after the vote had been counted, that Diego Gómez "took the word" and began his long harangue referring to the Precursor as "criminal," "traitor," and "bankrupt."[64] The voice was that of Gómez but the brain was the brain of Santander, who, though present until congress dissolved on October 14, was notably silent on the whole matter, apparently writing only two letters in the two-week period from October 3 to October 15, neither of them containing the slightest reference to the scandalous attack on Nariño by Gómez.[65]

In view of the prolific comment of Santander on other affairs of the same period, his silence in a matter which so directly concerned him is both significant and damning. As for the Gómez proposal, it was temporarily squashed, and its author condemned by several deputies. But others reserved judgment for the future. Ignacio Méndez and Antonio Briceño defended Nariño's election as senator on the grounds that he had been president of the state of Cundinamarca and second only to Bolívar in the republic of Colombia. Obispo, whom Azuero had suggested to prosecute Nariño on the charge of failing to pay debts incurred while treasurer of tithes, objected strongly to the charge. As judge in charge of the receivership of the tithing fund following Nariño's arrest in 1794, Obispo stated that Nariño had been declared bankrupt to the extent of eighty thousand pesos, that all his bondsmen had been duly paid eleven thousand pesos, through cruel sacrifices and great misery

---

63. *Ibid.*

64. Cortázar and Cuervo, *Congreso de Cúcuta*, p. 749. Both Hernández de Alba (1958) and Leopoldo Uprimny have rejected the bankruptcy charge in carefully reasoned and documented statements.

65. Santander, *Cartas y mensajes*, III, 382–86.

on the part of Nariño's family, and that the court did not declare Nariño an absconding bankrupt because the rest of the tithe money was uncollectable, having been used in farflung businesses in London, France, and Havana. The charge was not determined in the October 9 session, and the following day was passed in making the momentous decision to move the capital to Bogotá until such time as the new capital of "Bolívar" could be built.[66] On October 10, the persistent Gómez returned to the attack by proposing that Nariño's disqualification again be discussed. Senator Peña tried to postpone the issue by suggesting a motion that "Señor Nariño should present to the next senate the certification of the tribunal of tithes clearing him of the charge of being an absconding bankrupt, and documents concerning his military conduct in the south, and that, once accepted by the senate, he should be declared the duly elected senator from Cundinamarca."

A Counter-Proposal

Manuel Restrepo then made a counter proposal (approved twenty-one to twenty) that Nariño should continue as duly elected senator until the next senate disposed of the charges. Restrepo's proposal was accepted over the protests of Briceño and Méndez who claimed this irregular proceeding was highly unconstitutional. Diego Gómez then received approval for an amendment requiring that copies of the minutes relative to Nariño for October 9 and 10, 1821, be sent to the next congress.[67]

The remaining three days of the Congress of Cúcuta made no further reference to Nariño. Congress was too busy getting ready to dissolve itself, as it did on October 14, 1821, after reading some letters of congratulations from Abbé de Pradt, Henry Clay, Colonel William Duane, editor of the Philadelphia *Aurora,* and General Robert Wilson of the British army.[68] The field of battle between Nariño and the Gómez-Santander faction was now transferred to the new provisional capital, Bogotá, and to the new congress.

Santander himself was very busy governing the country and finding the troops and money to keep Bolívar in the field, "which, if you will permit me a little proud boasting in confidence, were miracles, considering the lack of means at hand."[69] Santander was not averse to bragging about his accomplishments, nor was he hesitant in condemning Nariño as a

---

66. Cortázar and Cuervo, *Congreso de Cúcuta,* pp. 748–51.

67. *Ibid.,* pp. 753–755.

68. *Ibid.,* p. 774.

69. Santander, *Cartas y mensajes,* IV, 66.

thorn in his flesh, and as "malicious, insolent, and more ungrateful than an Indian; I abhor this man to death and everything pertaining to him!"[70] This letter to Bolívar of February 20, 1823, was soon followed by a longer and stronger one, on March 17, 1823. In this letter, Santander called Nariño "a worm . . . who has come back to jeer and prepare public opinion to readmit him to congress."[71]

How many headaches he will give us! I will prevent any irregularities and advise you. I think it would be a good thing if from where you are you would write a letter throwing up in his face his past faults, his salvation by the Spanish power when others were dying at their hands, his propensity for disorder and opposition to the common wish . . . You should have copies of this letter printed in Quito or Guayaquil and signed by some public official of the same political views as his, then send me some copies from there.

You must know that this Nariño, with his family and friends, is dangerous under all circumstances and can be silenced only by indirect means. I am an enemy of these low contests against any person, but I fear much that Nariño will overturn us now that he finds himself pushed out of a position where he can command us and direct events according to his wishes . . .

In short, you shall see that . . . everybody here is your enemy and mine for the sole reason that you are president and I am vice-president. Since he who governs is most disliked, partisanship grows quickly. We are ripe for disunion . . .

Good-by my general, be happy and take care of your life for your life is the foundation stone upon which we will have to consolidate the edifice your genius created. Your most obedient friend.[72]

While secretly trying to undermine, blacken, and destroy Nariño in the eyes of Bolívar, and enlist Bolívar's sympathy and assistance in this work of destruction, Santander had openly tried a somewhat different tactic with the Precursor in Bogotá. To the unseated vice-president, Nariño, he offered several consolation prizes which Nariño at first accepted in good faith on October 16, 1822. One year and two days after the Congress of Cúcuta had dissolved without settling Nariño's qualifications as senator, Nariño was appointed by Santander to the office of "Commanding General of this department" and the next day, the additional title of "President of the Chief Commission for Reallotment of National Properties."[73]

Meantime, Santander was carrying forward both open and secret

70. *Ibid.,* IV, 69.

71. *Ibid.,* IV, 74.

72. *Ibid.,* IV, 75.

73. Posada and Ibáñez, *El Precursor,* pp. 543–44.

attacks on Nariño, about which Bolívar was briefly but directly informed by Nariño himself. After apologizing for taking valuable time needed to consolidate the great victories gained in the south, and for distracting his attention from the main object in view — victory for the armies of independence — Nariño described the tempest of criticism being stirred up by Santander in the official journals. Santander was not mentioned by name but referred to as one who "abhors me personally, but who should put the public interest first and not foment divisions prejudicial to the moment of consolidation of our new organization."[74] The Precursor then stated that, in spite of the attacks on him and his son, all his defenses were signed by himself and limited to defending himself. In spite of this restraint, anonymous attacks continued. He found himself continually insulted and calumniated by cowards; one of them reputedly a *godo,* who failed to accept his challenge to name themselves, and continued attacking from behind a mask of anonymity.[75]

The Precursor was further goaded by receiving an official reminder of the unsettled senatorship from Santander. This notice reminded him that when it came time for the new congress to meet in January, 1823, the case of his disqualification would have to be considered before he could accept the senatorship. Speaking out of both sides of his mouth, Santander at this very time was insisting to the public that his rivalry with Nariño was strictly political, not personal in the least. "It is quite natural for men of different opinions to disagree . . . and Colombia is no exception."[76] Santander, however, claimed that Nariño was opposed to the centralist system, a charge which could well be leveled at Santander, whether in 1812, 1822, or 1829, but which was never true of Nariño. Santander also charged that Nariño's project for "eight or ten states called 'equinoctials' which in urgent cases would call for a dictator, with himself firmly planted at the head of the state for many years"[77] was the chief reason for opposition to Nariño both at Cúcuta and Bogotá. This charge confused and misrepresented Nariño's plan of government, but contained just enough of truth concerning Nariño's desire to be chief executive to make it plausible to a gullible, misinformed public. However, in this same period of growing jealousy, even Santander would not accept the ridiculous charge of Gómez that Nariño had surrendered

---

74. *Ibid.,* pp. 544, 545.
75. *Ibid.*
76. *Ibid.,* p. 545.
77. *Ibid.,* p. 546.

willingly at Pasto. Instead, he said, ". . . abandoned in the Pasto campaign of 1814 by several of his officers, betrayed by some of his friends, Nariño always maintained the greatest serenity, so that he rose superior in stature to every misfortune."[78]

Santander's Ambition

Contrasting Santander's public praise of Nariño with the secret letters to Bolívar, we have a glimpse of the tragic depths to which ambition and jealousy were dragging Santander in 1823. Publicly, he admitted that Nariño was a great man who had sacrificed and suffered much for the cause of independence. Privately, he showed his jealousy and meanness toward Nariño in letters to Bolívar. To Nariño's protest that it was inconsistent to place the security of the nation in the hands of a general whom Congress considered unfit to be senator, a man accused of treason to his country,[79] Santander replied that he saw no impediment to Nariño's holding an interim military post, and three days later Nariño was given the further honor and responsibility of serving on a military commission with Urdaneta and others, to discuss the organization of Colombia's military forces. To this new honor, Nariño quickly replied that he was glad to help Urdaneta in such a capacity, but that when he had asked when and where the commission was to meet he received no answer. This letter was dated January 5, 1823. Two months later, on March 17, 1823, Santander was busy reminding congress that one of its first tasks was to try Nariño.[80]

Santander did not himself prosecute Nariño at the Congress of 1823. As we have already seen, he preferred to work through someone else. In this case the subterfuge was rather thin. The same Diego Gómez who had sponsored the D'evereux-English attack on Nariño at Cúcuta was in charge of the Bogotá attack of 1823. The hearings began with repetition of the three charges made by Gómez at Cúcuta in October, 1821. In the interim, Nariño had used his time to good advantage, and he gave a well-documented defense. In spite of the sickness which had nearly consumed his body, he showed his vast command of the facts concerned and much of his old skill in oratory. Some who were present described the scene. They spoke of his resonant voice, which made a powerful impression on their minds. They described his faltering

---

78. *Ibid.*
79. *Ibid.*, p. 547.
80. *Ibid.*, p. 549.

walk, hampered by the tyrants' chains, his very step a condemnation of his petty accusers. They spoke of the heads bowed in shame, the tears, and the handclapping which followed his speech.[81]

Defense of the Precursor

The speech was long, necessarily. The heavily documented defense fills fifty pages of *El Precursor*. In the words of the recorder, Rafael Urdaneta, it was "long and complicated" and occupied most of the special night sessions of April 24, 1823,[82] and May 15, 1823.

Captain C. S. Cochrane, a British naval officer who was present at Nariño's defense, described his speech as "showing great knowledge of men and events, a limitless fund of information, a truly distinguished orator who weighs his arguments and develops them with the decorum of a great gentleman. He is a man highly honorable in his private as well as in his public life." [83]

Apart from the long and well-documented summary of his life on the three occasions at issue in the charges, Nariño reserved a few blasts of withering scorn for the two Santander tools, Diego Gómez and Vincente Azuero, who were —

scarcely born when I suffered my first torture and jailing on behalf of my country . . . and what were Diego Gómez and Vincente Azuero in the year '94 when this bloody fight began which gave the first start to our ideas? Where were they? . . . But let's not go that far back. Where were they at the start of our transformation? Who knew them then? Were their names famous then? What services did they perform during those twelve years? What campaigns did they fight in? To what risks did they expose themselves to save their country? What personal and pecuniary sacrifices did they make then for which we owe them a debt; those two so worthy of each other? Listen then: their names began to be known beginning in the year '19. On the memorable day of the entry into this city of the liberating troops, while all the populace was rushing to arms to help them, to defend themselves, to chase out the enemy, who were not yet entirely destroyed, Sr. Diego Gómez ran to the botanic institute where the Spaniards had sequestered confiscated goods, broke open the windows of the floor where the Spaniards had been storing goods, and they loaded themselves with bundles and came out carrying them in their

---

81. Mariano Ospina Rodríguez, *El General Nariño* (1849), quoted in Henao and Arrubla, *op. cit.,* p. 369.

82. Posada and Ibáñez, *El Precursor,* pp. 549–92. Cortázar and Cuervo, *Congreso de 1823, Actas* (Biblioteca de Historia Nacional, vol. XXXVII Bogotá, 1926), pp. 60–62, 115.

83. Cochrane quoted in Posada and Ibáñez, *El Precursor,* p. xxix.

hands. Doesn't this seem to you gentlemen that this brilliant act merits the right for them to be seated in congress and obtain a toga? Doesn't this give a clear idea of their patriotism, their high ideals, their love of the holy cause while everyone was arming and fighting that day? Don't you think this was a meritorious citizen, a valiant athlete, the sort of man fitted to call me criminal? And why has no suit been brought against him? Let his friend answer that, his friend who was president of the *junta* of sequestered goods. And if he cannot answer, because they reciprocally aid eath other, let the fiscal who was named by the superior court of justice, who denounced him a few months ago, but with what result we know not yet, let him answer. And his friend, his worthy companion in accusing me, did he employ himself with better success, did he play a better part in the regeneration of his country? Ah, that he did, gentlemen! After the presidency of sequestered goods, about which I know of no account rendered yet of his conduct, he succeeded in getting himself named judge of tithes for Soatá. In only a year and a half in managing a fund of thirty-five thousand pesos, twenty-four thousand pesos was eaten up. And with this fraudulent bankruptcy, this true absconding bankrupt likewise sits here in congress and has the shamelessness to call me a liar to my face and accuse me of the crime of which he is guilty. To this very day while I stand here speaking, sirs, he has not paid a cent of this debt and you do not think for a moment that he has paid any debts from all that tithing money, no, in drafts to pay, issued by the government, with *novenos* from his brother, with salaries held back from his friends and their relations, with the income of investments, and for fear of not profiting from them or of losing them, that is how they were forced to calumniate me, so that I would never take my seat in the senate. Compare, I say, the rapacious plunders of these two men with the pecuniary sacrifices which my investments and business suffered as a result of my love of country. Here you see, on the one hand, Gómez and Azuero pillaging to clothe themselves in fine raiments and cut a figure in society and give themselves an importance they could not win through any service to their country. There, on the other hand you see me, sacrificing for the *patria* businesses which in less than ten years would have made me a millionaire. . . . Who now is the fraudulent absconding bankrupt?[84]

Most of the above passage was expunged from the record and not restored to the pages of history until 1903.[85] Only by agreeing to mutilate Nariño's testimony and erase the damning proof of Gómez' and Azuero's true baseness, were Nariño's friends able to get a motion to readmit the Precursor to the senate.[86] Some of the rest of Nariño's testimony attacking his calumniators, Gómez and Azuero, still remained openly in the records. For instance, in response to the second charge,

---

84. Posada and Ibáñez, *El Precursor,* pp. 570–72.

85. Cortázar and Cuervo, *Congreso de 1823,* p. 125. Posada and Ibáñez, *El Precursor,* p. xxix.

86. Cortázar and Cuervo, *Congreso de 1823,* pp. 125–26.

that his surrender at Pasto in 1814 was treason to his country and a voluntary act showing cowardice, he replied:

This second charge means then, that after twenty years of sacrifices and services rendered in the cause of liberty for my country, having been president-dictator of Cundinamarca, and general-in-chief of this expedition, always victorious, I purposely surrendered myself to the fury of the Pastusos and the Spanish government from whose bloody clutches I had miraculously escaped, not once but three times! And it will now be necessary for me to present myself, gentlemen, loaded down with documents, to disprove such a charge before I can clear myself before the senate? It would take a Diego Gómez or an Azuero to dare to stamp me with such an accusation before this congress with such shameless impudence! And what was I looking for at Pasto? What services was I supposed to render to the Spanish government? Did I have some treasury with me, some important personages? Did I surrender to them the army under my command? Was I carrying with me documents proving my great love for, and loyalty to the king? If I was not bearing any such things with me, what, then, was I doing in Pasto?

Men at such moments are not moved except by interest, ambition, glory, love of country. Let me ask my accusers, which of these motives would have led me to surrender voluntarily at Pasto? Would I have, perhaps, been going to seek my fortune among the Pastusos, whose cattle I had just destroyed, to support my troops? Would I be searching for higher employment than those I was just leaving in the bosom of my country? Or would I, perhaps, be seeking glory by abandoning my country, by making war on it to destroy its hard-won liberty for which I had sacrified so many years? Let us not search any further motive, for no matter where we seek it, it is always the same result, impossible. If love of country caused me to make the sacrifices I made, and to expose me to the risks to which I was exposed, each such act was a virtue and not a crime. And if one believes some motives to be impossible, certainly it was impossible that there could have been any reasons whatever for me to surrender voluntarily to my enemies? That I was afraid? But in that case no officer nor soldier could reproach me; it would be as silly as expecting a man afraid of fire to run toward the flames.

Very well then, what was the motive which led me to Pasto? You shall hear it. But not from my mouth, but from that of an impartial officer who was present, a witness there that day. Let me read you the official report of Major General Cabal to the electoral college of Popayán after I became a prisoner at Pasto. He says, "this was the moment in which I saw our general at his greatest heroism. He was everywhere, giving no thought to the danger, he rode up and down in front of all the divisions, he urged them on with his example, then at the front of the center division he attacked the chief enemy force, passing through their lines many times until they killed his horse. But always unperturbed, valiant, he faltered not an instant. He continued with the same impetuosity with which he started, driving them back completely!" Let me stop here for just a moment to ask what would the illustrious Diego Gómez have done had he been in such a situation? How could it be that my actions were considered noble and heroic in the middle of flying bullets, but now I am called criminal and traitor by those who were five hundred leagues distant from the enemy? . . .

With the enemy on top of me and around me I did not retreat. Retreat was impossible since none of my troops were left in sight. Gentlemen, shall I make it clearer? Was this surrendering voluntarily to the enemy? Or was it not rather being handed over by those who had deserted me? After they had deserted me I was alone; there was no way out. Yet for three days and nights I waited in vain for the return of my troops, and after I saw there were only two exits, to eternity or to Pasto, I chose the road to Pasto. I was determined to parley there with the president of Quito for a suspension of war, because I feared what could happen, what would inevitably happen if I did not appear in Pasto and ask them to stop the frightening tortures of our prisoners. I knew I would die in Pasto, but I could die still serving my fellow countrymen. That is what caused me to expose myself to die a useful death on the gallows rather than a useless one in the shade of the trees. Was this criminal, carrying out my duty to the end? [87]

Having disposed of the second charge "for the satisfaction of Diego Gómez, or so that his name shall live in eternal infamy," [88] the Precursor passed on finally to the last charge, so ridiculous and insulting that it must have made the senate squirm to think they had ever sanctioned it. In the third charge, Nariño was declared constitutionally ineligible to a senatorship because he could not meet the residence requirements, "having been absent, as Gómez says, 'by my own choice and not for the cause of the republic.' " [89]

This was a particularly idiotic, senseless, and ironic charge since the public well knew of the nine or more different jails where the Precursor had been for over twenty-one years rotting away in chains because of his persistent fight against Spain for independence. [90] Odd indeed, was it not, that if he had surrendered voluntarily at Pasto the Spaniards kept him hungry, starving, and in leg irons threatening to execute him, while the Pastusos yelled for his head? It was odd indeed that if he was a traitor, the forces he had supposedly deserted offered up to seventy colonels, lieutenant colonels and other officers to effect his exchange? For a traitor, what strange treatment as payment was given to Nariño by Montes and Aymerich and the royalists with whom he "chose to live," as Gómez said, "voluntarily," — oppression, jail, leg irons, manacles, no place to lie down or sit, no clothes but a *ruana* (shawl), no books, and no word from the outside world as the days passed into months, the months into years, and the ulcerated flesh rotted away under the iron chains; strange living conditions indeed for one to have chosen "voluntarily"!

---

87. Posada and Ibáñez, *El Precursor*, pp. 574–77.

88. *Ibid.*, p. 577.

89. *Ibid.*, p. 587.

90. *Ibid.*, p. 573.

Surely this was scarcely treatment for a traitor [to Colombia] and criminal . . .
a friend of liberty and justice and yet they dare make fun of me now for my
halting walk and the scars caused by the arm and leg irons of Pasto. . . . Can
you believe that such an accusation is meant to aid the safety of the republic?
No, gentlemen, the same causes which led me to Pasto today have led me
here to the senate; perfidy, malevolence, personal grudges of a few men. . . .
In Pasto it was the end of a campaign, it was the last enemy place that stood
between us and arrival at Quito. So they betrayed me, they cut me off, they
cut short the thread of victory, in order to sacrifice me, they sacrificed their
country. And what evils were to follow them! What tears, what blood was
soon to be shed! What calamities were to envelop the republic for this
imprudent, iniquitous, ill considered crime!!! I am not speaking, gentlemen,
before an audience uninformed of all this. I speak in the middle of the
republic, in the center of the capital, in view of the very people who suffered,
who are still suffering the evils brought on by that ill-omened day, that day
which shall be forever sad and mournful. I direct my words to you and to the
public now listening to me. Without the treason of Pasto would Morillo have
triumphed? Without it, would we have seen the atrocities which for three
continuous years afflicted this unhappy soil? Would Sámano and Morillo have
wallowed through the blood of our illustrious fellow citizens? No, gentlemen,
no! Always triumphant I would have arrived at Quito, reinforced the army,
returned to this capital, and blotted out the hallucinations of my enemies with
the testimony of their own eyes; we would have been strong and invincible.
Santa Marta, before Morillo could arrive, would have submitted to reason
and without this point of support, Morillo could never have taken Cartagena
and this capital would have escaped from the destructive scythe of the grim
reaper. Thus I was sacrified. Thus the *patria* was sacrified by vile jealousies
and ridiculous passions. . . .[91]

The Precursor concluded his attack on the third and last charge
by summarizing the paradox in which congress would be if it declared
him ineligible to hold office, for after all, he, Nariño, had installed
congress. Making him constitutionally ineligible would thus make them
and the Congress of Cúcuta and its constitution and the Congress of 1823
also ineligible, illegal, and unconstitutional. Thus in addition to being
doubly ridiculous, the third charge was the most unfounded and most
insulting. To describe twenty years of jails and exiles as something a
man would do "for pleasure" was utterly stupid, so Nariño rightly
wasted no documents and few words on this charge.

How could I be vice-president, but not eligible to be a citizen? . . . How could
I install congress but not sit in it? I was the same man when I installed congress
as when you confirmed me with unanimous vote. It was the same day you
made me vice-president that you elected me senator. If I cannot legally be
senator, or vice-president, then congress was not legally installed and does
not legally exist.[92]

91. *Ibid.,* p. 584.
92. *Ibid.,* p. 589.

CASA DE NARIÑO
VILLA DE LEIVA

Nariño spent the last days of his life in his home at Villa de Leiva, dying there on December 23, 1823, eight months after his final memorable address to the Congress in behalf of the young republic.

Final Words

Nariño's final peroration was a plea to congress to mend its ways, to consider the dangers of disunion which could destroy the new-founded republic if petty jealousies were not soon stopped. If such a scandalous accusation accompanied the first congress, where would the republic end?

What can we hope for the future if my accusers triumph or remain unpunished? ... This trial which seems of so little import in itself could well be the angle stone determining the future of the edifice of your reputation. Today, gentlemen, today each and every citizen will see how much security for his honor, his property, his person he can expect in the future; today the whole republic will see how much it can hope for from you of future glory. In vain, gentlemen, you will dictate decrees and promulgate laws full of wisdom, in vain will you have gathered together here in this august temple of the law, if the public continues seeing before its eyes a Gómez, an Azuero, seated in the first tribunals of justice, and a Barrionuevo insulting and threatening without impunity pacific citizens, honorable mechanics on the streets. In vain will your works, your hopes, be, no matter how just, no matter how well founded on your wisdom. If we see such examples in former republics, if we see them in Rome and Athens, we see them in their days of decadence, in the days of corruption to which their wealth led them. On the birth of the Roman republic, we see Brutus, sacrificing his own son out of love for justice and liberty; in its decadence we see Clodius, Catiline Marc Antony sacrificing Cicero to their personal interests. Athens was born under the head of wheat of Ceres, raised itself to the heights of the justice of the Areopagus and died with Milciades, Socrates, and Focion. What can we hope for, then, of our republic if it begins where those other ones ended? ... If you, sirs, do not in public present yourselves before the eyes of the world as legislators, as judges, as defenders of liberty and virtue, if you do not give an example of the integrity of a Brutus, of the disinterest of a Focion, of the severe justice of the tribunal of Athens, then our liberty will die at its very birth. From the hour in which the insolent, the shameless, the intriguing, flattering man triumphed, the reign of Tiberius began — that of liberty ended.[93]

Four days later, on May 19, 1823, the committee of three rendered its verdict, "not guilty," and congress voted by a three to one majority to seat Nariño as a senator. The sole victory of his enemies was a slight consolation to them. They managed, by a twelve-to-two vote, to erase, by legislative amendment, all references in Nariño's speech deemed personally offensive and injurious to the honor and reputation of his accusers, Azuero and Gómez.[94] However, this speech, his last effort, cost the Precursor his life.

---

93. *Ibid.,* pp. 590–91.

94. Cortázar and Cuervo, *Congreso de 1823,* pp. 115, 124–25.

At the conclusion of the Congress of 1823, on August 6,[95] the Precursor asked for and was granted, on August 8, 1823, permission to leave Bogotá and "travel wherever he needed in the department of Cundinamarca or Boyacá to reestablish his health, and for as long as necessary."[96] The Precursor was sinking fast, and even his bitter rival Santander was at last convinced that the end was in sight. After the May trial he wrote that Nariño had "quieted down a little," and that he had ordered his writers in the papers to "go easier, be less hard on Nariño."[97] By June he felt Nariño and Uribe were his sole opponents in congress,[98] and by June 21 he wrote that he and Nariño were "at peace," and that he would "leave him alone as long as he does not do anything to hinder my command of the government," but spoke scornfully of Nariño, *"not Mariño,* I don't care at all if anybody writes Nariño or not."[99] Briefly, in July, August, and September, the old hatred burned again when it looked as though Nariño had blocked the Revenga appointment as ambassador to England.[100] But by the time Nariño was definitely reported dying at Villa de Leiva (October, 1823), Santander at last felt sure enough of his power to relent and write a brief note of condolence.[101] This letter of condolence of October 22 had a ring of sincerity to it. However, less than a month earlier, on October 6, 1823, he had written Bolívar a letter in which he said of his relationship with the dying Precursor, "ostensibly, at least, we continue now in good harmony; for my part, at least I shall not pick on him any further."[102] In fact, Santander seemed very kind, friendly, and considerate to his old rival, now that it appeared certain that Nariño's great and effective popularity would soon be checked by death. In the letter of October 22, he said he expected no reply, knowing that the Precursor's eyes bothered him. He was writing only as a "proof of my friendship."[103] The rest of the letter was a chatty, informative one about the progress of Bolívar in Guayaquil, the decline of Canterac's royalists in Lima, the success of Sucre and Santa Cruz in the south, and the dangerous successes of

---

95. Cortázar and Cuervo, *Congreso de Cúcuta,* p. 632.

96. Posada and Ibáñez, *El Precursor,* p. 592.

97. Santander, *Cartas y mensajes,* IV, 144.

98. *Ibid.,* IV, 172.

99. *Ibid.,* IV, 180–81.

100. *Ibid.,* IV, 196, 217, 250.

101. Posada and Ibáñez, *El Precursor,* p. 593.

102. Santander, *Cartas y mensajes,* IV, 257.

103. Posada and Ibáñez, *El Precursor,* p. 593.

Ferdinand and the French against the liberal monarchy in Spain and the discouraging situation in England "from whom we must expect nothing of help."[104]

Not wishing to be unpleasantly surprised by any revival of health in Nariño, who had put off apparent death so often before, Santander kept close watch on the dying Precursor and was at least able to report with obvious relief, on November 6, 1823: "Nariño continues at Villa de Leiva and neither sleeps nor thunders."[105] In December, Santander's old fear of the Precursor briefly returned. It was with evident relief that he reported that "Nariño did not get to go to England, nor will go anywhere.[106] At last on December 13, 1823, Santander could rest easier in his vice-presidential chair. His dread rival was dead. But even the manner of the Precursor's death and his funeral did not suit Santander. He wrote Bolívar on December 16, 1823: "general [sic] Nariño died the thirteenth of this month at Villa de Leiva of hidropsy of the chest. His cadaver is being ordered brought here by his family so as to give us here in Bogotá the last tragic act of the life of this man."[107]

The Last Days

Friends closer to the Precursor gave a fuller, more generous summary of his last days, more in keeping with the high nobility, generous character, and driving energy of the man so well known, loved, and respected as a magnanimous leader throughout half a century in the making of Colombia. They described his continual efforts to remain physically and mentally active and of service to the last minute of his life. They told of his horseback rides around the country during the last week of his life, saying his final farewells to his friends and the country he loved so well. They described him spitting blood as he mounted his horse to visit his friends and neighbors, the friars of San Agustín, on the morning of December 9. In spite of fever and delirium, such as he said he had not since Cúcuta, he dressed each day of his last week, made confession, chatted, and sallied forth to see his friends. On the eleventh of December, 1823, they anointed him with holy oil at 9 a.m. but by 10 o'clock he was in the saddle again. In the afternoon the mail arrived, and he discussed the significance of events happening at Puerto Cabello. He seemed serene, and gave thanks to God that he could now pass to the

---

104. *Ibid.*
105. Santander, *Cartas y mensajes,* IV, 264.
106. *Ibid.,* IV, 278.
107. *Ibid.,* IV, 285.

other life willingly and freed of cares which had continually pained him. In spite of opposition, after a short rest he ordered a gentle slow she-mule saddled up for him. Everyone present objected but he insisted. He said he must hurry, time was short. Slowly he went out the gate. A friend accompanied him to the Carmelite friary. There he chatted with them at the gate, saying good-by and urging them to commend him to God, since his last moments were at hand. Then he passed to several houses saying good-by to friends. Upon his return, he said the exercise helped him; but he passed a bad night.

On the twelfth, he had no more desire to eat. Only a little goat's milk passed his lips. But, at eleven, he mounted the mule again, rode out of the house, then soon came back, riding slowly, very slowly. His pulse was fluttering weakly. He received a letter and the good wishes of Dr. Camilo Manrique while still mounted, which he answered very briefly upon sitting down. He stated that he would soon be seeing "what was offered in the land of the spirits, for he was already on his way." [108]

The morning of the thirteenth he was very low. He asked for music, then for some psalms, then asked the priest if the hour had struck yet. When they told him to be careful he laughed loudly and replied that was something he had never done. Then he took his watch in his hand, replied to the psalms while seated in his chair, received absolution, heard the *Pia Mater,* recited the *Miserere* and the penitential psalms, though in some agony. At 5 o'clock in the afternoon his face became serene. He had died. [109]

Envoi

Half a century later, in 1859, José Vergara y Vergara visited Villa de Leiva, scene of Nariño's last hours. There an ignorant or mocking sexton in the church pointed to an empty niche in the ground beside a small wooden casket which he said contained the remains of the illustrious Precursor. On the casket one could read only one word — the word "Fragile." [110]

In 1903 when Posada and Ibáñez gathered their monumental collection of documents, *El Precursor,* there was still no biography of the Precursor. A square in Bogotá, a village in Cundinamarca, a stone in the bridge of San Victorino, later destroyed, commemorating the triumph

---

108. Posada and Ibáñez, *El Precursor,* p. 594.
109. *Ibid.,* pp. 594–97.
110. *Ibid.,* p. xxxi.

of January 9, 1813, constituted the sole monuments to his glory at the beginning of the twentieth century.

In the last fifty years, however, there has been evidence of growing interest in the Precursor. Statues have been dedicated,[111] speeches delivered,[112] and books written.[113] A biography written by Soledad Acosta de Samper in 1910 became so scarce as to be almost unavailable, but the author of this volume finally found a copy in Bogotá in 1962. In 1936 was published Rivas' excellent biography of half of Nariño's life.[114] Colombia made a great and memorable occasion of the two hundredth anniversary of the Precursor's birth, on April 9, 1965. It may be that the time has at least arrived for fulfillment of Nariño's own prophetic words:

"Some day when I am no longer alive, the world will know how much I loved my country."[115]

---

111. Antonio Gómez Restrepo, "Discurso pronunciado ante la estatua de Nariño," *Boletín de historia y antigüedades,* IX (1913), 70–74. Speech given in 1913. Statue is now (1962) in plaza south of Capitol, facing the observatory.

112. Hernando Holguin y Caro, "Discurso pronunciado ante la estatua de Nariño," *Escritos en prosa, segunda serie, discursos* (Rome, 1929), pp. 27–31. Adolfo Leon Gomez, "Discurso frente a la casa del General Nariño al colocar allí una plaça conmemorativa," *Boletín de historia y antigüedades,* IX (1913), 66–70.

113. Gabriel Giraldo Jaramillo, *Bibliografía selecta de Nariño* (Bogotá, 1953), pp. 3, 10.

114. Rivas, *El andante caballero.*

115. Posada and Ibáñez, *El Precursor,* p. ix.

BIBLIOGRAPHY

Microfilm and Typescript Copies of Documents

The author of this volume was able to get from Spain in 1953 approximately 200 pages of documents and 50 pages of microfilmed documents dealing with Nariño, Miranda, Pedro Fermín de Vargas, and their plans for revolutionizing Latin America. The purchase was made possible through the cooperation of the Director of the Archives of the Indies in Sevilla, Jose Marca Peña de la Camara. The guide used to locate the documents desired was that invaluable work, *Independencia de America, fuentes para su estudio, catálogo de documentos conservados en el Archivo General de Indias de Sevilla,* by a former chief of the archives, Pedro Torres Lanzas (Madrid, 1912. 6 vols.).

Printed Documents, Correspondence, Memoirs, and Travels

Printed Documents of Greatest Value

The following collections of printed documents, largely published under the auspices of the Academia Colombiana de Historia in its series called *Biblioteca de Historia Nacional,* have proved invaluable in reconstructing the life and times of Antonio Nariño. They are listed below in the order of their importance as sources. The *Biblioteca* contained 87 volumes, mostly of documents on Colombian history in 1955, 91 volumes in 1958.

1. Posada, Eduardo, and Pedro M. Ibáñez, comps. *El Precursor; documentos* (Biblioteca de Historia Nacional, vol. II.) *sobre la vida publica y privada del General Antonio Nariño.* Bogotá, 1903. The editors of this magnificent collection of documents intended to write a biography of Nariño but never got around to it. In the process of collecting documents they searched the archives of Spain and Colombia, and included copies of documents in other valuable collections and some new materials not previously printed. Some of these other sources which they screened included the following:

   The diary of José Maria Caballero (contained in vol. I of Biblioteca de Historia Nacional), Bogotá, 1902.

Jorge Roa's collection of Nariño's writings in the Biblioteca Popular, Bogotá, 1897.

Reports of the viceroys contained in *Relaciones de mando,* Bogotá 1910 (Biblioteca de Historia Nacional), which is a reprint of an earlier collection of reports.

José Manuel Restrepo's *Historia de la revolución de la República de Colombia en la America Meridional,* Besançon, 1858, 4 vols.

J. Corrales, *Documentos para la historia de Cartagena,* Cartagena, n.d.

Bulletins and proclamations on the campaign of 1812–14.

Quijano Otero's *Campana de Pasto,* n.p., n.d.

Angostura hasta Cúcuta, n.p., n.d.

Pedro Ignacio Cadena, *Anales diplomáticos de Colombia,* Bogotá, 1878.

Marques de Mireflores, *Apuntes historico-criticos para escribir la historia de la revolución de España desde el año 1820 hasta 1823. Documentos, etc.,* London, 1834. 3 vols.

Pedro M. Ibáñez, editor, *Cronicas de Bogotá,* Bogota, 1908–11, 1923. 4 vols. (Biblioteca de Historia Nacional, vols. X–XII, XXXII.)

Captain C. S. Cochrane, *Journal of a Residence and Travels in Colombia During the Years 1823 and 1824,* London, 1825. 2 vols.

The Memorias of General Daniel O'Leary, 1823, reprinted in *Cartas y mensajes de Santander,* Bogotá, 1953–54. 7 vols. Vol. IV for portions referring to Santander.

L. Scarpetta and J. M. Vergara y Vergara, *Diccionario biografico de los campeones de la Nueva Granada,* Bogotá, 1879.

2. Many of the gaps remaining in the documentation of the trial and the jailings of Nariño have been filled by three books: one written by Hernández de Alba, in Bogotá, 1958, and two excellent documentary collections made by José Manuel Pérez Sarmiento.

José Manuel Pérez Sarmiento, *Proceso de Nariño,* Cádiz, 1914.

————. *Causas célebres a los precursores,* Bogotá, 1939. Vols .59 and 60 of Biblioteca de Historia Nacional. Vol. I of *Causas célebres* includes all of the *Proceso* plus additional documents numbered 75 through 195.

3. The third most valuable set of printed documents contains the writings of Nariño. Some are to be found in *El Precursor.* Of the others, the most easily accessible are contained in the works of José M. Vergara y Vergara, noted above, and in *La Bagatela,* reproduced as vol. 112 of the Biblioteca Popular de Cultura Colombiana, Bogotá, 1947.

4. A few valuable references have also been found in the monumental *Archivo Santander,* originally printed in Bogotá as a 22-volume set, 1913–1925, but more accessible now in two sets of which the first fifteen volumes were printed in Venezuela. Vols. 16–22, Havana, Cuba, now in University of Florida library (1962).

5. In 1958, Hernández de Alba printed a valuable set of documents on Nariño's Proceso. See annotated comments under his name. (Vol. XCI of *Biblioteca de Historia Nacional.*)

Bibliography of Primary Sources

Adams, John. *Works.* Boston, 1850–56. 10 vols.
Arboleda, Julio, editor. *Antonio Nariño y F. de P. Santander.* Bogotá, 1936. (Biblioteca Aldeana de Colombia, vol. 71 [Elocuencia].) Contains Nariño's defense before the senate and Santander's defense before the house.
Archivo Miranda. Edited by Vicente Davila. Caracas, 1929–50. 24 vols.
Archivo Santander. Edited by Ernesto Restrepo Tirado, Bogotá, 1913–27. 23 vols. (Publicacion hecha por una Comisión de la Academia de la Historia.
Bache, Captain Richard. *Notes on Colombia Taken in the Years 1822–23.* Philadelphia, 1827.
Good map of Bogotá, p. 223.

Biblioteca de Historia Nacional

VOL.   I   *La patria boba,* compiled by Eduardo Posada and Pedro M. Ibáñez, Bogotá, 1902.

VOL.   II *El Precursor,* compiled by Eduardo Posada and Pedro M. Ibáñez, Bogotá, 1903.

VOL.   IV *Los Comuneros,* edited by Eduardo Posada and Pedro M. Ibáñez, Bogotá, 1905.

VOL.   VIII *Relaciones de mando de los virreyes de la Nueva Granada,* compiled by Eduardo Posada and Pedro M. Ibáñez, Bogatá, 1910.

VOL. X–XII–

VOL. XXXII *Crónicas de Bogotá,* edited by Pedro M. Ibáñez, Bogotá, 1908–77, 1923. 4 vols.

VOL.   XVI *Bibliografia bogotano, by Eduardo Posada,* Bogotá, 1917.

VOL.   XXV *Congreso de Cúcuta, libro de actas,* compiled by Roberto Cortázar and Luis Augusto Cuervo, Bogotá, 1923.

VOL. XXXVII *Congreso, de 1823, actas,* compiled by Roberto Cortázar and Luis Augusto Cuervo, Bogotá, 1926.
            Catálogo del Fondo Anselmo Pineda, Bogotá, 1935, 2 vols.

VOL.   L   *El andante caballero Don Antonio Nariño, la juventud (1765–1803),* by Raimundo Rivas, Bogotá, 1936.

VOL. LIX–LX *Causas célesbres a los precursores,* edited by José Manuel Pérez Sarmiento, Bogotá, 1939. 2 vols.

Blanco, Jose Felix, and Ramon Azpurua. *Documentos para la historia de la vida publica del Libertador de Colombia, Peru y Bolivia.* Caracas, 1875–78. 14 vols.
Boletín de historia y antigüedades. Serial published by the Academia Colombiana de Historia. Bogotá, 1902.
Bolívar, Simón. *Selected Writings of Bolívar.* Compiled by Vicente Lecuña, edited by Harold A. Bierck, Jr., translated by Lewis Bertrand. New York, 1951. 2 vols.

Caballero, José Maria. "Dias de la independencia," *La patria boba,* vol. I of Biblioteca de Historia Nacional, Bogotá, 1902, pp. 75–274.
The second of three contemporary accounts contained in this volume. Cited in text of this work as Caballero, Diary.

Caycedo, Bernardo J. *Grandezas y Miserias de dos Victorias,* Bogotá, 1951.

Chastenet, Jacques. *Godoy Master of Spain, 1792–1808,* by J. F. Huntington, London, 1953.

Cochrane, Charles Stuart. *Journal of a Residence and Travels in Colombia During the Years 1823 and 1824.* London, 1825. 2 vols.
Vol. II contains good maps and a description of Nariño in his defense speech of 1823 before the senate, pp. 66–75.

Colombia, Being a Geographical, Statistical, Agricultural, Commercial and Political Account of That Country, Adapted for the General Reader, the Merchant, and the Colonist. London, 1822. 2 vols.

Cortázar, Roberto, and Luis Augusto Cuervo, comps. *Congreso de Cúcuta, libro de actas.* Bogotá, 1923. (Biblioteca de Historia Nacional, XXXV.)
Much of the lively debate occurring at the forming of the nation (1821) can be either read here, or inferred by reading between the lines. The year 1821 was an exciting one.

—————. *Congreso de 1823, actas.* Bogotá, 1926. (Biblioteca de Historia Nacional, XXXVII.)
This constitutes an invaluable source and record of the second major legislative and constitutional body of Colombia. In its pages can be seen some of the birth pangs of a great but argumentative people. As at Cúcuta, debate was often heated, ending finally in Nariño's resignation (see pp. 230–31).

Depons, Francois. *A Collection of Modern and Contemporary Travels.* Edited by Richard Phillips. London, 1806. 4 vols.

Documentos históricos de los hechos ocurridos en Pasto en la guerra de la independencia. Edición oficial. Pasto, Colombia, 1912.
These documents primarily present the royalist point of view for Pasto was ardently royalist, proving the downfall of Nariño in his hitherto victorious campaign of the south in 1814. They stress documents suggesting that Nariño finally became angry with Pasto's stubborn royalism and threatened them with total destruction, which may explain why they were able to defeat, not only Nariño, but many other republicans, including Bolívar. Contains letters to and from General Nariño and the officials of Pasto relative to Nariño's demands for surrender of Pasto in May, 1814.

Duane, Colonel William. *A Visit to Colombia, in the Years 1822 and 1823.* Philadelphia, 1826.
Another travel book by an intelligent observer from Philadelphia interested in the mineral and commercial possibilities of Colombia to the United States. Its main value is for background information.

Espinosa, José Marîa. *Memorias de un abanderado.* Bogotá, 1876.
Nariño's flag bearer covers 1810–19.

Franklin, Benjamin. *Autobiography.* New York, 1951.
This beautifully printed book purports to be the first exact copy, including

Franklin's orthographic mistakes and predilection for capitalization, edited by Carl Van Doren. Franklin's technique of organizing Juntos and subsidiary Juntos in 1727 (pp. 130–132) was clearly Nariño's model for organizing his "Casino" and his "Arcano Sublíme de la Filantropía." Franklin's Juntos also sound like Miranda's Logia Americana, if there ever was one.

Garcia y Garcia, Jose Antonio. *Relaciones de los vireyes del Nuevo Reino de Granada.* New York, 1869.

This immensely valuable book was written by a Colombian scholar-diplomat — not an unusual combination in that country. He began publishing reports of the viceroys of Colombia to their immediate successors. As he explains, the series is not complete as here printed. Amar's is missing. Montalvo's ends in 1818. The report of Montalvo's successor, Juan de Sámano, was to be separately printed as *Los últimos virreyes de Nueva Granada.* This early work formed the basis for most of Posada and Ibáñez' volume, *Relaciones de mando,* Bogotá, 1910.

Gibson, William Marion. *The Constitution of Colombia.* Durham, N. C., 1948.

Three-fourths of this represents a translation and reprint of Pombo and Guerra's (1911) work on the same subject. However, Professor Gibson has brought the work of Pombo and Guerra up to 1948, and introduced each constitution with an excellent summary explaining the historical and political background of each major change or new constitution. His index is thorough and accurate.

Gill, Conrad. *The Naval Mutinies of 1797.* Manchester, England, 1913.

Hall, Captain Basil. *Captain Hall's Extracts from a Journal Written on the Coasts of Chili, Peru, and Mexico in the Years 1820, 1821, 1822.* Edinburgh, 1824.

There is not much on Colombia in this official report. However, the frontispiece map is of considerable value and the introductory chapters on the weaknesses of the old colonial system of Spain are fair. This book is particularly good for its observations of customs.

Hall, Colonel Francis. *Colombia, Its Present State.* London, 1824. 2nd edition, 1827.

Another travel book — customs, resources, etc.

Hamilton, J. P. *Travels Through the Interior Provinces of Colombia.* London, 1827. 2 vols.

Helguera, J. León. "Tres Cartas de Nariño," *Boletín de historia y anti-güedadas.* Vol. 48. Bogotá, 1961 (pp. 112–16).

These three letters add to our rather inadequate information concerning Nariño's activities after his release from jail during the Riego revolt. The first letter from Paris is dated November 18, 1820. The second from Havre is dated December 19, 1820, and the third from Bogotá is dated June 16, 1822. These letters were found by Professor Helguera at Yale University in the Hiram Bingham Collection of Documents of the Venezuelan leader of independence, Don Francisco Ribas Galindo. They are printed in full, with photostatic copies of the original in the Boletín. They were called to my attention by Leon Helguera in the summer of 1962 in Bogotá. Professor Helguera who was then at North Carolina

State College, Raleigh, N. C., is now at Vanderbilt University, Nashville, Tennessee.

Hemingway, Joseph. *Story of the Spanish Revolution, Commencing with the Establishment of the Constitutional Government of the Cortes in the Year 1812 and Brought Down to the Overthrow of French Arms.* London, 1823. This work partakes of the character of both primary and secondary material. Though not footnoted in the modern sense, it contains much documentation such as the decree of July 21, 1814, establishing the Inquisition again; the edict reconstituting the Inquisition of January 12, 1815; and its order against Freemasonry. "An excess of oppression will ultimately produce reaction" (p. 88) is the main thesis of this book.

Hippisley, Gustavus. *A Narrative of the Orinoco Expedition of 1817.* London, 1819.
Hippisley gives a grim picture of the crude frontier conditions of the revolution in the *llanos* and of Colombia's first "capitals" on the Orinoco and Apure. Full title: *A Narrative of the Expedition to the Rivers Orinoco and Apure in South America: Which Sailed from England in November 1817, and Joined the Patriotic Forces in Venezuela and Caracas.* The work contains no specific mention of Nariño.

Ibáñez, Pedro M., editor. *Crónicas de Bogotá.* Bogotá, 1908–23. (Biblioteca de Historia Nacional, X–XII, XXXII.)
These four volumes contain a hodgepodge of primary, secondary material and comment, much of it found elsewhere in other volumes of the *Biblioteca.* Among its pages, however, there is included some data on the location of the houses of those three great rivals, Nariño, Baraya, and Santander:

Santander.	Calle 16,	No. 102
Nariño,	Calle 12,	No. 101
Baraya,	Calle 16,	No. 126

The fourth volume of the *Crónicas* concentrates largely on the years 1819–1845, thus shedding much light on the controversial last years of Nariño's life and of the important role he played in constitution making at Rosario de Cúcuta in 1821. Evidence presented here indicates that Nariño arrived in Cúcuta on April 27, 1821, and cut short the doubts of some as to the legality of his methods by installing congress and opening it on May 6, 1821, when some delegates had still not yet arrived due to war, bad roads, etc. This uncovers evidence that the writers of the *Correo de Bogotá,* which bitterly attacked Nariño and his *Toros de Fucha* were, primarily, Santander, V. Azuero, and D. F. Gómez. The last three years of Nariño's life were plagued by the machinations of Azuero and Gómez, but their mentor behind the scenes was Santander. (pp. 195, 196, 204, 230, 307, and 311–15.)

Index Librorum Prohibitorum Pii Sexti. Rome, 1786.

Indice último de los libros prohibidos y mandados expurgar. D. Augustín Rubin de Cevallos, Inquisidor General, y Señores del Supremo Consejo de la Santa General Inquisición. Madrid, 1790.

Juan, Jorge, and Antonio Ulloa. *Noticias secretas.* London, 1826.

This secret report, made as a result of an investigation initiated for Ferdinand VI in 1735, sheds much light on the weaknesses of the imperial system and the causes of colonial discontent. "Creoles are largely free of taxes because each one considers himself sovereign, they pay taxes when it suits them and only voluntarily, only the Indians pay rigorously, much of their disgust is due to poor governors. The biggest cause of creole hate for Spaniards is that the Spaniards monopolize all the highest jobs in church and state." (Pp. 440, 445–48.)

Manning, William R. *Diplomatic Correspondence of the United States Concerning the Independence of the Latin American Nations.* New York, 1925. 2 vols.

Miranda, Francisco de. *Diary of Francisco de Miranda.* Edited by William S. Robertson. New York, 1928.

This story of Miranda's tour of the United States in 1783–1784 suggests the reasons for Miranda's hopes for aid from Hamilton, Knox, and others in the United States at the time of the Nootka Sound crisis of 1790 and thereafter.

Mollien, G. *Travels in the Republic of Colombia, in the years 1822 and 1823.* Translated from the French. London, 1824.

This travel book contains maps, statistics, thumbnail sketches of leading Colombians, descriptions of cities and towns and their inhabitants, with frequent comments on events of the wars of independence, the leaders of both sides, and the difficulties they had to contend with in their campaigns. "The only mark of distinction between rich and poor, as elsewhere in the republic, is the wearing of shoes." (P. 203.) The frontispiece map is one of the best of Colombia for this date (1823) for quantity of details.

Mutis, José Celestino. *Archivo epistolar del sabio naturalista.* Edited by Guillermo Hernández de Alba. Bogotá, 1947.

These letters of the botanist and scientist, Mutis, reflect the names of creole revolutionary leaders who were *aficionados* of all new ideas of their times, including both ideas of reform and ideas of revolution. The Colegio of Rosario sponsored "New Learning" of Copernicus and the resulting arguments led to a viceregal plan sponsoring a program for making a "Public University." Out of such reforms, "the question of independence was initiated" (p. 23 of Alba's *Discursos sobre Nicolás Copernico,* Bogotá, 1943).

A letter of April 21, 1794, from Mutis to his sister, Doña Ignacia Consuegra, refers to suspicions he had that their relative, Sinforoso Mutis, was dangerously involved in "very delicate matters," that he was strongly suspected of plotting against the viceroy along with a French doctor (Rieux) since they had frequented the same *tertulias* as a known government spy named Cajigas. "In these *tertulias* are hidden some very secret spies and he will be named as an accomplice in these dangerous conversations" (pp. 194–96).

Nariño, Antonio. *La Bagatela.*
All thirty-eight copies of this political organ of Nariño, beginning with Sunday, July 4, 1811, and ending with April 12, 1812, are reproduced in Vergara y Vergara's *Vida y escritos del General Antonio Nariño* (1859, 1946) and as vol. CXII of the Biblioteca Popular de Cultura Colombiana, Bogotá, 1947.

—————. *Consideraciones sobre los inconvenientes de alterar la invocación hecha por la ciudad de Santafé en 29 de julio de 1810.* Bogotá, 1810.
Reproduced in Vergara y Vergara, *Vida y escritos del General Antonio Nariño,* Bogotá, 1859, pp. 88–97.

—————. *Declaración de los derechos del hombre y del cuidadano.* Bogotá, 1794.
No copies of the original printing have yet been found. Nariño himself reprinted it in 1811 as *Escrito presentado por don Antonio Nariño al Tribunal de Gobierno de Santafé de Bogotá el 17 de Abril de 1811.* This was reprinted in Vergara y Vergara's work of 1859 (pp. 9–11) and also in Posada and Ibáñez' documents in *El Precursor,* 1903 (pp. 45–48).

—————. "Defensa del General Nariño ante el Senado," April 24, 1823, in Posada and Ibáñez, *El Precursor,* pp. 551–91.
Documents presented on May 14, 1823, and voted on May 17, 1823. See vol. XXXVII of Biblioteca de Historia Nacional, pp. 60–62, 114, 125 *(Conreso de 1823, Actas).*

—————. "Dicurso del Vicepresidente interino de la Republica General Antonio Nariño, al Soberano Congreso Nacional, el día de su instalación en la villa del Rosario de Cúcuta, el 6 de mayo de 1821." Reprinted in *El Precursor,* pp. 297–508.
Probably copied from O'Leary, *Memorias,* XVIII, 166 ff.

—————. "Discurso para la apertura del Colegio Electoral pronunciado por el Excmo Señor Presidente de Cundinamarca, don Antonio Nariño en 13 de junio de 1813. En la Imprenta del Estado, Ano de 1813." Reproduced in *El Precursor,* pp. 398–412.
Earlier (1902) printed in the diary of J. M. Caballero, pp. 178 ff.

—————. "Escrito presentado al Tribunal de Gobierno de Santafé de Bogotá, el 17 de Abril de 1811." In *El Precursor,* pp. 305–15.

—————. "Manifiesto al publico de Cundinamarca," June 4, 1812, reproduced in *El Precursor,* pp. 340–54.

—————. "Manifiesto de la conducta del gobierno de Cundinamarca con respecto al congreso y al general de sus tropas en la guerra civil terminada el memorable nueve de enero de mil ochocientos trece." In *El Precursor,* pp. 359–94.
This manifesto includes some materials from the diary of J. M. Caballero and from other sources not listed.

—————. "Proyecto de constitución que el ciudadano Antonio Nariño presenta al Soberano Congreso General de la Republica de Colombia," Rosario de Cúcuta, May 29, 1821. In *El Precursor,* pp. 512–35.

—————. See also *Documentos historicos de los hechos ocurridos en Pasto,* listed above.

Palacio Fajardo, Manuel. *Outline of the Revolution in Spanish America, or an Account of the Origin, Progress, and Actual State of the War Carried On Between Spain and Spanish America: Containing the Principal Facts Which Have Marked the Struggle, by a South American.* London, 1817. This creole revolutionary, of Venezuelan origin, writes one of the best-balanced and original summaries of the Spanish colonial system, of the reforms made in it, and the reasons why, in spite of these reforms, the educated creoles chose to risk a prosperous, secure position, next to the top rank in the hierarchy, in a desperate effort to replace the Peninsular Spaniards at the very summit of the hierarchy. Though it does not contain footnotes in the modern sense, many citations are given within the body of this work. The *Recopilación de Indias* and the common law or *Siete Partidas* and the instructions for *intendentes* are all cited. This contains also a good discussion for the *real patronato* and its origins and significance in creating a state run church in America, wherein the Inquisition became a political extension of royal power and not vice versa as the Anglo-Saxon world usually believes. This work states that there were nine universities in Spanish America from which the future creole revolutionaries got their ideas and their doctor's degrees (p. 10). There is a good discussion of the mercantilist system, of the revolt against it, and of the revolt of Tupac Amaru. Governor Picton's proclamation from Trinidad of April 7, 1797, inviting the mainland to revolt with his help, and his further proclamation of June 26, 1797, are quoted in full. This writer states unequivocally that Spain greatly feared Nariño's uncommon powers of persuasion in the years 1797–1808 (p. 191). He gives Napoleon chief credit for destroying the Spanish Empire in America (p. 24).

Pérez Sarmiento, José Manuel, editor. *Causas célebres a los precursores: "Derechos del hombre," pesquisa de sublevación, pasquine ssediciosos; copias fieles y exactas de los originales que se guardan en el Archivo General de Indias.* Bogotá, 1939. 2 vols. (Biblioteca de Historia Nacional, vols. LIX, LX.)
This work continues and overlaps the archival discoveries made by the same author and printed while he was in the diplomatic service of Colombia in Cádiz in 1914, called *Proceso de Nariño.* The first 234 pages of *Causas célebres,* vol. I, is a complete reproduction of the 1914 work. Taken together, these documents from the Archives of the Indies throw much light on the trial of Nariño and of the royal government's continued surveillance of the Precursor throughout the rest of his life. By comparing with Torres Lanzas it can be seen that the latter not only did a brilliant analysis and summary of documents on independence but sometimes gave full quotation, or nearly so, of pertinent documents.

————. *Proceso de Nariño.* Cádiz, 1914. Tomo I.
There is no tomo II. *Causas célebres,* vols. I and II, continue this work. Taken together, the three volumes of Pérez Sarmiento perform the very important function of filling gaps which Posada and Ibáñez admitted they had been unable to fill in *El Precursor* (1903). Soledad Acosta de Samper wrote her biography (1910) before these documents were known in Colombia. Rivas, Vejarano, and Hernández de Alba all used the *Proceso* of 1914 but did not have the benefit of *Causas célesbres.* Any

future Colombian biographer with pretensions to scholarly accuracy will have to consider *Causas célebres* and its documents.

Pombo, Manuel Antonio, and José Joaquin Guerra, comps. *Constituciones de Colombia.* 2nd edition, Bogotá, 1911. 2 vols.
    This collection was the source of most of Dr. Gibson's *Constitutions of Colombia,* Durham, 1948.

Posada, Eduardo, and Ibáñez, Pedro M. *Los Comuneros.* Bogotá, 1905. (Biblioteca de Historia Nacional, vol. IV.)
    This is a scholarly work on the abortive revolts of 1781–1783 in New Granada. Later popularizers crib heavily from this standard work without fully indicating the extent of their borrowings (Arciniegas, and Henao and Arrubla). This is a mixture of original documents and essays interpreting the doings of Galán, Berbeo, and other *Comunero* leaders. The standard work on the *Comuneros* is that of Manuel Briceño (Bogotá, 1880).

Posada, Eduardo, and Ibáñez, Pedro M., compilers. *El Precursor; documentos sobre la vida publico y privada del General Antonio Nariño.* Bogotá, 1903. (Biblioteca de Historia Nacional, vol. II.)
    This set of 653 pages of carefully selected documents, chronologically arranged, contains the core of all information now available in print on Nariño. All biographers and critics of Nariño rely heavily on this rare work of which only 1,000 copies were printed. Duke University Library owns one copy. After five years of search, the present writer was able to locate and purchase a copy from a Buenos Aires dealer.

————. *Relaciones de mando de los virreyes de la Nueva Granada.* Bogotá, 1910. (Biblioteca de Historia Nacional, vol. VIII.)

Restrepo, J. M. *Documentos para la historia de la revolución de Colombia.* Paris, 1827. Volumes 8–10 of *Historia de la revolución de la republica de Colombia,* Paris, 1827.
    This work is a mixture of documents and historical analysis by a writer who lived through much of the events he describes. *El Precursor* relies on this work for comments on the controversial D'evereux-Mrs. English affair which proved Nariño's undoing in May and June of 1821.

————. *Atlas.* Paris, 1827.
    Excellent enlarged maps of the northern half of South America in color, by departments.

Santa Cruz y Espejo, Francisco Javier Eugenio de. *Primicias de la cultura de Quito.* Quito, 1792, reprinted in Quito, 1947.
    Reprint commemorates the bicentennial of the birth of the Indian savant, printer, and revolutionary who died in 1795 in jail as a result of the still-born revolution which he and Nariño plotted in connection with the printing of the *Rights of Man and of the Citizen.* The seven issues of this learned journal begin with January 5, 1792, and end with March 29. It is difficult to understand why this journal was considered dangerous to the security of the royal government unless for fear of what it *might* print. Earthquakes, better farming, better teaching, and the sort of moderate reforms discussed sixty years earlier by Franklin's Juntos in Philadelphia constitute the scope of these brief essays. This writer used the 1947 reprint.

Santander, Francisco de Paula. *Cartas y mensajes del General Francisco de Paula Santander*. Bogotá, 1953–54. 7 volumes. Edited by Roberto Cortázar. These seven volumes print many letters of Santander never previously printed as well as many that were formerly found widely scattered, especially in O'Leary's collection of Bolívar's letters. The first four volumes cover the last of Nariño's life, 1812-1823, and shed much light on the jealousy and fear of Nariño which Santander confided to Bolívar and others, especially in 1823. Volume IV is particularly valuable. I am indebted to John Tate Lanning for the loan of his copy of the set, as well as to him for calling it to my attention in June, 1955.

Turner, Frederick J. "Documents on the Blount Conspiracy, 1795–97," *American Historical Review*, X (April, 1905), 574–606.

Los ultimos virreyes de Nueva Granada. Relación de mando del Virrey Francisco Montalvo, y noticias del Virrey Sámano sobre la perdida del reino (1803–1810). Madrid, [1918].
These reports of the last two viceroys of New Granada help to explain from the royalist point of view how the wars of independence broke out and why; how Sámano and Morillo reconquered Bogotá in 1816, and how and why they began to lose again in the next year, 1817. Failure to win complete control of the Llanos, they felt, was a grave error.

Vergara y Vergara, José M. *Vida y escritos del General Antonio Nariño*. 2nd ed., Bogotá, 1946. Reproduction of 1859 ed.
This famous volume, reprinted in the Biblioteca Popular de Cultura as vol. CXII, contains the *Rights of Man and the Citizen*, all copies of the *Bagatela,* and Nariño's project for reforming the viceroyalty of New Granada. The last was written in jail in 1797 (Nov. 16, 1797) at the viceroy's request. Nariño hoped thereby to secure his release, but was unsuccessful. This 1859 work of Vergara marks the first real effort in print to give the Colombian Precursor the recognition he truly deserves, but is just now beginning to get in Colombia. Maybe in 1965 (200th anniversary of Nariño's birthday, according to most historians) Nariño will at least receive belated praise for his true genius.

Villaveces, Manuel. "El proceso D'evereux," *Boletín de historia y anti-güedades,* XIX (March 1932), 119–43.
This contains one of the most thorough discussions of the controversial question of Nariño, Mrs. English, and General D'evereux. Villaveces presents documents which in the main clear Nariño. He did *not* jail D'evereux in a *kitchen* as Nariño's enemies claimed. Part of the difficulty seems to have arisen because D'evereux was hot-headed and misunderstood Spanish. Nariño's chief fault seems to have been that he failed to pay the widow English back pay due her deceased husband out of the empty treasury at Cúcuta. Since this rejection followed a private interview with the vice-president, the author conjectures that the comely young Irish blonde may not have been above using her charms — unsuccessfully. D'evereux's official interpreter, Thomas William Yones — or Jones — claimed to know Spanish but does not appear to have improved relations much between Nariño and D'evereux. Just what Nariño said or did to Mrs. English in the private conference remains unanswered at the end of these documents. Probably nothing — which, along with no payment either, could be bad, too. "Hell hath no fury like a woman scorned."

Bibliography of Secondary Sources

Acosta de Samper, Soledad. *Biografía del General Antonio Nariño*. Pasto, Colombia, 1910.
> Up until 1910 there was no biography of Nariño. This book is now out of print and very difficult to locate. A search of five years in Colombia, Spain, Argentina, Mexico, and the United States failed until 1955 to locate a single copy for sale or for loan. A copy was finally listed in the files of the Pan American Union in July, 1955. This biography is good, but was written before Pérez Sarmiento made available his three volumes of printed documents covering Spanish materials in the Archives of the Indies (1794–1820) dealing with Nariño, his activities, and his trial and lawsuits. Located and purchased a copy in Bogotá in 1962. Documents in it settle April 9, 1765, as Nariño's birthday.

—————. *Biblioteca historica: epoca de la independencia*. Bogotá, 1909.

Alayza y Paz Soldán, Luis. *La constitución de Cádiz, 1812*. Lima, 1946.

Alison, Sir Archibald. *History of Europe from the Fall of Napoleon to the Accession of Louis Napoleon*. New York, 1852–60. 9 vols.
> Duke University owns volumes I and II of this very thorough work which appears to have been the source of Altamira, from whom Chapman borrowed. All appear to lean heavily on Hemingway for their information concerning Spain.

Altamira, Rafael. *A History of Spain from the Beginnings to the Present Day*. Translated by Muna Lee. New York, 1949.
> This is an excellent translation of an outstanding interpretation of Spanish history, which stresses the interpenetrations of culture. Chapter XIV is particularly good on social and cultural aspects. Pro-republican in bias, it nevertheless seeks and attains a high degree of objectivity and clarity. Of Spain's troubles he comments that the vertebration of Spain began in 1500 but is not yet solved (thesis of Chapter XVI).

—————. *A History of Spanish Civilization*. Translated by Leon P. Volkhov. London, 1930.
> Of the causes for independence, Altamira stresses the failure of the Bourbons to consider the real desires of American Spaniards. The Bourbon revival of 1701–1808 brought great prosperity but "the Bourbons, especially Charles III, were passionate imperialists even though influenced by liberal tendencies" (p. 161).

—————. See Chapman, *History of Spain*, below.

Amunategui, Luis Miguel. *Crónicas de 1810*. Santiago de Chile, 1876. 2 vols.

Aragón, Arcessio. "Battalla de Calibío," *Revista de Popayán* (January, 1914).

Arboleda Llorente, José María, "Carta de Justo Veraz," *Boletín de Historia y Antigüedades*. XLV, 1958, Bogotá.
> Vitriolic letter versus Nariño, written probably by José Ignacio Pombo of Cartagena in Feb., 1823. Handwritten letter is in Popayán Archives, beautifully arranged by Arboleda Llorente.

Arciniegas, German. *Los Comuneros*. Bogotá, 1938.
> A "popularized" version of Manuel Briceño's scholarly work of the same title. Contains no notes.

Armstrong, Martin. *Spanish Circus.* London, 1937.
A recent attempt to re-evaluate Charles IV, Godoy, and Maria Luisa. Sympathetic to the last named, but strongly biased against Godoy. Spain itself is characterized in 1700 as "overrun with an immense swarm of lazy nobles and priests and with little communication with the rest of Europe; Spaniards resented improvements forced upon them" (p. 10).

Azula Berrera, Rafael. "Nariño, padre nuestro," in *Poesia de la acción.* Bogotá, 1952, (Biblioteca de Autores Colombianos, vol. XXVII.)

Ballesteros y Beretta, Antonio. *Historia de España y su influencia en historia universal.* Barcelona, 1918–41. 9 vols.
The printing, illustrating, and binding is a work of art; the documentation is encyclopedic. Vol. V is good for the administrations of Charles III and Charles IV, and vol. VII covers the era of the wars of independence. Bibliographical essays at the end of each chapter appear to cover every conceivable source with citations and suggestions for further study.

Baralt, Rafael Maria, and Romon Diaz. *Resumen de la historia de Venezuela . . . de 1797–1850.* Curazao and Paris, 1887.
Contains references to early revolts, Nariño, Caro, and Miranda.

Baraya, José Marîa. *Biografías militaires, o historia militar del paîs en medio siglo.* Bogotá, 1874.
One of the first attempts to analyze objectively the military careers of Nariño and others.

Bernal Gamboa, Samuel. *El mártir de la cárcel.* Bogotá, 1951.
This brief interpretation (105 pages) is the beginning of what may become a flood of popular biographies praising the Colombian Precursor.

Briceño, Manuel. *Los Comuneros.* Bogotá, 1880.
Contains 40 documents on the great rebellion of 1781.

Brinton, Crane. *The Anatomy of Revolution.* New York, 1938.
This is a revolutionary work on the subject of revolutions. It attempts to use the techniques and language of medical diagnosis as applied to fevers to the study of revolutions. It is a provocative effort willing to risk criticism and the need for revision by including the Russian revolution in its attempted generalizations. (One revision has already been made.) It completely ignores, however, the fruitful field of Latin American revolutions.

Bulnes, Gonzalo. *Nacimiento de las repúblicas americanas.* Buenos Aires, 1927. 2 vols.
This excellent work deserves to be translated into English so that a largely unknown area of the American revolutions as a whole would be seen in proper focus and in their interrelated effects. Contains excellent brief study of the Quito Indian savant, Espejo, who tried to coordinate his plans with those of Nariño (vol. I, p. 69).

Bushnell, David. *The Santander Regime in Gran Colombia.* University of Delaware Press, Delaware, 1954.
Most of this book covers Santander after Nariño's death, but early chapters discuss the Nariño-Santander feuds of 1821–23.

Calvo, M. Charles. *Anales históricos de la revolución de la América Latina.* Paris, 1864–67. 5 vols.
This work of the famous Argentine legist and international law specialist

deals primarily with treaties and similar documents, but its bibliography in the introduction (pp. cvii–cxv of vol. I) contains a good *brief* summary of the revolutionary era up to 1810.

Cardenas, Acosta, Pablo E. *El Movimiento Comunal de 1781 en el nuevo reino de Granada.* 2 vols. Bogotá, 1960.

Supplements Briceño. Adds some new documents.

Cartagena, Acción Católica de, *Guía Turistica,* Cartagena, n.d. (probably 1961).

Excellent photos of Nariño's Inquisition jail and of his island prison of Bocachica which Nariño called San José, but is now designated San Fernando. Second cubicle on right as you enter from boat dock is where Nariño was jailed according to Cartagena historian Porras Troconis; shark moat is nearby.

Carrasquillo, Rafael M. "Oración pronunciada al inaugurar el sepulchro del Gen. Antonio Nariño," *Boletín de historia y antigüedades,* IX (1913), 90–98.

At first reading this oration in praise of the Precursor appears bombastic and exaggerated. However, upon second reading and check against the facts found in the documents, no untrue statements were uncovered. It just happens that Nariño is such a picaresque, fantastic, and dramatic figure that it is difficult to envision such a career outside the pages of fiction. Except for Vejarano, no writer has so far come away from a study of Nariño without admiration tinged by incredibility, and even Vejarano shares this reaction to Nariño throughout most of his biography. Nariño seems to have had during most of his life an almost magical ability of converting enemies into admirers and admirers into worshipers. Documents in *El Precursor* (pp. 598–99) fully support the orator's contentions that Santander so feared this magical power of the Precursor, even when dead, that he ordered the official funeral services in Bogotá to be cancelled, even after the notices had been printed. The priest scheduled to give the funeral oration wrote a letter apologizing for his refusal to conduct the service to Nariño's son on February 9, 1824, in which he gave as his excuse that the political rivals of the Precursor threatened to kill him if he were to carry out the proposed public funeral service.

Carreño, Manuel. "Defensa de Nariño ante el Senado," *Boletín de historia y antigüedades,* IX (1913), 642–49.

Caycedo, Bernardo J. *Grandezas y miserias de dos victorias.* Bogotá, 1951.

————. "La verdad sobre el federalismo de Nariño," *Boletín de historia y antigüedades.* Philosophizes on Civil War and Nariño as strategist. XLIII, 1956.

"Nariño never professed federalism!"

Chandler, Charles Lyon. *Interamerican Acquaintances.* Sewanee, Tenn., 1917.

The author, a former railroad man, used ship registers and logs to show an incredibly large number of Salem, Boston, and Philadelphia ships in Latin American ports as early as 1797. Its references to Nariño contain minor inaccuracies and there are unfortunately few footnotes, and no bibliography to this otherwise valuable study of hitherto underestimated and unknown contacts between the United States and Spanish America during and just before the wars of independence. E. T. Parks was kind enough to suggest that the author could still be reached at Ursinus College, Pennsylvania, for more information on this subject.

Chapman, Charles Edward. *History of Spain.* New York, 1918.

Founded on Altamira's *Historia de España y de la civilización española.* This is the best brief general work on the subject in English. Its chief defects result from excessive telescoping, especially for the period of modern times (18th and 19th centuries). Nevertheless, for the Napoleonic period, it gives a well-rounded picture, especially of the city of Madrid as improved by Charles III and Godoy. Its bias, when dealing with the Spanish-English struggles in the Americas is pro-Spanish. It is sympathetic to Spanish weaknesses and to the newly great writers and artists such as those of the "impressionistic" school. Its references to the new *Indice* of 1790 and its 1805 supplementary list clearly state that political and not religious reasons gave rise to this new wave of censorship. Political reactions of monarchist Spain, worried by the excesses of republican France, were the cause of the new censorship.

Chastenet, Jacques. *Godoy, Master of Spain, 1792–1808.* Translated by J. F. Huntington. London, 1953.

This little volume would be well worth while just for the Goya reproductions it contains. However, it is considerably more than just a discussion of Goya and his times. It is the only work in English able to give the devil (Godoy) his due. It is a genuine effort to consider the possibility that world and European situations in this critical period of Spanish history were often created and controlled outside of Spain, and that therefore a more moral and intelligent leader of Spain might not have been able to do much better than Godoy during the years he ran Spain, 1792-1808. Unfortunately, this English translation does not include the footnotes and bibliography of its French original. However, it approaches the question of the possible immorality on the downfall of the empire by quoting Albert Sorel: ". . . cette comedie aussi vieille que le vice et la bêtise, du mari debonnaire dupé par sa femme et de la vieille maîtresse exploitée par son amant. La pièce commence vers 1787, comme un chapitre de *Gil Blas* elle se terminera, vingt ans après, par un denouement à la Shakespeare!" (p. 12).

Childs, James B. *Colombian Government Publications.* Washington, D. C., 1941.

Clavery, Edouard. *El proceso de Nariño.* Quito, 1926. Reproduced in *Boletín de historia y antigüedades,* XV, 428–47.

Outside of the Spanish-speaking world, nobody has written more in admiration of Nariño than Edouard Clavery, a Frenchman with many South American connections. It is not surprising to find that he stresses the influence of the French Enlightenment, the French Revolution, and France and Frenchmen in general upon the Latin American revolutions and upon Nariño in particular. The occasion of this particular article was the publication by the consul general in Cádiz, José M. Pérez Sarmiento, of his volume of documents from the Archives of the Indies relating to Nariño's trial (1914). Of particular interest to Clavery were Nariño's Paris conferences of 1820 with Humboldt, De Tracy, the Geographic

Society, and some Napoleonic generals who all made suggestions for a projected constitution and gave books, agricultural machines, and scientific gadgets to Nariño to carry back to his struggling country.

—————. *Les droits de l'homme en Amerique Latine.* Paris, 1920.

—————. "La prensa de Nariño," *Boletín de historia y antigüedades,* XVIII, 67–70.

This article states that Nariño's press is now preserved on the fourth floor of the López building, Calle de Florian, Bogotá. In 1962 the press was on the second floor of The National Archaeological Museum, formerly a barracks. The press, a revered national relic, was a simple screw type. Few nations, he says, have a printing press as a symbol of their freedom. But Colombia still preserves the very press on which Nariño printed the *Declaration of the Rights of Man,* the very instrument of their freedom.

—————. "Une presse a imprimer, symbole nationale," *Journal des debats.* Paris, 1926.

—————. "Las repúblicas bolivianas y le declaración de los Derechos del Hombre," *Boletín de historia y antigüedades,* XV (1926), 483–86.

—————. "Simples observaciones sobre Antonio Nariño," *Boletín de historia y antigüedades,* XXII (1935), 355–62.

This article thoroughly destroys the accusations of the only biographer who seemed to dislike Nariño at times, Jorge Ricardo Vejarano. Vejarano's thesis, briefly, was that Nariño turned against Spain after he discovered that Spanish officials were about to uncover vast shortages and discrepancies in the funds entrusted to Nariño when he was royal treasurer of tithes (1789–1794). This charge, along with the charge that he voluntarily surrendered at Pasto are the same ones invented and hurled at Nariño by his two political enemies in the convention of Cúcuta; Azuero and D. F. Gomez. The new element arises from the fact that the accuser, Dr. Vejarano, acquired considerable prestige as historian and biographer of Nariño's wife, Magdalena Ortega. Clavery says the *Rights of Man* was printed secretly in the middle of December, 1793. His accounts were not under suspicion or investigation at that time. Vejarano vaguely says "in 1794" they were being investigated, but does not document any of his statements. Clavery agrees on 1794 but shows that the impounding of funds which prevented Nariño from liquidating any of his far-flung business investments *followed* the printing of *The Rights of Man.* This reversed chronology of events destroys Vejarano's thesis. Leopoldo Uprimny and Hernández de Alba both disproved Vejarano's thesis very thoroughly in 1958.

Clavery, Edouard. *Trois precurseurs.* Paris, 1932.

This work is not as good as Clavery's other writings. About a third of its two hundred pages is devoted to Nariño.

Colombia. Archivos Nacionales. *Indice.* Edited by Enrique Ortega Ricaurte. Bogotà, 1932–35, 4 vols.

Colombia. Archivos Nacionales. *Catalogo del Fondo Anselmo Pineda.* Bogotà 1935. (Biblioteca Nacional de Historia.)

This volume locates and briefly describes some of the source material on Nariño located in the National Archives of the Library in Bogotá. A portrait and a sample of Nariño's signature are indexed herein.

Cortázar, Roberto. "Acusación de Nariño en el Senado de 1823," *Santa Fé y Bogotá*, No. 10, pp. 203–18.

Dr. Cortázar, for many years a patient, thorough scholar and historian, editor of the *Boletín de historia y antigüedades,* and in 1953–54 of a seven-volume set of the letters and messages of Santander, gives a well balanced discussion of the heated controversy between Azuero and Gómez and the aging Precursor. Part of the heat resulted from the expunging from the records of some pretty harsh accusations which Nariño used against his young attackers. The question most debated was whether or not Nariño volunteered to have his angry words erased from the official records. The answer is no. He opposed the erasings and it was the senate that voted to eliminate from the record some of the harshest accusations, contrary to Nariño's wishes. In 1915, this question was fully debated by Manuel Carreño T. and others in the pages of the *Boletín de historia y antigüedades,* IX (March, 1915), 640–50.

Cuervo Marquez, Luis. *Independencia de las colonias hispano-americanas. Participación de los Estados Unidos: Legion Británica.* Bogotá, (1926?). 2 vols.

This is one of the few works on the subject in Spanish containing thorough footnotes, bibliography, and appendices. Considerable use of British Foreign Office notes is indicated. A valuable survey of the whole field of independence, its causes, and the major events leading to victory.

Depons, Francois R. J., *Travels in Parts of South America in 1801, 1802, 1803, and 1804.* Paris, 1806.

This is good on customs.

Dictionary of American Biography. Dumas Malone and Allen Johnson, editors. New York, 1928–37. 21 vols.

Vol. II, article on William Blount by Philip M. Hamer, describes (p. 390) the Blount plan to assist the British in an attack on Spanish Florida in 1796–97, the year the British captured Trinidad from Spain and encouraged the Venezuelan revolts which failed. Vol. XX, article on James Wilkinson, also by Hamer, describes some of the fantastic double dealings with Spain and against Spain of this arch-adventurer-general of the United States (pp. 222–26).

Dupre, Huntley. *Lazare Carnot, Patriot, 1753–1823.* Oxford, Ohio, 1940.

Lazare Carnot may have been involved in the strange doings of Pedro J. Caro, the mysterious agent who seems to have entered Miranda and Nariño's plots in Paris and London (1796–97) in order to betray Miranda, as he did after 1800, and perhaps all the time. A man named Villery or D'haussonville, who made contacts with the Spanish ambassador in Vienna, the Count of Campo de Alange, on June 10, 1797, via Augsburg, then via Hamburg, acquired some of Miranda's papers obtained from Caro. On April 5, 1800, Villery-Villely-Haussonville passed some more of Miranda's papers to the Spanish ambassador in Vienna. (Torres Lanzas, *Independencia de America*, I, 270) Carnot is vaguely mentioned. His part is still not clear.

Enciclopedia universal ilustrada europeo-americana. Madrid, n.d. 72 vols. ("Espasa Calpe")

Espinosa, José María. *Memorias de un abanderado. Recuerdos de la Patria Boba, 1810–19.* Bogotá, 1876.
A valuable account of an eyewitness. Very loyal to Nariño. Short clear sentences. Written 50 years after the events by Espinosa, Nariño's flag-bearer at Pasto in 1814.

Ferrer del Río, Antonio. *Historia del reinado de Carlos III en España.* Madrid, 1856. 4 vols.
Contains footnotes but no bibliography. A well balanced survey.

Fuente, Vicente de la. *Historia de las sociedades secretas antiguas y molernas en España y especialmente de la francmasonería.* Vol. I, Madrid, 1874; vols. II–III, Lugo, 1870.
Background of masonry in the Riego revolt of 1820 is discussed in this work.

Garcia Chuecos, Hector. *Estudios de historia colonial venezolana.* Caracas, 1937–38. 2 vols.
This contains material on the abortive revolt of 1797 and its chief leader, Juan Mariano Picornell (I, 44, 331, 332; II, 228).

Gillett, C. R. *Burned Books, Neglected Chapters in British History and Literature.* New York, 1932. 2 vols.
American and British readers should peruse this work before throwing stones at the Spanish Inquisition. They will probably be surprised and not a little shocked to see a long list of over three hundred titles of books burned by protestant England in the days of Queen Elizabeth and after. The author was librarian of Union Theological Seminary in New York City.

Giraldo Jaramillo, Gabriel. *Bibliografía selecta de Narino.* Bogotá, 1953.
This work was not available to this writer until July, 1955. It would have been most helpful six or seven years earlier. Its author is now (September, 1955) professor and director of college extension work of the National University system of Colombia.

Gómez Restrepo, Antonio. "Discurso pronunciado ante le estatua de Nariño," *Boletín de historia y antigüedades,* IX, 70–74.
This speech, delivered in 1913 in Bogotá at the dedication of a statue commemorating the Precursor, Nariño, is rather short as such speeches go and not too flowery. He is described as a man of both the pen and the sword but primarily a civilian in thought and action and "a giant in a generation of giants." "Let us not make of the rights he gained a delirium."

Gómez Restrepo, Antonio. *Historia de la literatura colombiana.* 2nd ed., Bogotá, 1945.

Gonzaga, Luis. *Efemerides colombiana.* Bogotá, 1920.

Groot, Jose Manuel. *Historia elclesiástica y civil de Nuevo Granada, escrita sobre documentos auténticos.* Bogotá, 1869. 3 vols.
Contains brief comments on Nariño, neither panegyric nor critical.

Gutiérrez, Miguel L. "Antonio Nariño," in *Biografías de hombres notables de Hispano-America.* Collected by Ramon Aspurúa. Caracas, 1877.
Pages 101–11 contain brief biography of Nariño.

Haggard, J. Villasana. *Handbook for Translators of Spanish Historical Documents.* Austin, 1941.
Very helpful!

Hankins, Frank. "Masonry," *Encyclopedia of the Social Sciences,* IX, 177–178. Contains brief references to Latin America.

Haring, Clarence H. *The Spanish Empire in America.* New York, 1947.
In common with other writers, he comments on the rapid growth of prosperity between 1765 and 1800 which resulted from reforms and led to a growing spirit of independence among the American Spaniards and finally to secession when the opportunity offered in 1808.

Hasbrouck, Alfred. *Foreign Legionaries in the Liberation of South America.* New York, 1928. Young foreigner, Macaulay won victories near Pasto, captured by Indians near Pasto, executed by Spanish Gen. Tomás Santa Cruz on 26 Jan. 1813, was one of few U.S. citizens fighting for Colombia. This Ph.D. thesis explains the origins and victories and defeats of the "Irish Legion" and the "English Legion" and of a few North Americans like Macauley — a motley lot that fought with and for and sometimes against Bolívar. They were exceedingly quarrelsome, rowdy, drunken, and rank conscious, yet this brave handful of men weighted the scales in favor of independence in spite of their few numbers. For John D'evereux, recruiter of the Irish Legion, the man whose offer to duel with Nariño destroyed the Precursor as vice-president at Cúcuta in 1821, he has nothing good to say.

Henao, J. M., and Gerardo Arrubla. *History of Colombia.* Translated by J. Fred Rippy. Chapel Hill, N. C., 1938.
This one volume condensation and translation of a longer Colombian work is particularly valuable because of its excessive emphasis on the colonial and independence periods of Colombian history. It covers very little of the twentieth century. Its chief defect is that it fails to indicate that it is more than a selection and arrangement of source material. In many cases, whole chapters are almost verbatim reproductions of valuable sources. More complete footnoting would more accurately reveal the true nature of this so-called textbook of Colombian history.

Hernández de Alba, Guillermo. "A proposito de una biografía de Nariño," *Boletín de historia y antigüedades.* XXVI (1939), 410–19.
This article contains a strong blast at the iconoclastic biography of Vejarano "who seems to belong to the impressionistic school and does not support his views with a single document" (p. 413).

————. "Diez anos desconocidos de la vida de Nariño," *Boletín de historia y antigüedades,* XX (1933), 601–23.
This speech covers Nariño's life from 1800 to 1810 and draws heavily from the documents of Pérez Sarmiento for its proof. This was an initiation speech required of new members of the Colombian Academy of History.

————. El Proceso de Nariño a la luz de documentos inéditos. Bogotá, 1958.
Valuable documents from Madrid Archives.

Herr, Richard. *The Eighteenth Century Revolution in Spain.* Princeton, New Jersey, 1958.
This was originally printed in 1954 as a Ph.D. dissertation just before the publication of Jean Sarrailh's great work in French, printed in Paris on the same subject. Herr says his work is not superseded by that of Sarrailh

because it (Herr) "dealt more directly with the changing effects on Spain of foreign enlightenment and the French Revolution."

Holguin y Caro, Hernando. "Discurso pronunciado ante la estatua de Nariño," *Escritos en prosa, segunda serie, discursos.* Rome, 1929, pp. 27–31.

Hume, Martin. *Modern Spain.* London, 1923.

Hussey, Roland D. "Traces of French Enlightenment in Colonial Hispanic America," in *Latin America and the Enlightenment,* edited by A. P. Whitaker. New York, 1942.

Jijón y Caamaño, Jacinto. *Espejo y Nariño.* Quito, 1922.
    A letter from the *alcalde* of Cuenca (August, 1955) to this writer stated that this work is extremely rare and impossible to find in Ecuador.

Kaufmann, William W. *British Policy and the Independence of Latin America.* New Haven, Conn., 1951.
    This young man draws the startling conclusion concerning the Venezuelan revolt of 1810 that "as far as the British were concerned the vagueness of the whole thing was a splendid innovation . . . lots of commerce, yet they kept their treaty obligation to Spain . . . ignorance, silence and inactivity seemed for once the ideal components of policy" (p. 49). (Since when is this a *new* policy?)

Laprade, W. T. *England and the French Revolution, 1789–97.* Baltimore, 1909.
    This highly documented thesis shows that the violent aspects of the French Revolution made it possible to set back trends of reform in England at least a quarter of a century by associating reforms in the minds of the public with the bloody excesses of the Jacobin head-choppers. Much the same effect is visible in Spain beginning with the *Indice* of 1790. Unfortunately for Spain, however, she was not able to imitate later English reforms of the nineteenth century in a peaceful fashion. Violent reforms followed by violent reactions seemed to be her lot throughout the nineteenth century.

Lea, Henry Charles. *The Inquisition in the Spanish Dependencies.* New York, 1922.

Lefebvre, George. *The Coming of the French Revolution.* Princeton, 1947.
————. *Le Directoire, 1795–99.* Paris, 1946.

Leguía, Jorge Guillermo. *Historia de America, texto para los colegios de segunda enseñanza, segunda parte.* Lima, 1929.
    Well organized text, particularly good on the rivalry of creole *cabildos* against the *audiencias.*

Leon Gómez, Adolfo. "Discurso frente a la casa del General Nariño al colocar alli una placa conmemorativa," *Boletín de historia y antigüedades,* IX, 66–70 (1911).

Lievano, Roberto. *Viejas estampas.* Bogotá, 1948.

López Alvarez, Leopoldo. *Campaña del sur y destruccion del ejercito patriota.* Pasto, 1914.

McCabe, Joseph. *Spain in Revolt, 1814–1931.* New York, 1932.

Madariaga, Salvador de. *Anarchy or Hierarchy.* New York, 1937.

————. *Fall of the Spanish Empire.* London, 1948.
    In general Madariaga praises Nariño. However, he considered the confessions of 1797 Nariño's one great flaw (p. 98).

Madariaga, Salvador de. *Simón de Bolívar.* London, 1952.

Marquez, Ezequiel. *El Arbol de la libertad plantado por el General Nariño en 1813.* Cuenca, 1936.

Marroquín, Lorenzo. *Precursores: Nariño y los Ricaurtes.* Bogotá, 1913.

Marsland, William D., and Amy L. Marsland. *Venezuela Through Its History.* New York, 1954.
> A good recent study. Good on Miranda and Gual.

Mecham, J. Lloyd. *Church and State in Latin America.* Chapel Hill, N. C., 1934.

Medina, José Toribío. *Historia del Tribunal del Santo Oficio de Cartagena de las Indias.* Santiago de Chile, 1899.

——. *La imprenta en Bogotá.* Santiago de Chile, 1904.

——. *La imprenta en Cartagena de las Indias.* Santiago de Chile, 1904.

Menéndez y Pelayo, Marcelino. *Historia de los heterodoxos españoles.* 2nd ed., Madrid, 1911–32. 7 vols.
> A massive scholarly work which in spots sounds like Burke on the French Revolution; he is anti-Rousseau, anti-Voltaire, anti-Beccaria, anti-agricultural and economic and Basque societies. Heterodoxies soon lead from reform to revolution, that is his thesis.

Mesanza, Fray Andres. "Casas de Nariño y de Ricaurte en Leiva," *Boletín de historia y antigüedades,* XIV (1923), 383–384.
> Discusses country homes of Nariño and the Ricaurtes in Leiva.

Michelet, Jules. *History of France.* Paris, (1872?).

Miramón, A. *Los precursores.* Bogotá, 1950. A secondary school text.

——. *Nariño.* Bogotá, 1960. A well-balanced recent biography, somewhat overly rhetorical but sound interpretation. No footnotes, but extensive quotations in the body of the text.
> Good bibliography. No footnotes, but tells in text where some of his quotations come from in the National Archives, Bogotá.

Mitre, Bartolomé. *Emancipation of South America.* Translated by William Pilling. London, 1893.
> Although the stress of this work is on Mitre's beloved Argentina and upon his hero, San Martín, it also contains well-balanced generalizations and evidence concerning events further north. He stresses fundamental principles rather than taxes as causes of the revolutions of 1808–23. He believes there really was a secret society in London called the Gran Unión Americana in which Nariño, Miranda, and others coordinated plans in the 1790's (pp. 12–17).

Mitre, Bartolomé. *Historia de Belgrano y la independencia.* Buenos Aires, 1913.

Monsalvo, Jose Dolores. "Nariño," *Boletín de historia y antigüedades,* XX, (1933), 419–25.

Moreno Arango, Sebastiano. *Biografía del General Antonio Nariño.* Bogotá, 1913.
> This little sixteen-page primary school biography of the Precursor caused a furor which echoed through the pages of the *Boletín de historia y antigüedades* for several issues. The proposal to print and distribute it throughout the elementary schools of Colombia caused the descendants of Nariño's accusers of 1821–23, D. F. Gómez and Vicente Azuero, to get very angry. After a hot debate in the National Academy of History

in 1913, it was decided to censor the offending parts of the pamphlet. The Gómez and Azuero families did not think it proper for school children to read these harsh charges which Nariño cast against their ancestors in response to their attacks upon him in 1821 at Cúcuta and in 1823 at Bogotá. Ancestors and politics were soon hopelessly involved in the moral question of censorship and the arbitrary alteration of unpleasant aspects of the national history. A compromise was finally reached for partial censorship.

Moses, Bernard. *The Intellectual Background of the Revolutions in South America*. New York.

————. *The Social Revolution of the Eighteenth Century in South America*. Washington, 1917. (Annual Report of the American Historical Association for the Year 1915.)

————. *Spain's Declining Power in South America, 1730–1806*. Berkeley, 1919.

————. *Spanish Colonial Literature in South America*. New York, 1922.

————. *South America on the Eve of Emancipation, the Southern Spanish Colonies in the Last Half of Their Dependence*. New York ,1908.

O'Leary, Daniel F. *Gran Colombia y España, 1819–22*. Madrid, 1919.

Ortíz, Sergio Elias. *En el centenario de la muerte de Nariño*. Pasto, 1927.

————. *Franceses en la independencia de la Gran Colombia*. Bogotá, 1949. (Academia Colombiano de Historia, Biblioteca Eduardo Santos, vol. I.)

Osorio, Alejandro. "Campaña de Nariño en el sur," *Boletín de historia y antigüedades,* VIII, 735–46.

Otero Muñoz, Gustavo. "Don Antonio Nariño," in *Semblanzas colombianas,* vol. I, Bogotá, 1938.

————. *Historia del periodismo en Colombia*. Bogotá, 1936.

Ots Capdequi, José María. *Instituciones de gobierno del Nuevo Reino de Granada durante el siglo XVIII*. Bogotá, 1950.
Madrid, 1958, extension of this work concentrates on independence era, especially 1810.

Pacheco Quintero, Jorge. *Influencia de masonería en la emancipación de America*. Bogotá, 1943.

Parks, E. Taylor. *Colombia and the United States, 1765–1935*. Durham, N. C., 1935.

Pasto, Departmento de, *Documentos historicos de los hechos occurridos en Pasto*. Pasto, 1912.

Paxson, Frederick L. *The Independence of the South American Republics*. Philadelphia, 1916.

Pereyra, Carlos. *Historia de America española*. Madrid, 1871–76. 8 vols.

Pérez Marchand, Monelisa Lina. *Dos estapas ideológicas del siglo XVII en Mexico a través de los papeles de la Inquisición*. Mexico City, 1945.

Plaza, José Antonio. *Memorias para la historia de Nueva Granada desde su descubrimiento hasta el 20 de julio de 1810*. Bogotá, 1850.

Porras Troconis, Gabriel. Calle Real de Manga 25–01 Cartagena. *Historia de la cultura en el Nuevo Reino de Granada*. Sevilla, 1952. (Publications of the Escuela de Estudios Hispano-Americanos de Sevilla.)

Posada, Eduardo. *Bibliografía bogotana*. Bogotá, 1917. (Biblioteca de Historia Nacional, vol. XVI.)

————. "Nacimiento de Nariño," in Apostillas colombianas, pp. 106–109.

————. "El Proceso de lost pasquines," *Boletín de historia y antigüedades,* VIII, 721–28.

Restrepo Canal, Carlos. *Nariño Periodista.* Bogotá, 1960.
Contains all 38 issues of *La Bagatela, The Rights of Man,* and Nariño's *Diálogos.*

Restrepo, Sáenz, J. M. and Raimundo Rivas. *La familia de Nariño,* Bogotá, 1928.

Restrepo Canal, Carlos. "La nueva obra de Raimundo Rivas," *Boletín de historia y antigüedades,* XXVI, 232–36.

Restrepo Tirado, Ernesto. "Informe sobre el folleto, *Biografía del General Nariño," Boletín de historia y antigüedades,* IX, 650–54.

————. "Nariño y el Duque de Frias," *Boletín de historia y antigüedades,* XXX, 926–29.

Ribas, Lincoln Machado. *Movimientos revolucionarios en las colonias españolas de America.* Montevideo, 1940.
"Nothing more false than the idea that revolts of 1810 were preceded by three hundred years of lethal enervation." (p. 11).

Rippy, J. Fred. *The Rivalry of the United States and Great Britain over Latin America, 1808–30.* Baltimore, 1928.

Rivas, Raimundo. *El andante caballero Don Antonio Nariño; la juventud (1765–1803).* Bogotá, 1936. (Biblioteca de historia nacional, vol. L.)

————. "En defensa de Nariño," *Boletín de historia y antigüedades,* XXVI (1939), 137–62.

————, and José María Restrepo Sáenz. "La familia de Nariño," *Revista del Colegio Mayor de Nuestra Senora del Rosario,* VI (1910), 45–55.

————. "La ultima palabra sobre el nacimiento y el matrimonio del General Nariño," *Revista del Colegio Mayor de Nuestra Senora del Rosario,* XI (1917), 288 ff.

Rivera, Rodolfo Osvaldo. "Francisco de Paula Santander: His Role in the Making of Colombia." Unpublished Ph.D. thesis, Duke University, 1932.

Robertson, William Spence. *France and Latin American Independence.* New York, 1939.
Discusses among other topics, the Brissot-Dumouriez plan to place Miranda in charge of Saint Domingue, 1792–93. From this base he was to assist Genet in revolutionizing Spanish America, including possibly Florida and Louisiana.

————. *The Life of Miranda.* Chapel Hill, N. C., 1929. 2 vols.
This biography represents a life work. No new biography is apt to uncover much that is new very soon. This is truly "definitive."

Robertson, William Spence. *Francisco de Miranda and the Revolutionizing of Spanish America.* Washington, 1908. (Annual Report of the American Historical Association for the year 1907.)
This highly documented study of Nariño's Venezuelan counterpart was expanded in 1929 into a two-volume biography of the Venezuelan Precursor. This 1907 study represented a pioneer work into what was, at the time, an untouched (for United States scholars) personality in a frontier area of research. Dr. Robertson's deductions finally led to the uncovering of the original bound volumes of documents of Miranda which

had been put aboard a British vessel at the time of Miranda's capture by the Spanish.

Rojas, Ulises. *El Profesor Dr. Juan Gualberto Gutiérrez, medico del Precursor General Antonio Nariño y del ejercito libertador de la Nueva Granada.* Tunja, 1940. 59 pp.

Romoli, Kathleen. *Colombia, Gateway to South America.* New York, 1942.

Roth, Cecil. *The Spanish Inquisition.* London, 1937.

    Thesis: Spain gained the world and lost its soul. Fairly objective work.

Rourke, Thomas (pseudonym of Daniel Joseph Clinton). *Man of Glory, Simón Bolívar.* New York, 1937.

Sarrailh, Jean. *L'Espagne eclairée de la seconde moitie du XVII e siècle.* Paris, 1954.

    Sarrailh's monumental economic study includes references to the founding of Basque societies and "friends of the country" of the type that demanded reform and, later, revolution in Mompox and Bogotá. Lower taxes and better farming methods sound echoes of Franklin's Junto of 1727 and thereafter.

Scarpetta, L., and José M. Vergara y Vergara. *Diccionario biografico de los campeones de la Nueva Granada, Venezuela, Ecuador y Peru.* Bogotá, 1879. Pp. 383–385 on Nariño.

Schons, Dorothy. *Book Censorship in New Spain.* Austin, Texas, 1950.

Shafer, Robert Jones. *The Economic Societies in the Spanish World.* Syracuse, New York, 1958.

    Monumental notes! Some on Mompox and Bogotá; used and praised Sarrailh, but condemns Emilio Novoa's 1955 work on the same subject.

Spell, Jefferson Rea. *Rousseau in the Spanish World before 1833.* Austin, Texas, 1938.

    More proof Spanish censorship was very weak in this period at the end of the eighteenth and the beginning of the nineteenth century.

Torre Revello, J. *El periodismo en America durante la dominación española.* Buenos Aires, 1940.

    Continues the work of J. T. Medina.

Torres, Carlos Arturo. *La estatua del Precursor.* Liverpool, 1907. 24 pp.

Tovar, Manuel Maria, and Osorio Umaña, A.M. "Estudios históricos, 1765 y No 1760," *Revista del Colegio Mayor de Nuestra Señora del Rosario,* Ano III, No. 23, pp. 166–69.

Turberville, A. S. *The Spanish Inquisition.* New York, 1932.

Turner, Frederick Jackson. "The Policy of France Toward the Mississippi Valley in the Period of Washington and Adams," *American Historical Review,* X (January, 1905).

Uprimny, Leopoldo. "El Proceso de Nariño a la luz de las leyes de Indias," *Revista Rosario,* Bogotá, October, 1958. Says Nariño was *not* an "absconding bankrupt."

    ————. "El Problema de Nariño con la Caja de Diezmos a la luz de las Leyes de Indias." *Revista del Colegio Mayor de Nuestra Señora del Rosario,* Año LIII, Nos. 447–48, Agosto-Octobre, 1958. Bogotá, Colombia. Pp. 114–29. Demolishes Azuero-Gómez charges of 1823.

Vejarano, Jorge Ricardo. "Carta sobre Nariño," *Boletín de historia y antigüedades,* XXVI (1939), 478–83.

————. *Nariño, su vida, sus infortunios, su talla historica.* Bogotá, 1938. Reissued in 1945 as vol. III of Biblioteca Popular de Cultura Colombiana. Like Rupert Hughes, "humanizes" his subject by stressing his weaknesses. In important points disagrees with other biographers. No footnotes. Insists Nariño was a "deudor fallido." Disproved by documents of G. H. de Alba and by analysis of Leopoldo Uprimny in 1958.

————. "La vida extraordinaria de Nariño," *Boletín de historia y anti- güedades,* XXII (1936), 255–71.

Vergara y Vergara, Jose M. *La historia de la literatura en Nueva Granada.* Bogotá, 1931. 2 vols.

Villaveces, Manuel. "Historia anecdótica, tradiciones de la familia Nariño sobre el Precursor," *Boletín de historia y antigüedades,* XXIII (1936), 177–92.

Warren, Harris Gaylord. "The Early Revolutionary Career of Juan Mariano Picornell," *Hispanic American Historical Review,* XXII (February, 1942), 56–81.

————. *The Sword Was Their Passport.* Baton Rouge, La., 1943.

Webster, Charles K. *Britain and the Independence of America. Select Docu- ments, 1812–30.* New York, 1938.

Whitaker, Arthur P., editor. *Latin America and the Enlightenment.* New York, 1942. John Tate Lanning describes the ineffectual nature of the censorship of the Inquisition and states that the cultural lag which had earlier existed ceased to exist between 1780 and 1800. Other scholars say the same thing yet all of them shouting together will have a hard time undoing the black legend. It dies hard! The public does not love those who try to change their preconceived beliefs. However, the growing mass of evidence will eventually make an impression and force a revision. College texts have accepted some revision.

INDEX